ORDNANCE SURVEY MEMOIRS OF IRELAND

Volume Five

PARISHES OF COUNTY TYRONE I
1821, 1823, 1831-36

Published 1990.
The Institute of Irish Studies,
The Queen's University of Belfast,
Belfast.
In association with
The Royal Irish Academy,
Dawson Street,
Dublin.

Grateful acknowledgement is made to the Economic and Social Research Council and the Department of Education for Northern Ireland for their financial assistance at different stages of this publication programme.

Copyright 1990.

Reprinted 2024 by Ulster Historical Foundation
www.ulsterhistoricalfoundation.com

All rights reserved. No part of this publication may be reproduced, stored in a retrieval system or transmitted, in any form or by any means, electronic, mechanical, photocopying, recording or otherwise, without the prior permission of the publisher.

ISBN: 978-0-85389-362-2

Reprinted by LightningSource, 2024

Ordnance Survey Memoirs of Ireland
VOLUME FIVE

Parishes of County Tyrone I
1821, 1823, 1831-6

North, West & South Tyrone

Edited by Angélique Day and Patrick McWilliams.

The Institute of Irish Studies
in association with
The Royal Irish Academy

EDITORIAL BOARD

Angélique Day (General Editor)
Patrick S. McWilliams (Executive Editor)
Dr B.M. Walker (Publishing Director)
Professor R.H. Buchanan (Chairman)

CONTENTS

	Page
Introduction	ix
Brief history of the Irish Ordnance Survey and Memoirs	ix
Definition of terms used	x
Note on Memoirs of County Tyrone	x

Parishes in County Tyrone

Aghalurcher	1
Ardstraw	2
Cappagh	15
Clogher	24
Donacavey	62
Donaghedy	88
Dromore	93
Drumragh	104
Kilskeery	113
Leckpatrick	117
Longfield (West)	127
Longfield (East)	131
Longfield (Lower)	134
Skirts of Urney and Ardstraw	136
Termonamongan	142
Miscellaneous Papers	146

List of selected maps and drawings

County Tyrone, with parish boundaries	vi
County Tyrone, 1837, by Samuel Lewis	viii
Gold ornament from Tulnafoile townland	34
Earthen vase from Ardunshion townland	39
Brass ornament found on Knockmany	40
Tracing of Manor of Cecil	48

List of O.S. maps, 1830s

Castlederg	137
Clogher	25
Fintona	63
Fivemiletown	31
Newtownstewart	3
Omagh	105
Strabane	118

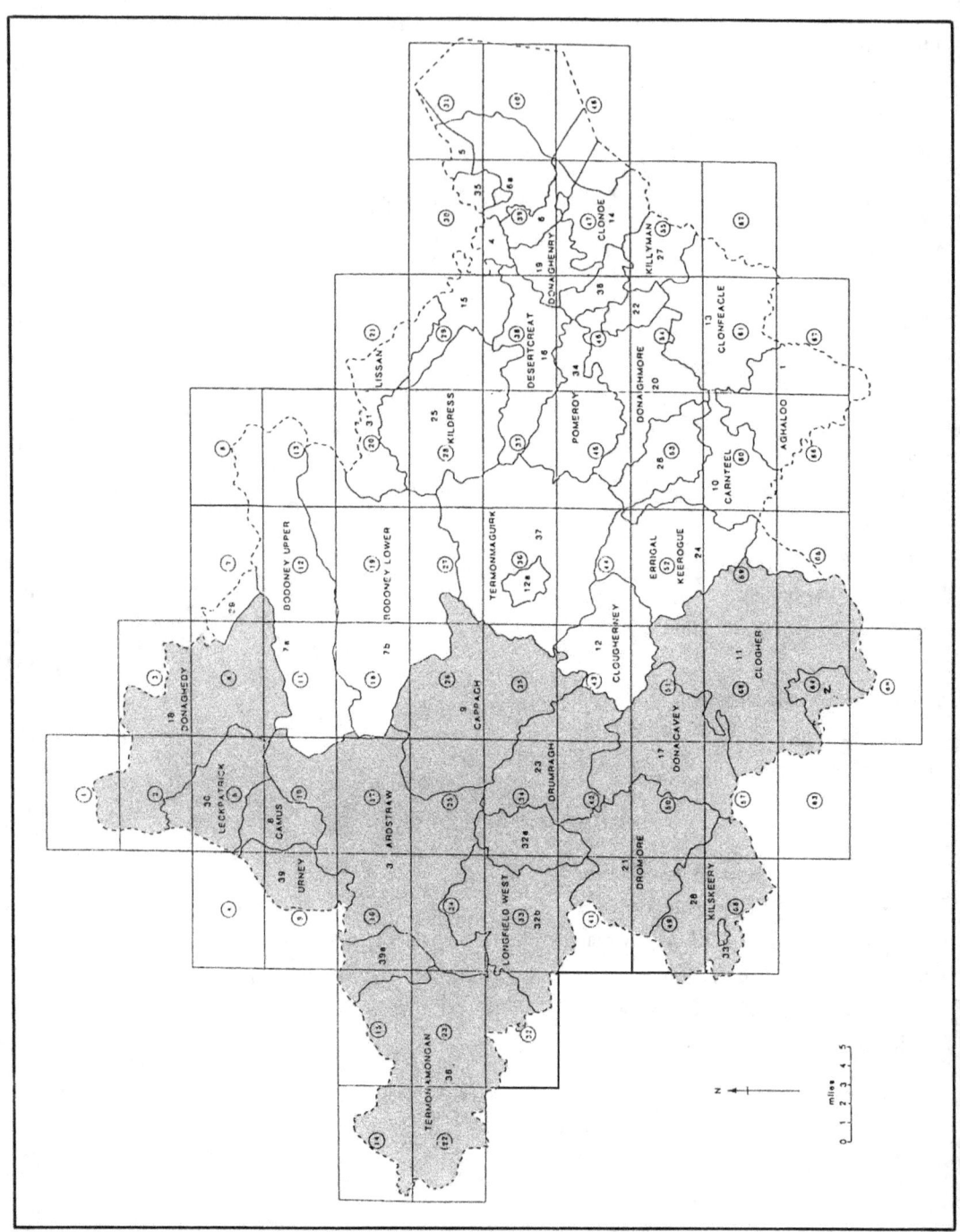

ACKNOWLEDGEMENTS

During the course of the transcription and publication project many have advised and encouraged us in this gigantic task. Thanks must first be given to the Royal Irish Academy, and the library staff, particularly the librarian, Mrs Brigid Dolan, for making the original manuscripts available to us.

We should like to acknowledge the following individuals for their special contributions. Dr Brian Trainor led the way with his edition of the Antrim memoir and provided vital help on the steering committee. Dr Ann Hamlin also provided valuable support, especially during the most trying stages of the project. Professor R.H. Buchanan's unfailing encouragment has been instrumental in the development of the project to the present. Without Dr Kieran Devine the initial stages of the transcription and the computerising work would never have been completed successfully: the project owes a great deal to his constant help and advice. Dr Kay Muhr's continuing contribution to the work of the transcription project is deeply appreciated. Mr W.C. Kerr's interest, as well as his own work on the Memoirs, gave inspiration. Professor Anne Crookshank and Dr Edward McParland were most generous with practical help and advice concerning the drawings amongst the Memoir manuscripts. Finally, all students of the nineteenth century Ordnance Survey of Ireland owe a great deal to the pioneering work of Professor J.H. Andrews, and his kind help in the first days of the project is gratefully recorded.

The essential task of inputting the texts from audio tapes was done by Miss Eileen Kingan, Mrs Christine Robertson, Miss Eilis Smyth, Miss Lynn Murray, and, most importantly, Miss Maureen Carr.

We are grateful to the Linen Hall Library for lending us their copies of the first edition 6" Ordnance Survey Maps: also to Ms Maura Pringle of QUB Cartography Department for the index maps showing the parish boundaries. For providing financial assistance at crucial times for the maintenance of the project, we would like to take this opportunity of thanking the trustees of the Esme Mitchell trust and The Public Record Office of Northern Ireland.

Left:
Map of parishes of County Tyrone. The area described in this volume, the parishes of North, West and South Tyrone, has been shaded to highlight its location. The square grids represent the 1830s 6" Ordnance Survey maps. The encircled numbers relate to the map numbers as presented in the bound volumes of maps for the county. The parishes have been numbered in all cases and named in full where possible, except those in the following list: Aghalurcher 2, Longfield East 32a, Magheracross (no Memoir) 33, Skirts of Urney and Ardstraw 39a.

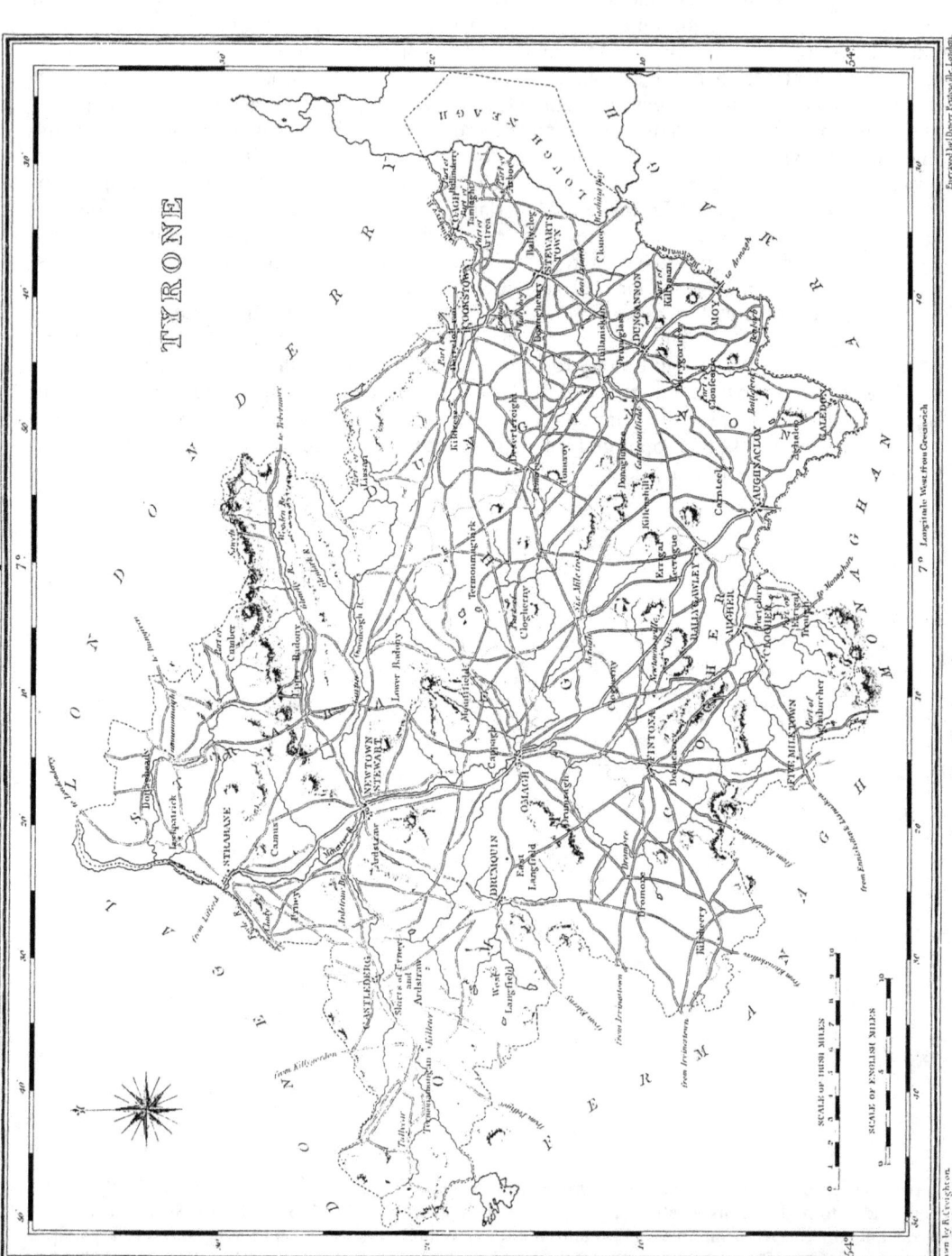

Map of County Tyrone, 1837, from Samuel Lewis' *Atlas of the counties of Ireland* (London, 1837)

INTRODUCTION AND GUIDE TO THE PUBLICATION OF THE ORDNANCE SURVEY MEMOIRS

The following text of the Ordnance Survey Memoirs was first transcribed by a team working in the Institute of Irish Studies at The Queen's University of Belfast, on a computerised index of the material. For this publication programme the text has been further edited. Spellings have been modernised in all cases except for townland and other place-names, although where the original spelling was thought to be of any interest it has been retained and is indicated by angle brackets in the text. Punctuation has been modernised and is the responsibility of the editors. Editorial additions are indicated by square brackets. Original drawings are referred to, and some have been reproduced. Original page references have been omitted from this series. Because of the huge variation in size of Memoirs for different counties, the following editorial policy has been adopted: where there are numerous duplicating and overlapping accounts, the most complete and finished account, normally the Memoir proper, has been presented, with additional unique information from other accounts like the Fair Sheets entered into a separate section, clearly titled and identified; where the Memoir material is less, nothing has been omitted. To achieve standard volume size, parishes have been associated on the basis of propinquity, although where there is less material, parishes of one county have been included in one volume. There are considerable differences in the volume of information recorded for different areas: counties Antrim and Londonderry are exceptionally well covered, while the other counties do not have the same detail. This series is the first systematic publication of the parish Memoirs, although individual parishes have been published by pioneering local history societies. The entire transcriptions of the parish Memoirs made in the course of the indexing project can be consulted in the Public Record Office of Northern Ireland and the library at the Queen's University of Belfast. The manuscripts of the Ordnance Survey Memoirs are in the Royal Irish Academy, Dublin.

Brief history of the Irish Ordnance Survey in the nineteenth century and the writing of the Ordnance Survey Memoirs

In 1824 a House of Commons committee recommended a townland survey of Ireland with maps at the scale of 6", to facilitate a uniform valuation for local taxation. The Duke of Wellington, then prime minister, authorised this, the first Ordnance Survey of Ireland. The survey was directed by Colonel Thomas Colby, who had available to him officers of the Royal Engineers and three companies of sappers and miners. In addition to this, civil assistants were recruited to help with sketching, drawing and engraving of maps, and eventually, in the 1830s, the writing of the Memoirs.

The Memoirs were written descriptions intended to accompany the maps, containing information which could not be fitted on to them. Colonel Colby always considered additional information to be necessary to clarify place-names and other distinctive features of each parish; this was to be written up in reports by the officers. Much information about parishes resulted from research into place-names and was used in the writing of the Memoirs. The term "Memoir" comes from the abbreviation of the word "Aide-Memoire". It was also used in the 18th century to describe topographical descriptions accompanying maps.

In 1833 Colby's assistant, Lieutenant Thomas Larcom, developed the scope of the officers' reports by stipulating the headings under which information was to be reported, and including topics of social as well as economic interest. By this time civil assistants were writing some of the Memoirs under the supervision of the officers, as well as collecting information in the Fair Sheets.

The first "Memoirs" are officers' reports covering Antrim in 1830, and work continued on the Antrim parishes right through the decade, with special activity in 1838 and 1839. Counties Down and Tyrone were written up from 1833 to 1837, with both officers and civil assistants working on Memoirs. In Londonderry and Fermanagh research and writing started in 1834. Armagh was worked on in 1835, 1837 and 1838. Much labour was expended in the Londonderry parishes. The plans to publish the Memoirs commenced with the parish of Templemore, containing the city and liberties of Derry, which came out in 1837 after a great deal of expense and effort.

Between 1839 and 1840 the Memoir scheme collapsed. Peel's government could not countenance the expenditure of money and time on such an exercise; despite a parliamentary commission favouring the continuation of the writing of the Memoirs, the scheme was halted before the southern half of the country was covered. The manuscripts remained unpublished and most were removed to the Royal Irish Academy, Dublin.

The Memoirs are a uniquely detailed source for the history of the northern half of Ireland immediately before the Great Famine. They document the landscape and situation, buildings and antiquities, land-holdings and population, employment and livelihood of the parishes. They act as a nineteenth century Domesday book and are essential to the understanding of the cultural heritage of our communities. It is planned to produce a volume of evaluative essays to put the material in its full context with information on other sources and on the writers of the Memoirs.

Definition of descriptive terms.

Memoir (sometimes Statistical Memoir). An account of a parish written according to the prescribed form outlined in the instructions known as "Heads of Inquiry", and normally divided into 3 sections: Natural Features and History, Modern Topography and Ancient Topography, Social and Productive Economy.

Fair Sheets: "Information gathered for the Memoirs", an original title describing paragraphs of additional information following no particular order, often with marginal headings, signed and dated by the civil assistant responsible.

Statistical Remarks/Accounts: Both titles are employed by the Engineer officers in their descriptions of the parish with marginal headings, often similar in layout to the Memoir.

Office Copies: These are copies of early drafts, generally officers' accounts and must have been made for office purposes.

Ordnance Survey Memoirs for County Tyrone

This volume, containing the Memoirs for 13 parishes around Omagh and Clogher, is the first for county Tyrone and the fifth in the present series. Answers written in response to a questionnaire sent out by the North West Society of Ireland, a society formed to promote improvements in agriculture during the early nineteenth century, often accompany the Memoir proper and, although dating from the 1820s, provide valuable comparative information to the reports written by officers working on the Ordnance Survey between 1831-36. Of this type is the Memoir of Leckpatrick, which details the area surrounding Strabane but not the town itself. Drawings are listed below and are cross-referenced in the text; some are illustrated. Ground plans are referred to in the text only. The manuscript material is to be found in Boxes 51 and 52 of the Royal Irish Academy's collection of Ordnance Survey Memoirs and box references are given beside each parish below. The editors have incorporated

Parishes of County Tyrone

all material relevant to a particular parish into the Memoir of that name, and this is indicated in the text. The Fintona Memoir has been incorporated into that of Donacavey. Some material within the reports has been rearranged to conform with the original Heads of Inquiry.

Box 51		Box 52	
Aghalurcher	III	Donacavey	I
Ardstraw	V	Donaghedy	II
Cappagh	VIII	Dromore	IV
Clogher	X	Drumragh	VI
		Fintona	IX
		Kilskeery	XII
		Leckpatrick	XIV
		Longfield	XVI, XVII, XVIII
		Skirts of Urney and Ardstraw	XXIV
		Termonamongan	XXI
		Miscellaneous Papers	XXV

Drawings

Clogher:

Stone with indented ornament called the Clogher stone. Detail drawing showing where tablet may have been removed.

Stone with sculpted head and hollow built into churchyard wall (for curing headaches and warts).

Another stone with sculpted head built into wall (reputed to cure warts).

Plan of 2 forts on Castle hill close to the palace, showing planted trees in main fort.

Plan of Augher Castle showing outer walls and star shaped dungeon.

Tracing of the manor of Cecil, belonging to the Rev. Francis Gervais [illustrated].

Ground plan of the castle of Aghentain or Ochenture, and front elevation showing turrets [text drawing].

Earthen vase showing incised decoration found in Ardunshion [illustrated].

Gold ornament [lunula] belonging to Rev. Francis Gervais, showing detail of terminal ornament, March 1833 [illustrated].

Rough sketch of watch dated 1603.

Brass or copper ornament, double pronged with handle, found on Knockmany near the Druid's Altar [illustrated].

Parish of Aghalurcher, County Tyrone

Memoir for part of the parish by J.R. Ward, (before) September 1835

MEMOIR WRITING

Comment on Front Cover of Memoir

Slight and imperfect. Refer to Mr Boyle, [initialled] R.K.D. [Dawson], 24 September 1835.

NATURAL FEATURES

Hills

The southern part of the parish is mountainous. The principal point, Altaveedan, is situated near the eastern boundary. It is part of a large mountain district which borders the south of the county. It is 976 feet above the sea and there is broken fall north west by west nearly as far as the high road between Clogher and Fivemiletown.

Lakes

Cullentra lough, which is partly in the townland of the same name and part in Tattanellan, is 325 feet above the sea [and] contains 11 acres 3 roods. Its depth is unknown.

Curlough, partly situated in Kill townland (the remaining part being in the adjacent parish of Clogher), is about 765 feet above the sea. Its content is about 10 acres and its depth is unknown.

Lough Natroy in Kill townland is 909 feet above the sea and contains about 3 acres Irish. Its depth is unknown.

Crockacleaven lough, situated in the townland of the same name; it is 591 feet above the sea. Its content is 10 acres and is said to be upwards of 40 feet in depth.

Rivers

There is no considerable river in the parish but there are a great number of streams, the principal of which is the [blank], which takes its rise in the parish of Clogher, and it is usefully situated for drainage.

Bogs

The southern part of the parish is of a boggy nature and there is very good turf for fuel to be met with in all parts of it. In the townlands of Beagh, Kill and Mullaghmore there is a large tract. The height above the sea varies from 310 to 320 feet and the depth of the bank is from 3 to 7 feet. There are a few trunks of oak and fir and birch scattered indiscriminately through this tract.

MODERN TOPOGRAPHY

Towns and Buildings

Towns, public buildings, gentlemen's seats and bleach greens: none in that part of the parish which is in this county.

Mill

Corn mill, Cullynane townland, breast wheel, 16 feet diameter, 3 feet 6 inches broad.

Communications

Part of the main road between Clogher and Fivemiletown traverses the northern part of the parish for about 2 miles. It is 28 feet broad. For particulars see parish of Clogher.

The road between Fivemiletown traversing from north to south for [blank] miles in the parish; it is apparently a new road, the breadth is 27 feet.

ANCIENT TOPOGRAPHY

Standing stone

There is an old "clogh" or standing stone in Timpenny townland.

SOCIAL ECONOMY

General Remark

Same as the parish of Clogher.

School

[Table] Cullynane townland, Protestants 55, Catholics 21, males 52, females 24, total 76 [pupils]; supported by the Hibernian Society, not known when established.

Manor of Blessington: Townlands

Reheck, Relessey, Teircare, Beagh, Colenane, Mullaghmore, Crockaleven, Kananelly: [proprietor] N. Montgomery Esquire.

Parish of Ardstraw, County Tyrone

Memoir by John Fleming Tait and J. Hill Williams, January 1831

Natural Features

Hills

The principal hills in the parish of Ardstraw are Bessy Bell, Ligfordrum, Mary Gray and Magheracreggan. The most prominent of these is the mountain of Bessy Bell. Its height is 1,386 feet above the level of the sea and 1,000 feet above the adjacent valleys and streams. This mountain at first sight appears to be an isolated feature, but is found on further examination to form a connection between the Sawel range of hills and those of Lough Derg. It is of a oval form and runs north and south, and consequently the steepest banks are the eastern and western. Its southern base is terminated by the Fairy water, its eastern and northern by the Strule river and its western by lakes Catherine, Fanny and Mary in Baronscourt demesne.

Bessy Bell is 6 miles long from the northern to the southern base and 4 miles from the eastern to the western. It is cultivated in some parts to the height of 800 feet above the level of the sea. It is situated on the eastern boundary of the parish and is partly in the adjoining parish of Cappagh. That part of it which is in Ardstraw is principally the property of the Marquis of Abercorn, who has lately much improved it by planting 5 acres with larch, beech and fir trees.

Mary Gray is situated 1 mile to the east of the town of Newtownstewart, and is separated from Bessy Bell by the River Strule. Properly speaking it is not a hill, being only the termination of a ridge of the mountain of Mullaghcarn which runs in a north westerly direction. The height of the part called Mary Gray is only 626 feet above the level of the sea and 500 feet above the adjacent country. Its breadth from base to base is 2 miles and it is washed on the north side by the Glennelly river. There are no plantations on this hill, the ground being very rocky and broken. It is principally the property of Arthur W.C. Hamilton Esquire.

Ligfordrum mountain is situated 6 miles northward of the town of Newtownstewart, the summit being the extreme northern point of Ardstraw parish. It is the termination of the range of mountains running from Sawel in a westerly direction, and is 1,343 feet above the level of the sea and 1,200 feet above the country to the west and north.

Lakes

There are [5] lakes in this parish, viz. Lough Catherine, Lough Fanny, Lough Mary, Maghera lough, Emvagh lough. Lough Catherine is situated in the demesne of Baronscourt, 190 feet above the level of the sea. It is 1 mile English long, 300 yards broad, varies in depth from [blank] to [blank] feet and contains 106 superficial acres. In the middle of this lake lies Island McHugh, which is flat and of an oval form, 180 feet from north to south and 132 from east to west. It is planted and it adds much beauty to the appearance of the surrounding scenery.

Lough Fanny, in the demesne of Baronscourt 154 yards south west of Lough Catherine and connected with it by a channel, is 190 feet above the level of the sea. It is [blank] long, [blank] broad, from [blank] feet to [blank] feet deep and contains [blank] superficial acres.

Lough Mary, in the demesne of Baronscourt [blank] south west of Lough Fanny and connected with it by a stream, is [blank] feet above the level of the sea. It is [blank] long, [blank] broad, from [blank] feet to [blank] feet deep and contains [blank] superficial acres.

Maghera lough is situated in the townland of Creery at an elevation of 300 feet above the level of the sea. It is 33 acres 3 roods 3 perches in extent and from 10 to 30 feet deep.

Woods

At Woodhills in the townland of Birnaghs there remains a quantity of brushwood, part of a natural wood (oak) which was cut down in the year 1810 by Mr Knox, late Bishop of Derry and sold. There are remains of natural oak in the townlands of Mulvin and Lisky.

Modern Topography

Towns

The principal town in this parish is Newtownstewart. In addition to the above there are several villages, viz. Ardstraw and Magheracreggan. Magheracreggan is a small village situated near the western boundary of the parish, containing 9 houses of 2-storeys and 6 of 1-storey, all of which are thatched and present a dirty appearance. It

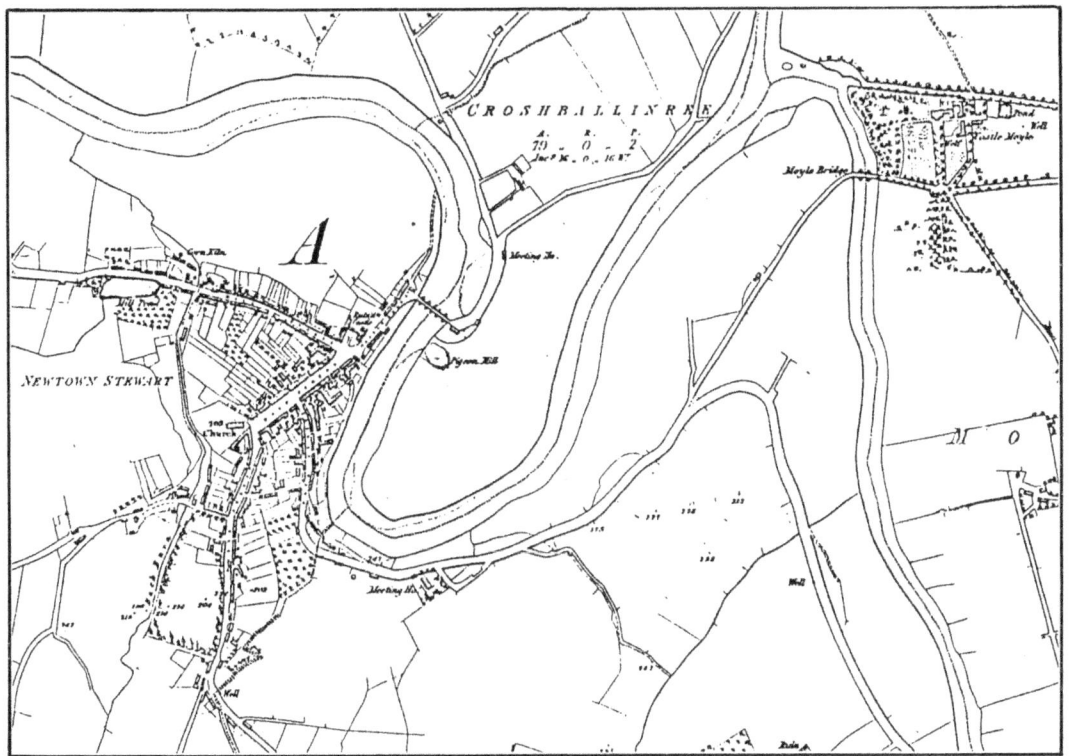

Map of Newtownstewart from the first 6" O.S. maps, 1830s

contains no public buildings. There are 2 fairs held there annually but no markets. The inhabitants are farmers or labourers. Customs are paid to the Marquis of Abercorn. The traffic of the town is cattle, pigs and sheep. List of trades: grocer 1, spirit dealer 1.

Public Buildings: Presbyterian Meeting Houses

The Presbyterian meeting house, situated in the village of Ardstraw, is a rectangular building of unhewn stone and in good repair, 79 feet long and 33 feet broad. It was rebuilt in the year 1796. The present minister is the Reverend Mathew Clarke.

A Presbyterian meeting house is situated in the townland of Drumlegagh. It is a plain stone building of the following shape and dimensions: [ground plan, main dimensions 60 by 42 feet, "T" shape]. It accommodates 450 persons and the average attendance is from 200 to 400. It was built in the year 1785 at an expense of 410 pounds, defrayed by the congregation. The present minister is the Reverend Andrew Maxwell, with an income of 110 pounds per annum, of which 70 pounds are regium donum and 40 pounds stipend.

Altaclady meeting house is situated in the townland of Clady Blair on the road between Strabane and Ardstraw, at the distance of three-quarters of a mile from the latter. It is a plain slated building, 60 feet long and 28 feet broad, lighted by 10 windows. The present minister is the Reverend Thomas Kernaghan.

Gentlemen's Seats

Cross House, the residence of Alexander William Colqhoun Esquire, is a good 2-storey house situated in the townland of Crosh, on the road between Newtownstewart and Tobermore at the distance of three-quarters of a mile from the former. It was built in the year 1835 by A.W. Colquoun Esquire on the site of the old house erected by Major Colquoun, the great-grandfather of the present proprietor.

Woodbrook, the residence of William Tagert Esquire, is a good 2-storey house built of stone, situated in the townland of Birnaghs on the road between Newtownstewart and Castlederg, 1 and three-quarter miles from the former. It was built about the year 1765 by Samuel Tagert Esquire, the father of the present proprietor. There is a garden annexed and it has been improved and ornamented with planting by William Tagert Esquire within the last 20 years.

Mulvin Parks, the residence of William Auchinleck Esquire, situated in the townland of [blank] on the new road between Newtownstewart and Strabane at the distance of 3 and a half miles from the former, is a simple 1-storey house built of unhewn stone. It was built by the proprietor William Auchinleck Esquire in the year 1827 and cost 200 pounds. The grounds were at the same time improved and planted with spruce and larch fir at an expense of about 2,000 pounds. It has 1 large garden.

Mills

[Table contains the following headings: situation and description, date of erection, proprietor, type and dimensions of wheels, fall of water, single or double geared, type of machinery, observations].

Flax mill in the townland of Ballyrennan, on the coach road from Enniskillen to Derry, 2 miles from Newtownstewart, in good repair, erected about 1825, proprietor John [McCreary, McCreavy or McEreavy]; breast wheel, 10 and a half feet by 14 inches, cog wheel 6 feet, fall of water 9 feet, single geared, wooden machinery; supplied by the Pulrory burn, which rises in the bog on Bessy Bell mountain and falls into Lough Catherine; works only about 6 months in the year on an average, the supply of water failing in summer.

Corn mill in the townland of Ballyrennan, 70 yards [?] west on the road from Drumquin to Newtownstewart, 2 miles from the latter, in good repair, erected about 1750, proprietor John [McCreary, McCreavy or McEreavy]; breast wheel, 12 feet by 18 inches, diameter of cog wheel 7 feet, fall of water 10 feet, single geared, wooden machinery; water supplied by the Pulrory burn, works about 6 months during the year.

Saw mill in the townland of Ballyrennan, on the Pulrory burn 300 yards west of corn mill, built of wood and in good repair, cost 700 pounds, erected 1834, proprietor the Marquis of Abercorn; breast wheel, 15 feet by 4 feet 6 inches, diameter of cog wheel 5 feet, double geared, cast iron machinery with 3 circular steel saws, 2 feet in diameter; water supplied by the Pulrory burn, works on an average 7 months during the year.

Flax mill in the townland of Milltown, 300 yards south west of bridge over the River Derg on the road from Strabane to Newtownstewart, 2 and a half miles from the latter, in good repair, built about 1780, rebuilt in 1825, proprietor John Smith; breast wheel, 13 feet by 2 feet 8 inches, diameter of cog wheel 6 feet, fall of water 9 feet, single geared, wooden machinery; water supplied by the outlet of Lough Catherine which discharges itself in the River Derg, works on an average 8 months during the year, supply of water not constant.

Newtownstewart corn mill is in the town, off Mill Street; it is in good repair, date of erection not known, proprietor King Barton Esquire, breast wheel 14 feet by 24 inches, diameter of cog wheel 7 and a half feet, fall of water 9 feet, single geared, wooden machinery; water supplied by the Back burn, which rises in the townland of Newtownstewart and falls into the Strule; the supply is not good during the summer and it works on an average 8 months in the year.

Woodbrook flax mill, in the townland of Birnaghs north of Woodbrook House, extensive and in good repair, erected in 1765, changed from a bleach mill into a flax mill in 1835, proprietor William Tagert Esquire; breast wheel, 14 feet by 3 feet, diameter of cog wheel 7 feet, fall of water 6 feet, double geared, machinery wooden and cast iron; water supplied by the outlet of Lough Catherine, works during the whole year.

Ardstraw corn mill, in the townland of Milltown, in good repair, erected in 1740, repaired in 1835, proprietor John Chambers; breast wheel, 14 feet by 14 inches, diameter of cog wheel 7 feet, fall of water 8 feet, single geared, wooden machinery; water supplied by the outlet of Lough Catherine, works only 3 months in the year.

Tuck mill, in the townland of Birnaghs 3 and a half furlongs south of Woodbrook in the open air, erected in 1808, proprietor John Baskin, breast wheel, 13 feet 4 inches by 14 inches, no cog wheel, fall of water 7 feet, only 1 wheel, wooden machinery; nearly a constant supply of water from Lough Catherine, works during 9 months (there being no cloth to dress from the 1st of May to the 1st of August).

Corn mill, in the townland of Killymore, 70 yards north of road between Newtownstewart and Cookstown 2 miles distant from the former, in good repair, erected in 1826, proprietor John Buchanan, breast wheel, 13 feet by 1 foot 9 inches, diameter of cog wheel 7 feet 6 inches, fall of water 7 feet, single geared, wooden machinery; water supplied by a stream which rises in the mountain in the townland of Dunbunrawer in the parish of Lower Bodoney.

Drumlegagh corn mill, 1 foot 4 and a half inches by 12 feet, breast wheel.

Drumlegagh flax mill, 1 foot 4 inches by 12 feet, undershot wheel.

Magheracreggan flax mill, 1 foot 6 inches by 12 feet, undershot wheel.

Parish of Ardstraw

Magheracreggan corn mill, 1 foot 10 inches by 12 feet, undershot wheel.

Scarvagherin flax mill, 1 foot 6 inches by 12 feet, undershot wheel.

Crew Upper corn mill, 1 foot 4 inches by 12 feet, undershot wheel.

Communications

There are several principal roads in this parish. The first of these is the line from Newtownstewart to the city of Londonderry. Its length in the parish is 5 miles and its average spread with the footpath is 36 feet. It is a macadamised road, is well and judiciously laid out and is kept in repair at the expense of the county. It was made at the expense of the county. Its direction is north west.

The road from Newtownstewart to Omagh runs in a southerly direction for 2 miles in this parish. Its average breadth is 21 feet. It is a well laid out road and is also macadamised. It is kept in repair by the county. It was made at the expense of the county and forms along with the above mentioned road part of the line between Derry and Dublin.

The road from Newtownstewart to Drumquin runs in a south westerly direction in the parish for 6 and a half miles. Its average spread is 21 feet and it is kept in repair by the county, as most of the roads in this county are. It is macadamised.

The road from Newtownstewart to Castlederg runs in the parish in a westerly direction for 7 and three-quarter miles. It is a handsome and well laid out road and was made at the expense of the county. It is repaired by the county. Its average breadth is 20 feet.

The line from Newtownstewart to Cookstown and Gortin runs in an easterly direction for 2 and a half miles in the parish. It is very well laid out and is a gravel road. Its average breadth is 16 feet.

There is a line of road from Strabane to Drumquin running north and south in the parish for 8 and a half miles. Its average breadth is 20 feet.

The road from Newtownstewart to Tobermore runs for 3 miles in a north east direction through the parish, [made] by the county and repaired by the county, in very bad condition, [blank] broad.

The crossroads are not unnecessarily numerous. They are, however, in general not in very good order. They are sometimes made at the expense of the county and at others of the landed proprietors through whose farms they run.

Bridges

There are several bridges of a considerable magnitude in this parish. One of the principal of these is that over the River Strule at Newtownstewart: it was built about the year 1727. It is in bad condition and is very narrow, the breadth being only 13 feet. The length is 300 feet. It is built of unhewn stone and has 6 arches. The approach to it is by a narrow street called Castle Road. This bridge is situated on the road from Newtownstewart to Tobermore in the county of Londonderry. Its height above the water is 20 feet. The breadth of the river at this part is 270 feet. It was made by the county and kept in repair at the expense of the county.

Ardstraw old bridge is situated on the road from Newtownstewart to Castlederg and passes over the River Derg which is there 180 feet broad. It is an old structure of unhewn stone, with 6 arches, built about the year [blank], total length 270 feet, breadth 12 and a half feet. It is kept in repair at the expense of the county.

Ardstraw new bridge is situated on the road between Strabane and Newtownstewart at the distance of 2 and a half miles from the latter. It passes over the River Derg, the breadth of which is there 160 feet. It is a good modern structure of unhewn stone with 5 arches. It was built in the year 1814 at the expense of the county and cost above 1,200 pounds. In the middle of the western parapet there is a stone with the following inscription: "This bridge was built under the inspection of Sir John Burgoyne, James Sinclair, William McClintock and Jones Crawford Esquires. John Quin, overseer, G.S. Arnold and John Campbell, architects, 1814." Its total length is 290 feet and breadth 40 feet.

Moyle bridge, on the road between Newtownstewart and Cookstown, is thrown over the River Strule before its junction with the River Glennelly. It is 280 feet long and [blank] broad. The Strule is 165 feet broad at the bridge, which is built of unhewn stone, consists of 3 arches and is kept in good repair. It was built by the county in 1750 and is kept in repair by it.

SOCIAL ECONOMY

Local Government

The following are the magistrates in this parish (none of them are stipendiary): Major Crawford J.P., lives at Newtownstewart; Major John Humphreys J.P., Baronscourt; William Tagert Esquire, J.P., Woodbrook; Alexander William Colqhoun Esquire, J.P., Cross House.

The usual number of constabulary police stationed in Newtownstewart is four, who are under the orders of Lieutenant Fitzmaurice, Strabane. There are no revenue police nearer than Gortin, 5 miles from Newtownstewart in the parish of Lower Bodoney.

Petty sessions are held in Newtownstewart one Thursday in every month, in the petty sessions room hired for the purpose near the post office. There are generally 3 of the above named magistrates in attendance. The number of outrages committed is small, and they are generally the result of drunken riots. Illicit distilling has been decreasing for several years since the establishment of the revenue police and also by the exertions of the magistates, so that there is little or none now carried on in this parish.

School Statistics

[Table contains the following headings: name, situation and description, income and expenditure, physical, intellectual and moral instruction, number of pupils subdivided by age, sex, religion, name and religious persuasion of master and mistress].

Parochial school, Mill Street in Newtownstewart, established 1820 and given for a parish school by the ancestors of the present Charles Gardener Esquire; income: the Reverend Doctor Nash 5 pounds per annum, Charles J. Gardener Esquire 6 pounds 6s per annum, from pupils 20 pounds per annum; intellectual education: books not furnished by any society, Bible and testament, arithmetic, mensuration and English grammar; moral education: pupils are examined in the Holy Scriptures by the rector and curate; number of pupils: males, 19 under 10 years of age, 15 from 10 to 15, 6 above 15, 40 total males; females, 6 under 10 years of age, 3 from 10 to 15, 9 total females; 49 total number of pupils, 30 Protestants, 16 Presbyterians, 3 Roman Catholics; master William Noble, Protestant.

Newtownstewart national school, situated on the high road to Omagh (slated), established August 1835; the income from the board is not yet known; intellectual education: geography, geology, history, physiology, natural philosophy and the whole course of an English, mercantile and mathematical education; moral education: each child catechised according to the directions of its parents, Authorised and Douay Version; number of pupils: males, 55 under 10 years of age, 38 from 10 to 15, 18 above 15, 101 total males; females, 41 under 10 years of age, 28 from 10 to 15, 16 above 15, 85 total females; 186 total number of pupils, 60 Protestants, 38 Presbyterians, 88 Roman Catholics; master and mistress: P. O'Brien, Roman Catholic and Sarah Hopkins, Roman Catholic.

Mercantile and classic school in the Main Street, Newtownstewart, established July 1834; income: none from public societies or benevolent individuals, 20 pounds per annum from pupils; intellectual education: the Scriptures of the Old and New Testament, Kildare Place books as far as the teacher can influence the parents to procure them; moral education: visited by the rector and Presbyterian clergymen; number of pupils: males, 4 under 10 years of age, 11 from 10 to 15, 15 total males; females, 2 under 10 years of age, 1 from 10 to 15, 3 total females; 18 total number of pupils, 7 Protestants, 7 Presbyterians, 4 other denominations; master the Reverend D. Fulton, Seceding minister.

Ardstraw school, in the village of Ardstraw, connected with the London Hibernian Society in 1822; income: 1d per week from each pupil who is able; expenditure: 8 or 9 pounds paid by the society and 9d for every pupil that has acquired proficiency; intellectual education: books furnished by the Hibernian Society, Bible, testament and spelling books; moral education: visited by the Reverend John Martin, Seceding minister, and the Reverend Thomas Kernaghan, Presbyterian minister, Protestant version; number of pupils: males, 30 under 10 years of age, 15 from 10 to 15, 45 total males; females, 24 under 10 years of age, 10 from 10 to 15, 5 above 15, 39 total females; 84 total number of pupils, 7 Protestants, 58 Presbyterians, 15 Roman Catholics, 4 other denominations; master is Presbyterian.

Drumleggagh, at the back of Drumleggagh meeting house, established 1824; income: London Hibernian Society 12 pounds 12s per annum and Lord Abercorn 5 pounds per annum, from pupils 7 pounds per quarter; intellectual education: spelling, reading, writing and arithmetic; moral education: the Reverend Andrew Maxwell, Presbyterian minister visits, the Scriptures are read; number of pupils: males, 23 under 10 years of age, 45 from 10 to 15, 5 above 15, 73 total males; females, 45 under 10 years of age, 25 from 10 to 15, 2 above 15, 72 total females; 145 total pupils, 2 Protestants, 98 Presbyterians, 45 Roman Catholics; master Arthur Foster, Presbyterian.

Erganagh, 2 miles from Castlederg on the high road to Newtownstewart, established 1825; income: Lord Abercorn 5 pounds per annum, from pupils 1s per quarter each; intellectual education: general school books; moral education: the Scriptures are read and catechisms are taught; number of pupils: males, 33 under 10 years of age, 27 from 10 to 15, 3 above 15, 63 total males; females, 18 under 10 years of age, 11 from 10 to 15, 1 above 15, 30 total females; 93 total number

Parish of Ardstraw

of pupils, 9 Protestants, 66 Presbyterians, 28 Roman Catholics; master John McEwen, Presbyterian.

A neat cottage in Magheracreggan townland, established July 1833; income: Lord Abercorn 5 pounds per annum, from pupils 1s 1d per quarter each; intellectual education: books furnished by the Kildare Street Society; moral education: the Scriptures are read and catechisms taught; number of pupils: males, 27 under 10 years of age, 31 from 10 to 15, 1 above 15, 59 total males; females, 31 under 10 years of age, 3 from 10 to 15, 34 total females; 93 total number of pupils, 25 Protestants, 55 Presbyterians, 13 Roman Catholics; master John Forbes, Protestant.

A cabin in Priestsessagh townland, established 1835; income: Lord Abercorn 5 pounds per annum, from pupils 1s 3d per quarter; intellectual education: general school books; moral education: the Scriptures are read and catechisms taught; number of pupils: males, 27 under 10 years of age, 10 from 10 to 15, 37 total males; females, 28 under 10 years of age, 28 total females; 65 total number of pupils, 51 Presbyterians, 14 Roman Catholics; master James Dogherty, Roman Catholic.

Sunday Schools

[Table with headings: situation and average attendance].

1 in Newtownstewart church, attendance 100.

1 in Presbyterian meeting house, Newtownstewart, attendance 50.

1 in Seceding meeting house, Newtownstewart, attendance 40.

1 in Wesleyan Methodist chapel, Newtownstewart, attendance 100.

1 in Ardstraw schoolhouse, attendance 80.

1 in Drumclanf, attendance 70.

1 in Drumclanf, attendance 80.

1 in Seceding meeting house, Drumleggagh, attendance 200.

1 in Altacladdy Presbyterian meeting house.

1 in Kilstrawl, attendance 46.

1 in Killane, attendance 30.

1 in Roman Catholic chapel near Newtownstewart, attendance 100.

NATURAL STATE AND SOCIAL ECONOMY

Newtownstewart: Locality and Extent

Newtownstewart is 96 miles distant from Dublin, in latitude [blank] north and longitude [blank] west, in the diocese of Derry, province of Ulster, county of Tyrone, parish of Ardstraw and north west circuit of assize. It is situated on the left bank of the River Strule, on the road between the cities of Dublin and Londonderry. Its extreme length from north east to south west is 3 furlongs and its extreme breadth from east to west is 2 and one-third furlongs. It is 200 feet above the level of the sea and pleasantly situated.

Population and Religion

According to the census taken by the government commissioners in 1831, the population of Newtownstewart was Protestants 811, Roman Catholics 636, Presbyterians 353, total 1,800.

MODERN TOPOGRAPHY

Principal Buildings

The principal buildings and public institutions in the town are the church, the Methodist meeting house, the hotel, the bridge, [blank] schoolhouses and the private residence of Major Crawford, the post office, police barracks and dispensary.

Church

The church, a plain rectangular building with a square tower and spire 93 feet long and 31 feet broad, is situated at the south western end of the Main Street. It contains a gallery on the north side and is lighted by 7 windows, 2 of which are on the north side, 3 on the south, 1 at the east and 1 small one at the west. The average attendance is [blank] people, and it accommodates [blank]. It was erected in the year [blank] and rebuilt in the year 1727 by Dr John Hall, then rector of this parish, and previously vice-provost of Trinity College Dublin.

Inscriptions in Church

It contains 5 marble monuments with the following inscriptions on white marble tablets.

1, "To the memory of the reverend Gerald Fitzgerald, late rector of this parish, and formerly vice-provost of the University of Dublin, descended from John, first Lord Decies and Desmond, AD 1250" etc. He died on the 10th of March 1519, in the 80th year of his age. "Also to the memory of his wife Elizabeth" who died on the 14th of September 1818 aged 60 "this monument is placed by the piety of their children in testimony of their love, respect and sorrow."

2, "Underneath are deposited the remains of Frederick Fitzgerald Esquire, son of the rector of this parish and lieutenant in the 20th regiment of foot. The baleful effects of the Walcheren expedition and his subsequent exertions in the Peninsular War, terminated by slow degrees his pure and honourable life on the 6th day of March 1817, in the 25th year of his age. This monument was erected in memory of his many estimable qualities as a son, brother, relative and friend."

3, "The Reverend Thomas Wilson D.D., formerly a senior fellow of Trinity College Dublin and rector of this parish, died on the 22nd day of September 1790 in the 75th year of his age."

4, "Sacred to the memory of the Right Reverend George Hall D.D., formerly rector of this parish, this tablet is inscribed by the desire of the inhabitants." (He became provost of the University of Dublin, and afterwards Bishop of Dromore, which last dignity he only enjoyed for 5 days; he died on the 23rd of November 1811, in the 59th year of his age).

5, This monument was taken down on building the gallery, it contains the following inscription: "Here lieth the body of John Hall D.D., who died on the 13th day of April in the year of Our Lord 1735, and the 78th year of his age. He was son of William Hall, gentleman, and grandson of Sir William Hall of the county of Kent. He was born in the county of Cork, and educated there until he entered Trinity College near Dublin, of which in the year 1685 he was chosen fellow, and in the year 1697, vice-provost." In this station he remained 16 years, and was presented to this living of Ardstraw in the year 1713. "This church was rebuilt under his care" etc. "He left an estate of 120 pounds per annum for the educating 2 young men in the college and other charitable uses mentioned in his will, and his library, a very valuable collection, to the diocese of Raphoe <Rapho>. This monument was erected to his memory by his grateful wife Mrs Susanna Hall, daughter of Mr Richard Harvey, late merchant in Cork."

Presbyterian Meeting Houses

The Presbyterian Synod of Ulster meeting house, situated in Back Street, is a plain building 72 feet long and 26 feet broad, lighted by 13 windows. It was built in the year 1802 at an expense of about 400 pounds (no accounts were kept), raised by private subscription. It was repaired in 1828 at an expense of 50 pounds supplied by the congregation, and the green was ornamented with shrubs and flowers by voluntary work performed by the members of the congregation. The average attendance is 230 and the building accommodates 500 persons. The present incumbent is the Reverend Charles Adams, with an income of 100 pounds per annum, regium donum included.

The Seceding Presbyterian meeting house, situated near the bridge at Newtownstewart on the road to Tobermore, is a simple building in good repair, 50 feet long and 28 feet broad. It accommodates 240 persons and the average attendance is 130. It was built in the year 1828 and cost 273 pounds, raised by private subscription. Incumbent the Reverend John Martin, income regium donum 50 pounds Irish, stipend variable.

Methodist Chapels

The Wesleyan Methodist chapel in Back Lane is a plain building in tolerable repair, lighted by 4 windows and 41 feet long by 27 feet in breadth. It was built by private subscription in the year 1792. It accommodates 150 persons and the numbers in attendance varies from 50 to 80. The ministers are the Reverend John Jebb (Newtownstewart), income 50 pounds per annum, the Reverend Edward Hazleton (Omagh).

The Primitive Wesleyan Methodist chapel in Back Street is a building in good repair, 52 feet long and 28 feet broad, erected by subscription in the year 1818 at an expense of 300 pounds. It accommodates 230 persons and the average attendance is 130. The ministers are Mr Adam Ford and Mr John Hurst.

Roman Catholic Chapel

The Roman Catholic chapel, situated in the townland of Glenknock or Cloghogle, 75 yards north west of the road between Newtownstewart and Tobermore and at the distance of 5 furlongs from the former, is a rectangular building in the form of the letter T, 72 feet in length and 57 feet in extreme breadth, containing 3 galleries and lighted by 12 windows. It accommodates 1,500 persons and the average attendance is 1,000. It was built by private subscription about the year 1785, and repaired with additions in the year 1823 at an expense of 150 pounds, raised by private subscription. In the year 1834 a temporary wooden steeple and belfry, resting upon a square brick base, was erected at the side of the chapel. Its total height is 53 feet and it contains a bell weighing 330 pounds. Incumbent the Reverend Philip Porter P.P.

Rectory and Glebe House

The rectory or living of Ardstraw was presented to Trinity College Dublin by King James I, probably at the commencement of the year 1639

Parish of Ardstraw

as the first incumbent was nominated on the 11th February of that year. It was formerly said to be worth 1,800 pounds per annum, but of late years has been considerably reduced. It is still, however, one of the most valuable in the province of Ulster.

The Glebe House is commonly called Moyle House or Moyle Castle. It receives the latter name in consequence of being built close to the ruins of an old castle which formerly belonged to a branch of the O'Neill family. This ruin was converted into a summer house by one of the former incumbents. The present dwelling house was built in the year 1727 by Dr John Hall. It has a solid old-fashioned but comfortable appearance, is surrounded with a few trees and is situated half a mile to the east of Newtownstewart at the junction of the Strule and Glennelly rivers.

SOCIAL ECONOMY

Incumbents of Ardstraw

The following is the list of the former incumbents of this living:
1, Richard Winter, nominated the 11th February 1639.
2, Caesar Wilkinson, nominated the 15th February 1660.
3, Adam Usher, nominated the 19th August 1680.
4, John Hall, nominated the 14th September 1713.
5, Robert Shaw, nominated in 1740.
6, John Palisier, nominated the 16th March 1758.
7, Thomas Leland, nominated the 27th May 1781.
8, Thomas Wilson, nominated the 28th January 1786.
9, George Hall, nominated the 27th February 1800.
10, Gerald Fitzgerald, nominated the 27th August 1806.
11, Richard Herbert Nash, the present rector, nominated the 18th August 1819.

In the above list there are the names of 2 or 3 men eminent for their talents. The first of these is Thomas Leland, whose eloquence in the pulpit was only surpassed by his powers of writing. He was the author of the *History of Ireland* and of the *Life of Philip of Macedon*, and was also the translator of Demosthenes and several other works. Dr George Hall, Bishop of Dromore, was celebrated as a linguist and as a preacher. He resided in the parish for 5 years.

Coaches

[Table contains the following headings: coaches, from, to, days of passing, hours, proprietors, when established]. The following coaches pass through Newtownstewart.

Royal Mail from Londonderry to Dublin, passes every day at 10 a.m., from Dublin to Londonderry every day at 4 p.m.

Shareholder (day coach) from Strabane to Dublin, passes on Monday, Wednesday and Friday at 6.40 a.m. and returns the other days except Sunday at 8.30 p.m.; [owned] in 500 shares, established September 1835.

Wonder (day coach) from Omagh to Londonderry, passes every day (Sunday excepted) at 7.30 a.m., returns same evening 7.30 p.m., proprietors Mr Clarke Mathewson and James Wilson, Strabane, established 1829.

Eclipse (day coach), from Omagh to Londonderry, passes every day (Sunday excep-ted) at 7.30 a.m., returns same evening 7.30 p.m., proprietor John Harkin, Omagh, established 1833.

There are 6 cars kept for hire.

Dispensary Reports in 1834 and 1835

A copy of surgeon's report of the Ardstraw dispensary from 5th March 1834 to 11th March 1835: remaining on books 5th March 1834, 167 patients, since which 1,420 have been recommended, viz. 98 cases of fever, 80 rheumatism, 96 accidents, 152 obstipates and its consequences, 115 catarrhal complaints, 102 smallpox, 97 stomach complaints, 121 worms and other intestinal disorders, 48 whooping <hooping> cough and 511 other complaints; of which number 149 remain on the books at present, 30 have died, 1 sent to the county infirmary and the remaining 1,407 have been cured or relieved. [Signed] J.W. Hamilton, surgeon R.S.

Copy of surgeon's report of the Ardstraw dispensary from 11th March 1835 to 31st December following: remaining on books 11th March 1835 149 patients, since which time 1,096 have been recommended, viz. 87 cases of fever, 43 rheumatism, 104 dyspepsia, 124 obstipates and its consequences, 14 measles, 6 smallpox, 31 whooping cough, 129 worms and other intestinal disorders, 93 itch, 91 catarrhal complaints, 87 wounds and accidents, 416 other complaints. Of the above number, 2 have been sent to hospital, 19 have died, 95 are on the books at present and the remaining 1,129 were cured or relieved. [Signed] J.W. Hamilton, surgeon R.S.

Statistical Report by Lieutenant W. Lancey, 4th February 1834

NATURAL STATE

Locality and Extent

Ardstraw is situated in the barony of Strabane, county Tyrone and diocese of Derry. It is a very extensive parish, having its northern mearing within 3 miles of the canal head at Strabane [and] its southern within 3 miles of Omagh, the county town. On the east it approaches within 3 miles of Gortin, on the south west 2 of Drumquin, on the west 1 of Castlederg. [It] possesses in itself the market town of Newtownstewart within 2 miles of its south eastern boundary and contains 44,974 acres of land, the greater part of which is under cultivation and a considerable portion of it valuable.

Mountains

The mountains of Mullacroy, Bessy Bell, Mary Gray and Ballinatibert run through the southern end of the parish; those of Gallon and Craignatogue bound it on the east, Ballycarney, Douglas, Koram, Meenyshesk, Claddy hill, Whiskey hill and Priestsessagh on the north and the lowlands of the parish of Skirts on the west.

Rivers

The Fairy water, flowing from the west, divides the southern part of this parish from East to West Longfield and Drumreagh, and falls into the Strule <Strewel> about a mile and a quarter north of Omagh at the Poe bridge over the mail road.

The Strule here about [blank] feet in breadth and flows pleasantly through Mountjoy forest until it again meets the parish of Ardstraw about [blank] miles from the rectory at Moyle Glebe, where it receives from the east the Glennelly draining the mountains of Badoney. The Strule is now about [blank] feet in breadth and winds under the town of Newtownstewart which stands on its left bank. At the townland of Birniaghs it receives from the west the river which drains Lough Derg and the greatest part of Termonmaguirk, Skirts and all the central parts of this parish west of the Strule and Mourne <Morne>, the latter name being given to the great stream now [blank] feet wide after its confluence with the Derg. The Mourne continues through the rest of the parish and receives the drainage of the Lisfordrum mountain district through the channel of the Douglas burn, a stream of small importance.

Lakes

There are 5 lakes in the parish, 3 in the demesne of Baronscourt, called Catherine, Mary and Fanny, the names of the late marquis's daughters; 1 at Magheracriggan and 1 at Envagh. The principal one at Baronscourt is upwards of a mile in length <lenth>. That at Magheracriggan contains 33 acres, but that of Envagh is of small dimensions <dimentions>.

General Appearance

In a hilly country of such extent its appearance <apperance> varies considerably, but as a whole it is one of the best and most fertile parishes in the northern portion of Tyrone. The central and western districts are well cultivated and present an appearance of wealth and independence not usually met with. Enlivened with the beautiful demesne of Baronscourt, the strikingly situated town of Newtownstewart, the rectory and several gentlemen's houses, good farming establishments and bleach greens, bounded with belts of plantations or studded with trees, this parish with its rivers, mountains and woods presents a cheerful and interesting landscape.

MODERN TOPOGRAPHY

Gentlemen's Seats: Demesnes and Buildings

Baronscourt, the Marquis of Abercorn's demesne, lies in a valley between the mountains of Bessy Bell and Mullaghcroy. The mansion is built of freestone and is a modern building erected by the present nobleman's grandfather [marginal note: date ?]. Considerable improvements and alterations are about to be made to it immediately. It stands on the east bank of Lough Mary and is embosomed on 3 sides with trees, the fourth being a terrace and parterres of flowers. The landscape is very limited, lying in a narrow valley, and the woods embracing the loughs in broad belts extending 3 miles in length, the greatest breadth being about [blank] miles. The present marquis has given directions to fill up with plantations the arable spaces between the demesne and the roads, which run nearly parallel with it, leading from Drumquin to Newtownstewart. The demesne is kept in neat order and no persons are allowed to enter its gates unless by written permission of the agent.

The Glebe House, an old building, is pleasantly situated to the east of Newtownstewart at the meeting of the waters of the Glennelly and Strule. It was built by Dr Hall in 1725. It is surrounded with old trees and wears an aspect of comfort and retirement.

There are several smaller snug residences in the parish, but none that require particular description, being farmhouses of a better kind, inhabited by persons who appear not to be dependent altogether on the produce of the soil. Deerpark, Malvin Parks and Mr Colhown's in Croish are amongst this class.

Towns: Newtownstewart

Newtownstewart, the property of William Gardiner of Mountjoy forest, is strikingly situated on the left bank of the Strule at the foot of Bessy Bell. The mail road from Dublin to Derry passes through it. It is a second class town for this part of the north of Ireland. It contains [blank] inhabitants and has a good market on Mondays, every alternate week being a cloth market. It contains no private residence of any consequence, but there are some families residing in it not in trade. Major Crawford, a magistrate and proprietor of land in the neighbourhood, is the principal resident. No chaises or post horses are kept in the inn, which is an inferior establishment.

Places of Worship: Church

The church stands on an eminence at the west end of the town and was rebuilt by Dr John Hall in 1724. It is capable of containing with its gallery [blank] and is generally well attended. The curate also conducts divine service in Drimclamp schoolhouse very frequently.

Methodist Meeting Houses

Two congregations of Methodists, one Wesleyan, the other Church, have their meeting houses in the town. Each will contain 200 persons on forms. These Dissenters have also a house of worship at Lisleen.

Presbyterian Meeting Houses

The old Presbyterian meeting house, lately repaired, stands within a quarter of a mile of the south end of the town on the Dublin road. There are 4 others in the parish. The principal one is at Ardstraw <Arstraw> bridge, fully pewed and lately galleried, another at Garvetagh with pews and galleries. Douglas and Altaclady houses are partly pewed and will shortly be completed. These 5 places of worship adhering to the Synod of Ulster will contain about 1,600 persons.

Seceding Meeting Houses

A Seceders' meeting house stands within a short distance of Newtownstewart on the road to Gortin. It was built in 1828 and cost 273 pounds, obtained by subscription. It is the only ceiled meeting house in the parish. It has pews but no gallery and will contain upwards of 200 persons.

There is another Seceders house at Drimleaghan, capable of holding 200 persons. It is well attended and had an aisle added last summer.

Roman Catholic Chapels

There are 3 Roman Catholic chapels, 1 near Newtownstewart on the Gortin road, 1 in Envagh and the third in Glenrock. These houses are tolerably large, but as they have no pews an estimate of the numbers they will contain cannot be made, but about 500 in each would not be too great. Besides these, the neighbouring towns and adjoining places of worship afford accommodation to those who may be too far from their own immediate pastors.

ANCIENT TOPOGRAPHY

Castles

The sites of 6 castles are still known in the vicinity of Newtownstewart, one in the demesne of Baronscourt built with gables lying on the east of Lough Catherine, the second in the island in the lough, both belonging to the ancient <antient> family of McHugh. Harry Avery's Castle, beautifully situated for prospects and defence and one of the most ancient and principal residences of the O'Neill <O'Neil> family, stands west of north above Newtownstewart. The 2 round towers of the gateway and the platform on which the castle stood only remain. A fourth is now occupied by the ruins of a more modern building with gables thus: [small sketch], erected by Lord Mountjoy and burnt down by King James' forces retreating from the walls of Derry. One of the gables and some chimneys of this castle yet remain, and its walls form portions of modern buildings. The yard is now appropriated to the potato and corn markets.

The fifth site is in the holme across the river near the old bridge. Nothing remains but the small eminence on which the castle stood to secure it from floods. It is now called Pigeon Island.

The sixth castle was situated in Castle Moyle in the grounds of the present Glebe House. No vestige of the building is to be found but the supposed site is still shown near an arbour on the bank of the river.

Tradition regarding Castle

The same tradition respecting the daughter of O'Neill mentioned by Dr Fitzgerald is kept up, to which may be added the following: a person desirous of the exalted alliance with the child of O'Neill demanded her hand. He was informed it should be given, if he could provide a castle for her dwelling in one night. Overwhelmed with distress, he wandered on Bessy Bell to relieve his tortured mind, when a fairy promised him he should have a house for his bride if he would visit the summit of the mountain at midnight. He obeyed and found a magnificent castle, and hastened down for O'Neill. When he was conducting him into the place it all fell together and buried Donald Gorm alive. This accounts for the cairn so called on the summit of the mountain. Dr Fitzgerald states it was a place of worship dedicated to the [blank].

There is no doubt from the large stones that some place of superstition or defence existed there; but a holy well with a penance to carry up a stone not later than 30 years ago easily accounts for the accumulation of smaller fragments of rock, several of which are [? simnite], the hill being of gneiss and talc slate.

Ruined Churches

The ruins of Scarvagherin church are next in importance. The walls and gables remain and the ground is used as a burial place. It is strikingly situated on the right bank of the Derg river. Tradition states it was a monastery.

An old burial ground now divided into 2 portions, one for the Catholics, the other for the Protestants, stands on the left bank of the Derg at Ardstraw bridge. Tradition says there was a church here, and some show its remains built up in the enclosure wall.

There is also an old burial ground at Pubble, with the ruins of an old church on the right bank of the Strule, the gable yet standing.

Cloghogle Stones

There are many forts in the parish and some cloghogle stones. The most perfect of the latter is a slab supported by 3 upright stones at Glenrock, one fallen down near the fort in Croish, a third at Meachy, with only one stone in an upright position called the Giant's Den, one in Castey, a giant's grave at Derrygoon and standing stones in Lower Crew.

Forts

The forts are situated thus: 1 in Archill, 1 in Aghassissy, 1 in Envagh, 1 in Lisnacreaght, 2 in Lisaburny, 1 in Puble, 1 in Lisnafin, 1 in Croish, 1 in Erginagh, 2 in Lislymore, 2 in Teevery, 4 in Knockroe, 1 in Bunderg, 1 in Shannony [marked with an "A"], 1 in Urbalreagh, 2 in Cladyblair, 1 in Killen and Brucklass, 1 at junction of Cladyhallyday and Arstraw, 1 in Lower Crew, 1 in Whitehouse, 1 in Magherycriggan, 4 in Meaghy, 3 in Moyle Glebe, 1 in Strahulter, 2 in Killimore, 1 in the Deerpark, 1 (White Fort) in Magheracotton, 1 in Milltown, 1 in Lisnaferty, 1 in Largybeg, 1 in Baronscourt (Lislea Fort), 3 in Karnkenny and 1 in Kilstrool.

SOCIAL ECONOMY

Inhabitants: Habits of the People

The Marquis of Abercorn is the only nobleman who occasionally resides in the parish. His income, said to be derived from his Irish estates which stretch to New Buildings, including Strabane, amounts to 34,000 pounds per annum. There are no other residents that can be called wealthy, but many who are independent. The farmers have good houses and the inhabitants appear to be equal to if not above the general run of persons of the same rank in the adjacent parishes. The same mistake is made here as elsewhere: short leases with old lives to enable the tenants to vote and the landlords to keep them in subjection.

The morals of the peasantry are not so good as might be wished. Drunkenness and party spirit still abound to a considerable extent, but cock-fighting and private distillation are on the decrease and almost wholly confined to the dregs of the people. The valleys are filled with Protestants, chiefly of the Scotch churches, the mountains are tenanted by Catholics. English is spoken by all but the vernacular tongue of the highlands is Irish, but is on the decrease.

Their dress varies according to their wealth. They are generally well and comfortably clothed. Potatoes and milk with herrings are their chief food. They seldom eat meal; loaf bread is more consumed than formerly, but meal is scarcer as the chief part of the oat crop is exported. The poor usually keep a cow.

The places of worship are much better attended than formerly, and, religious education being more general amongst the present than the last generation, it is hoped morality will assume a higher standard than heretofore.

Schools

The people are generally anxious to educate their

Parish of Ardstraw

children. There are 28 schools in the parish, 7 of which are in Newtownstewart. Mr McElroy teaches the classics in the town and has about 14 scholars at 3 pounds per annum. Mr Noble has the parochial school and is a good English teacher. There are London Hibernian schools in Ardstraw, Drimclamp, Drimlegagh, Lisatunny and Baronscourt. Those of Drumnabony, Erginagh, Foyfin, Tamnagh and Coolaghy are under the Kildare Street Society. The national system is in operation in Tillymark, Teeveny, Golan and Galen, whilst others unconnected with any society are established at Douglas Bridge, Ballyreanan, Birnaghs, Crosh, Kilstrol, Priestsessagh and Glasmullin. The schools at Clare and Magheralough are also under the Hibernian or Kildare Society.

The best schoolhouse is that of Baronscourt, built by the late Marquis of Abercorn and overlooks the demesne. It has a male and female teacher who reside. It is supported by the marquis, who also gives an annuity of 5 pounds to 5 other schools on his estate, each of which is under the Hibernian or Kildare Street Society.

The Drimlegagh school seems to merit the second place. It is also the retiring house of the session of Seceders and stands in the meeting house yard. It was erected by subscription. The Kildare Place Society assisted in the building of Erginagh, Foyfin and Drimclamp houses, and Dr Nash the present rector subscribed to several others.

The number of scholars is not known. Those of Tillymuck amount to 85, principally Catholics. The school at Ardstraw bridge has 70 Protestants, that of Drimlegagh 60, 50 of whom are Protestants. That at Douglas bridge consists of 50 children, two-thirds of whom are Protestants. Knockroe school has only 20 scholars, mostly Catholics, and on an average the schools may be said to educate about 50 each, making a general total of 1,400 children. The terms of education are very low. The masters under the Kildare and Hibernian Society having had their salaries reduced obliged the other masters to lower theirs, and the usual sums now paid vary from 2s 6d to 3s a quarter. The schoolhouses generally are moderately good, but the teachers of the society schools seldom reside in them as there are no accommodations.

Dispensary

This institution is in Newtownstewart. It is the means of relieving annually about 2,000 patients, whose prevailing diseases are fever, rheumatism and stomach complaints. The grand jury gives 30 pounds and 70 pounds are raised from the resident gentry to defray expenses. Dr Hamilton, a naval surgeon, has the charge of it; he resides in town. No persons are relieved who hold lands, however small in quantity.

PRODUCTIVE ECONOMY

Size of Farms and Rent

The farms vary much in size. Those along the banks of the Derg, the most fertile part of the district, run from 40 to 60 acres, the marquis' tenants paying 20 shillings an acre, the bishop's land 7 pounds for 40 acres. Mr Patrick of Ardstraw bridge holds 200 acres churchland, farms 50 and lets the rest. Mr Love of Crew mill has 70 acres from the marquis.

Manures and Farming Societies

The chief manure is lime with compost. The former is obtained from the marquis' quarries at Magheralough for his own tenants, who may raise any quantity for their own use only. The other farmers purchase theirs in West Longfield, 7 miles distant from Ardstraw bridge.

Farming societies are doing some good in the parish.

Prices of Produce

Prices of produce in Strabane market in 1833 are 7d a stone for oats, 15s a barrel for barley, 2d farthing a stone for potatoes, clover hay 35s a ton, meadow hay 25s a ton, wheat 23s a barrel. [Insert marginal note in different hand: this is not an average as 1833 was a remarkably cheap year].

Crops

The usual method of cropping a lea field is first oats, then flax, potatoes, then wheat or oats or barley with clover, clover lea for 2 years, then again wheat. Not much forced grasses yet sown, but wheat is rapidly increasing in the fertile parts of the parish.

Cattle and Horses

Cows worth 5 to 8 guineas are plentiful. The farmers rear the calves, but there is no breeding or grazing farms to any extent. Butter and pigs abound; the immense number carried to Derry in winter from this and the adjacent parishes is surprising.

Good horses for country purposes are common, and some better description of cattle can always be purchased at Mr Colhown's near Newtownstewart. Sheep are scarce.

Fish and Game

There are salmon and trout in the rivers, and hares, partridge, woodcock and grouse on the hills and mountains. The Marquis of Abercorn is raising pheasants in a preserve close to the mansion.

Orchards

Common fruit in the market of Newtownstewart is plentiful in the season, and there are several orchards in the parish.

Mills and Bleach Greens

There is a spade foundry in town, 1 in Aghassey, 1 in Miltown and 1 flax mill; 1 flax mill and 2 corn mills in Drimlegagh, 1 corn mill in Lisnacreaght, 1 flax mill in Knockaniller, 1 corn mill in Upper Crew, 1 flax mill in Killen, 1 flax mill in Knockroe, 1 corn and 1 flax mill in Magheracriggan, 1 flax mill in Magheralough, 1 in Killymore, 1 corn mill on the Glennelly river, 1 corn and 1 flax mill in Ballyreanan, 1 tuck mill in Birnaghs, and 2 bleach greens, 1 at Woodbrook, the other at Skinbwee close to Douglas Bridge.

Woodbrook is not worked; that at Skinbwee is doing little except keeping the machinery in order. Its water wheel is 21 feet in diameter. Only 7 men are now employed in this green. The water wheels of the corn mills are from 10 to 15 feet in diameter, those of the flax mills smaller. The hammers of the spade foundries are worked by water wheels. The number of spades manufactured has not been ascertained.

Manufacture of Cloth

In addition to the spades mentioned above linen is woven in most parts of the parish. This branch of industry has so much fallen into neglect by reason of its very small profits that a journeyman weaver can earn more money at daily wages than those who grow and prepare the flax. A weaver can earn 12 to 25 shillings for 52 yards of linen in 3 weeks according to the quality. The usual cloth runs 9 to 11 hundreds and sells from 8d to 15d a yard. There from 150 to 200 webs sold every Monday in Newtownstewart market. Common cloth for home use is also manufactured, but not to any great extent as sheep are scarce.

Price of Labour

The price of labour varies from 8d to 10d a day. A farm servant usually receives 3 pounds a half-year with diet, female house servants about 30s for the same period.

MODERN TOPOGRAPHY

Roads

The mail road from Dublin to Derry runs through the parish from south to north for about 7 English miles. Leading roads to Gortin and Castlederg branch from it to the east and west. They are all in a tolerable state of repair as are all the other principal crossroads in the parish.

Bridges

The bridges are good. Those thrown over the Strule are the Castlemoyle and the ancient one from Newtownstewart to the old castle in the holme. Those over the Derg are the new bridge, over which passes the mail road, the ancient one at Ardstraw at the foot of the old burial ground, and Lower Crew bridge, one of a single arch at Douglas, Drumshanbow bridge leading to Drumquin, Monaghan's and the Priest's bridge over the Fairy water, the latter being a plank for foot passengers.

NATURAL FEATURES

Woods and Plantations

There is little natural wood in the parish, but extensive plantations at Baronscourt. Only an old wood stood in the memory of man in the western side of the loughs. There are also belts of plantations and some old trees about many of the farmhouses.

Fuel

The chief fuel is turf. Coals could easily be obtained from Strabane but turf is procured by the farmer for the trouble of cutting it. Bog wood is found in the turf bank, but is not generally allowed to be raised except by permission.

NATURAL HISTORY

Geology

The geology of this parish will be found in its proper place. Suffice it to say that the mountains are of gneiss and talcose slate and the valleys of sandstone. A few veins of primitive blue limestone are quarried, and on the southern boundary are seen the lowest beds of the old red sandstone belonging to the Longfield coal measures. [Signed] William Lancey, Lieutenant Royal Engineers, 4 February 1834.

Parish of Cappagh, County Tyrone

Memoir [by George Scott ?]

Natural Features

Hills

Mullaghcarn, the highest point of which is 1,778 feet above the level of the sea; about three-fourths of this mountain is in the parish of Cappagh <Cappa>, the remainder in the adjoining parish of Lower Bodoney. The top is within 6 miles of Omagh and 2 and a half miles from Mountfield. It forms part of an extensive range of mountains which run north west of the trigonometrical point on this top until it joins Mary Gray's mountain, which is 826 feet above the level of the sea and about 2 miles a little to the south, if east, of Newtownstewart <Newtown Stewart>. This mountain appears chiefly to consist of mica slate, great quantities of which may be found where the streams have formed a chasm for themselves. It is frequently found mixed with carbonate of lime and in many cases fragments of the latter are to be found separate. The church of Mountfield and some of the houses in the neighbourhood are built of this stone.

Lakes

Lough-a-terrive, a small lake situated at the east end of the parish; it is surrounded with mountain, some portion of which is prettily planted. There is generally a small boat kept on the lake for the convenience of fishing which is in some degree preserved. It is a romantic lake, and when viewed from the easterly point appears to some perfection. It abounds with trout but they are so capricious that it is almost impossible to land them with a fly.

Bogs

There is a great quantity of uncultivated ground in this parish, but as it is chiefly mountain ground the heights of the various portions of bog cannot be very well given, as there is not any extent of flat ground on the mountain. There is not more turf cut than will supply the farmers and cotters that live convenient to it.

Woods

In the eastern portion of this parish there is scarcely a tree to be seen. There are some round the shooting lodge belonging to J. Stack Esquire of Dublin, also a small plantation round Faccary Lodge which belongs to Sir William MacMahon of Dublin and a young plantation surrounding the house of the Reverend M.J. Taylor. The former and the latter are within half a mile of Mountfield, the one belonging to Sir W. MacMahon about 2 and a half miles from Mountfield on the Omagh road.

Natural History

Zoology

There are some rivers in the adjoining parishes of Lower Bodoney and Termonmaguirk that afford a good supply of trout.

Modern Topography

Towns: Mountfield

Mountfield is a small village situated on the eastern side of the parish. It has completely been rebuilt in the last 6 or 7 years. It consists of 12 houses, all of which are slated and of equal size. There is but one side to the village, fields being opposite to all the houses. It is a neat little place and generally kept clean.

Public Buildings: Church

The church, which was built in the year 1828, is the only public building in the surrounding country. Its architecture is of the plainest description. It cost 900 pounds which was granted by the Board of First Fruits. It is extremely small and would not accommodate more than 100 persons.

Gentlemen's Residences

The residence of the Reverend M.J. Taylor; shooting lodge belonging to [blank] Stack Esquire; shooting lodge belonging to Sir William MacMahon.

Bleach Mills and Manufactories

Corn mill belonging to Mr McFarlin, overshot wheel, fall of water 4 feet, diameter 15 feet, breadth of buckets 3 and a half feet, townland Faccary, parish of Cappagh.

Communications

The main road from Omagh to Mountfield passes through this parish for the distance of 6 miles by the new road, which is now always travelled by carts, and cars. It is 5 and a half miles by the old road but it appears that in laying out the old road the chief aim was to make a straight line. The new road runs through an extensive bog almost pursuing a level throughout. A portion of this belongs to Sir W. MacMahon, who has used his influence in causing this new line of road to be continued from Mountfield through a very extensive bog until it meets the Cookstown and Gortin road, a distance from Mountfield of 10 and a half miles. The object in laying out this line of road is to change the course generally adopted between Omagh and Belfast. It is in contemplation that a coach will drive daily from Omagh to Cookstown on this road.

The main road to Gortin passes through this parish for a distance of 7 miles, the main road to Sixmilecross for 1 and a half miles.

General Appearance and Scenery

The north eastern portion of the parish presents one continued scene of mountain and uncultivated ground without anything pleasing that the eye can touch upon. From an eminence may be seen mountains looming one above another and in the low ground numerous quick hedges without a sign of a green leaf on the 23rd April. The only plantation in the country that has arrived at maturity is Faccary, the shooting lodge of Mr Stack.

SOCIAL ECONOMY

Evaluation

Mountfield and the evaluation of the adjoining country is of so late a state [date] that it leaves little to be said on this head.

Local Government

There is a court baron held every third Friday in the month by the seneschal (Mr Wilson), [who] resides at Omagh, 6 miles from Mountfield. He is much respected by the people. There are 12 revenue police and 1 officer stationed at Mountfield, also 3 of the constabulary. Outrages are unfrequent in this part of the country. Illicit distilling is not carried on in the immediate neighbourhood on account of the revenue being stationed in the village. The houses are not insured.

Dispensaries and Poor

Dispensaries none. There is not any provision for the poor more than what is collected in the church on Sundays which seldom amount to 1s. It is divided between 3 old women.

Religion

The greater number of persons in this country are Catholics.

Habits of the People

The general style of the cottages are 1-storey, built of stone, mostly thatched with small glass windows. Food, chiefly potatoes and milk. Fuel, turf. Dress, no way remarkable. There are generally from 5 to 7 in a family. The Catholics marry aged 17 to 20, the Protestants from 24 to 30. The peasantry generally make a holiday on St Patrick's Day by dancing and drinking. Legendary tales are recited among the Catholics. Funeral cries are sometimes heard but not so much as formerly. The females mostly wear a kind of homespun woollen yarn for gowns.

There is a great deal of class reading on the eastern side of the parish particularly among the Methodists. They assemble together at each others' houses, appoint a leader, who reads a portion of Scriptures and then explains each text according to his idea on the subject. They appoint as many as 2 or 3 leaders at each assembly, which takes place about twice a week. It was much more general about 2 years ago [insert lines crossed out: but since the Reverend M.J. Taylor of Mountfield came to officiate among them, by devoting his whole time and attention to his parishioners he has in some degree diverted them from these meetings].

PRODUCTIVE ECONOMY

Trades and Occupations

Grocers 2, public house 1, smiths 1, baker 1.

Statistical Report by Lieutenant W. Lancey, 26 Februry 1834

NATURAL STATE AND NATURAL FEATURES

Locality and Extent

The parish of Cappagh is situated in the baronies of Omagh and Strabane, county Tyrone and diocese of Derry. It is an extensive parish, surrounded by Drumragh, Ardstraw, Lower Bodoney <Badoney>, Termonmaguirk, Clogherny. Its extent is about 11 miles from north to south and about 10 from east to west. The summit of Bessy Bell mountain divides it from Ardstraw and its mearing <mering> runs from thence along the watershed line of

Parish of Cappagh

the Mary Gray range by the gap of Gortin to the top of Mullaghcarn. From thence it takes the fall of the mountain to the east of the village of Mountfield and then the general direction of the Cloghfin river to the Camowen <Cammon>. It runs west of this last river towards Omagh and then takes again the centre of the Camowen to the Poe bridge. The Fairy water to the west then bounds it to the parish of Ardstraw when the common mearing runs nearly north to the top of Bessy Bell.

This extent comprises 37,661 acres, about half of which is under cultivation and wood.

Mountains

The only mountains are Mullaghcarn, Bessy Bell and the Mary Gray range which embrace the northern and eastern sides of the parish. The rest of the land is generally low and very easy of access.

Rivers

The Cloghfin river on the south eastern boundary is a small stream which falls into the Camowen, which receives the Drumragh river at the town of Omagh. The stream at the bridge is [blank] feet wide and flows quietly past the town and gaol bounding plantations, fertile meadows and fields until it receives the Fairy water at the Poe bridge. It then is called the Strule <Strewel> and turns sharply to the right and winds through Mountjoy forest to the parish of Ardstraw.

Lakes

There are no lakes of any importance in the parish except that at Mountfield called Attirrive. There are 2 small ones in the forest and one called Lough Skit near Omagh.

General Appearance

The extensive and very beautiful demesne of Mountjoy forest, with plantations of Lisanelly and Mountpleasant render the central part of Cappagh more than ordinarily interesting. The lowlands are under good cultivation and the mountains which surround the northern part of it, by contrast, add to the general effect. Near Mountfield the country is in a less advanced state of civilisation, but great progress has lately been made under the new possessor of the soil, the present Master of the Rolls. The village of Mountfield has been rebuilt, and with its neat new church and the lately erected mansion at Faccary this otherwise bleak place is much enlivened.

MODERN TOPOGRAPHY

Gentlemen's Seats: Demesnes and Buildings

Mountjoy forest: the principal part of the north of Cappagh belongs to Mr Gardiner of Mountjoy forest. The demesne comprises 3,000 acres of undulating parkland, about one-third of which is planted with trees of about 25 years growth. The parish church stands near its centre. Its spire, rising above the wood, is seen from most of the eminences of the adjacent country and adds considerably to the landscape. The Strule <Strewel> meanders very prettily through the plantations and glades and nothing is wanting to render the demesne one of the first in Ireland but a suitable mansion. The present house called "the cottage" is an inferior erection, room having been added to room, which do not form any regular suite.

There are plenty of deer, rabbits, hares, partridges, woodcock and a few pheasants in the forest and Mr Gardiner keeps a small pack of hounds for his own amusement. He has also introduced an annual race in the demesne which tends, as all such amusements do, to bring a number of idle persons into the country and lowers the state of public morals.

Lisanelly joins the forest and derives much of its beauty from it. The pleasure grounds occupy 100 acres of land lying on the right bank of the Camowen between Mountjoy and the town of Omagh, from which it is only half a mile distant. The house is large but in bad repair and everything is falling into decay since the late possessor's death, the property being in chancery. There is a good garden and many requisites for a family of wealth. The former proprietor was killed in this house by lightning, [insert crossed out words: the last destroyed himself by whiskey].

Mountpleasant, the residence of the Reverend Mr Criggan, stands on the mail road 1 mile north of Omagh on the left bank of the Camowen. It is a small place with a good substantial modern house with a flat roof, from which is a beautiful view of the forest and adjacent country.

Faccary, the seat of Sir William MacMahon, Master of the Irish Rolls, is a modern building near the village of Mountfield. It is a new place, built and planted within these last 6 years and has nothing very striking about it except its size, contrasted with the neighbouring habitations, bleak mountains and bogs with which it is surrounded.

Mountfield Lodge at Lough Atterrive is a pretty little wild place in summer and let for a shooting lodge to the Reverend Joseph Stack.

Mullaghmore House is a substantial dwelling.

The Glebe is an old house, very uninteresting and is shortly to be pulled down and a new one erected. The site, however, is good as it commands an extensive view of the forest.

There are some substantial farmhouses in the parish but few equal those of the better class in Ardstraw.

Places of Worship

The parish church was built by Doctor Gibson (rector) in 1780. It is a neat erection of cut stone with a spire and will contain about 300 persons. It has no gallery and is warmed by flues lately put up by Mr Hart, the present rector. It is prettily situated in Mountjoy forest.

Mountfield church was built in 1827 by the Board of First Fruits and 14 townlands given to the superintendence of a perpetual curate who resides near the village and receives 75 pounds per annum. There are also 4 schoolhouses in which divine service of the Established Church is performed.

Meeting Houses and Roman Catholic Chapel

There is 1 Presbyterian house at the crossroads north of Omagh and 2 Catholic chapels, one at Killyclogher, the other in Knockmoyle, north of the demesne. I have not been able to ascertain the numbers these places of worship will contain or the expense incurred in their erection.

A Baptist meeting house stands in Camowen, capable of holding 400 persons on forms. It was built by Mr Buchanan, the present consul at New York.

Towns

There are no towns in Cappagh, but Omagh stands on its western mearing. The village of Mountfield consists of a few houses only.

ANCIENT TOPOGRAPHY

Antiquities

The same antiquities are found in Cappagh as in most of the parishes around Omagh: an old church, of which no person can give the least information, and a number of forts. These latter were certainly not all built for defence as their situations plainly indicate. In the old churchyard are some tombs of 200 years old, whose inscriptions are in a raised character. Coins have also been taken out of the fort at Castleroddy (?) but I could get no information respecting them. Indeed, total ignorance of these matters appears equally to be the fate of peasant and proprietor.

SOCIAL ECONOMY

Inhabitants

Of the present inhabitants, Mr Gardiner possesses the greatest influence. His rent roll from his Cappagh and Ardstraw estates amounts to 9,000 pounds a year. The Master of the Rolls resides for a few weeks during the summer, but with the exception of the rector and Mr Criggan, there are no persons of very independent property who live in the parish. There are, however, some very respectable farmers, and in general those who occupy the soil appear to be in tolerable circumstances. The people are quiet as the Protestant party is equal in number to the Roman Catholic.

Language

The Irish language is very little spoken and is principally confined to the Roman Catholics who occupy the mountains.

Dress, Food and Religion

Their usual dress and food are of the same coarse materials as the adjacent country. The dress of the women is much gayer than it used to be, and young women going to market with lace veils and fine ribbons, with their shoes and stockings tied up in a handkerchief, is still an everyday sight. Manufactures being at present so cheap and the passion for dress being uniform, the peasant women have learnt to deck their persons with finery without confining themselves to real comforts, as the contrast fully proves when seen in their own cabins.

The parish of Cappagh has been for some years badly neglected by ministers of religion, but since the appointment of the new rector, Mr Hart, who has added 2 curates, a spirit of enquiry has been set on foot.

Schools

Education is very general. There are 15 schools under the following control <controul>: Capel Street Association for Discountenancing Vice 1, Kildare Street Society 5, London Hibernian Society 4, New National Society 4, parish school supported by the rector 1. These schools educate 750 children, three-fourths of whom are Protestants. The houses are built partly by subscription and partly by the societies, and the teachers seldom reside. There is also an extensive Sunday school at the Camowen meeting house which has the merit of being the first established in Tyrone, about 30 years ago. A Sunday school is also held in the mill

Parish of Cappagh

at Mullaghmore, one near the curate's house at Newlands and one in Mayne. Indeed, no poor persons anxious to educate their family need send them far from home in this parish.

Dispensary

The inhabitants apply to Omagh and Newtownstewart for medical relief. There is no dispensary in Cappagh.

PRODUCTIVE ECONOMY

Farms

There are some large and old farms in the parish, tenanted by independent yeomen whose ancestors have resided on the land for some generations. Many of the farmhouses are large and commodious, but the usual buildings consist of a kitchen, parlour, bedroom and loft. The extent of land in each farm varies from a few acres to 30 or 40.

There are a few grazing farms, the principal belonging to Mr Scott of Straughroy <Straughrog>, an extensive one in Glenhordial held by Roddy Donald, tenant of Mr Gardiner, and the chief part of the demesne of Mountjoy forest let to Mr Quinn, who exports a number of cattle by Belfast annually. There are considerable tracts of good pasturage on the mountains, where the tenants graze a limited number of beasts.

Rents

The rent of land of course varies considerably. Near Omagh it lets as high as 3 pounds an acre but the arable parts of the parish are average 15s to 25s. The general soil of the parish being of an inferior quality, this sum is considerably higher than the same rate in Drumragh, Clogherny or Ardstraw.

Manures

Lime procured from Tatteraconaghty near the crossroads 3 miles north of Omagh and from the quarries at West Longfield, mixed with compost form the principal manures. The tenants of Sir William MacMahon procure lime from a quarry he purchased for their use in Kilmore in Drumragh near Omagh. They pay 5d for 8 cwt of stone and usually return laden with it every market day.

Farming Societies

There are no farming societies in the parish.

Prices of Produce

The prices of produce are much the same in Omagh as in Strabane. The following may be taken as a fair average last autumn. Prices of produce: oats 7d per stone, 15s a barrel for barley, 1d ha'penny a stone for potatoes, forced grass hay 2 pounds a ton and meadow hay 25s. Wheat has not yet become general in the Omagh market.

Crops

The same method of cropping as in the adjacent country prevails in Cappagh. First oats then flax, potatoes, oats or barley, then lea for 1 or 2 years. There is little or no wheat sown in the parish.

Livestock

There are plenty of good cows to be obtained, worth from 4 pounds to 7 pounds. Mr Buchanan of Straughroy keeps a dairy and supplies the gaol with milk. Mr Quin has always a large number of cattle grazing in the forest for the English market. Roddy Donald grazes to some extent in Glenhordial. Mr Scott of Straughroy also has a considerable number of cattle feeding on his lands. The farmers as usual raise a few calves and a good supply of cattle can at all times be obtained.

Pigs abound from 40s to 50s. Horses for country work are plenty, from 5 to 10 pounds apiece but there are none for road or light work. Sheep brought from Fermanagh and fattened for the Omagh market are principally obtained from Mr Scott's farm at Straughroy from 35s to 50s apiece, but country bred sheep are not plentiful. Their average price varies from 12s to 20s.

Fish and Game

Salmon and trout, hares, partridges, woodcock and grouse are not scarce, particularly hares which abound in the townlands of Mayne and adjacent country.

Fruit

Common fruit abounds in the Omagh markets in the summer. There are no very extensive orchards in the parish but most of the respectable houses have fruit trees. The principal orchards are those in the forest at Straughroy, Lisanelly and Mountpleasant.

Mills

There are [blank] mills in the parish, [blank] being corn, the rest flax mills. The leap mill on the mearing of Clogherny, a new slated mill in Mullaghmore, 2 in Faccary.

Bleach Green

Machinery of an old bleach green in Mullaghmore has gone to ruin, not having been worked for some years.

Brewery

There is an extensive brewery quarter of a mile from Omagh in Lisnamallard, the property of Falls, Peebles and Co., who possess the distillery at Dungannon and principally supply Omagh with spirits. This firm also deals in wines. They have an oat mill with fans on the premises, which is much frequented as the meal is made in a superior style.

Manufactures

The only manufacture of consequence is linen which will be treated of at large in the statistics of Drumragh. Common country cloth is also occasionally woven and sells from 2s 6d to 4s a yard. In Lurganbouy blue and white check for women's aprons is also made and sold at 10d a yard. The weavers purchase cotton dyed and prepared for their use in Scotland. Woollen stockings are knit in almost every farmhouse and when sold bring from 12d to 24d a pair.

Price of Labour

The wages of labourers is nearly the same in all the districts around Omagh. Men receive from 15s to 3 guineas the half year and female servants from 24s to 30s. Daily wages vary from 8d to 12d a day.

MODERN TOPOGRAPHY

Roads

The Dublin mail road passes through this parish for a considerable distance and is now in tolerable repair. Turnpikes were erected on it in 1832 but as it has not been properly attended to until lately, they have not been the means of keeping it in a better state of repair than heretofore.

The principal crossroads are to Cookstown by Mountfield, 1 to Castlederg and 1 to Gortin. The former when completed, it is said to have a stage coach put on it, if not a mail. The latter is a good hard road running through the gap of Gortin, a passage in the mountains of some picturesque beauty. The rest of the roads are all passable and in tolerable repair.

Bridges

The bridges thrown over the Camowen are those of Lisbwee, Bloody bridge, Campsie and Omagh. Those over the Drumragh river are the new and the Cranny bridges. The wooden and stone bridge cross the Strule, and the Poe and Calkill the Fairy water. These are all of substantial stone work except the wooden bridge, which is fast falling into decay.

NATURAL FEATURES

Woods and Plantations

There are no natural woods in Cappagh. Those already alluded to in Mountjoy forest, with the plantations of Lisanelly, Faccary and Mountpleasant <are> the only ones of any extent. Oak, fir, beech, sycamore and larch can be purchased in the proper seasons from the forest and an annual sale of bark usually takes place.

Fuel

Turf and bog fir are the only fuel in Cappagh, except perhaps in 2 or 3 houses where coal may be occasionally used. Turf in Omagh sells for 5d a box which measures 3 feet 10 inches by 2 feet 6 inches by 1 foot 10 inches in breadth. Bog wood when brought into market sells for about 3s a car load.

Geology

The mountains are of gneiss and talc slate. Near Mountfield church greenstone commences, which spreads itself over the eastern portion of Termonmaguirk. The eastern fall of the mountain of Aghalane is old red sandstone and it is seen in large quantities in Killyclogher. Silicious sandstone occupies much of the lowlands about the Strule river and clay sandstones are found to the south of Omagh. Primitive blue limestone is quarried on the southern foot of Bessy Bell but in no other parts of the parish. An attempt to raise lime from a vein of talc slate in Mullaghmore was made by the Reverend Thomas Stack, but it proved to be too silicious to be useful.

MODERN TOPOGRAPHY

Projected Canal

The late Lord Blessington wrote a pamphlet to show the practicability of running a canal from Strabane to Lough Erne, which would pass along the banks of the Mourne and Strule rivers through the forest. The expense deterred from the undertaking those interested about it. A railroad would be a far more preferable method of rapid and easy

Parish of Cappagh

communication, and as stone is so abundant would probably cost far less money. The traffic between Omagh and the canal head at Strabane is in certain seasons considerable; but it is much to be doubted if any undertaking of the above nature would pay its expenses where food and labour are so cheap and money so scarce. [Signed] William Lancey, Lieutenant Royal Engineers, 24 February 1834. Forwarded to the O.S. Office, 1 March 1834, [signed] W.W. Waters, Captain Royal Engineers.

Answers to Statistical Queries of the North West Society of Ireland, by Samuel Cuthbertson [1820s]

NATURAL STATE

Locality, Ministers and Proprietors

[Query number in brackets].
(1) County of Tyrone.
(2) Omagh, Londonderry [towns].
(3) Cappagh, Mr Ormsby, rector, Messrs McCintock and Cuthbertson, Presbyterian ministers.
(4) Earls Belmore and Blessington, not at home at present, Mr Bateson and Mr McCausland, townlands of Cuingnary, Terraquin and [blank]. Parish large but very mountainous and uncultivated.

PRODUCTIVE ECONOMY

Size of Farms, Crops and Stock

(5) From 20 to 30 acres, some hawthorn hedges old mode. Very little improvement. Oats for the most part, a little barley is sown, rye occasionally. If rents and tythe [underlined] were lower, capable of improvement.
(6) Being mountainous, considerable quantities of young cattle and sheep grazed. Much improvement might be made if lime could be easily procured.
(7) Railagh, Glenherdel, Enniskillen [mountains] grazed on even to the tops by sheep and not capable of much further improvement without lime, by fogs and cold.

Bogs

(8) Great quantities of bog. Principal moors Killycuiragh and Mayne, much fir found, not very deep.

Woods and Trees

(9) Mountjoy forest and nursery, one orchard the property of Mr Scott of Strochroy.

(10) In west [wet] lands, larch, fir and elder, in dry land, oak and ash thrive tolerably.

Rents

(11) From 1 pound to 2 pounds per acre. Best land 2 pounds, middling 1 pound, 15s inferior. Considered too dear [all underlined].
(12) In some places 6s paid for a day's cutting but for the most part nothing paid for bog as the tenants are so taxed with dear land and tythe as to be able to bear no more burdens.

Improved Farming Techniques

(13) Very little improvement has been recently made except the introduction of the Scotch plough, considered as useful for the stiff lands.

Fencing

(14) Here and there hawthorn, which mixed with elder and birch might make a good fence.

Employment and Wages

(15) In spring and harvest chiefly. If small farms were let in mountainous parts at a cheap rate, general employment might be given to idle begging fellows.
(16) From 2 pounds to 2 pounds 5s 6d [per year]. In spring and harvest 10d per day and 5d for the remainder part of the season.

Crops and Grasses

(17) None except a few kale plants for private use and some turnips by Lord Mountjoy for sheep.
(18) In some places rye and timothy are sown.

Drainage, Manure and Irrigation

(19) Underdraining for the most part.
(20) Mire clay occasionally which answers meadows better than lime, but not so useful for stiff moory lands [manures].
(21) Not frequently, as water put on wet meadows <meddows> causes rushes and spits to rise up.

Dairies and Oxen

(22) No great encouragement, the farms being rather small. Young cattle more valuable.
(23) None [oxen].

Crops

(24) For the most part potatoes set in drills at Lord Mountjoy's place [spade husbandry].

(25) Oats, rye, from 10d to 1s per stone of 14 lbs. Provision generally plenty, little barley sown.

(26) Mostly by the Irish [measure] in the estates of the Earls of Belmore and Blessington and Mr Bateson.

Livestock

(27) The same kind that was reared near a century ago, not the longhorned Devonshire.

(28) Sheep, black cattle and sometimes goats in the craggy mountainous parts.

(29) Small little sheep fitting for coarse pasture. Mr Scott of Straughroy <Strakroy> feeds good weathers and excellent mutton is raised in Mountjoy Park. The sheep mostly brought from Connaught.

(30) In some places little Scotch ponies and shelties. In lower grounds tolerable good horses. No good stallions are scarcely ever seen here unless brought occasionally from the county Fermanagh.

(31) Not a good breed. The best kind brought from the county Fermanagh, no encouragement [swine].

(32) Cannot say [number of stock]. Some improvement might be made both in black cattle and in sheep if landlords would keep or encourage farmers to keep bulls and rams pro bono publico.

(33) Very little as far as I know [improvements in stock].

NATURAL FEATURES AND NATURAL HISTORY

Rivers and Loughs

Camowen <Common> water, which takes its source from Lough Fingain, and near which is a cottage of the Right Honourable Sir J. Stewart. No loughs of any consequence. No production.

Mines, Quarries and Minerals

(35) None [mines].

(36) No quarries of any value. No place even if there were for exportation.

(37) Sometimes blue, sometimes grey burned with peat [limestone]. Not very expensive, peat plenty.

(38) No coal has been searched for, the peat being plenty throughout the parish.

(39) No mineral springs.

(40) I have not heard of any kind of marl being found.

SOCIAL ECONOMY

Habits of the People

(41) As the inhabitants in general are industrious, they who have long leases live tolerable comfortable, but vice versa they earn their bread with the sweat of their brow.

(42) They practise that which Aristotle called a virtue, namely cleanliness, and if encouragement were given to procure lime, their houses would be whitewashed.

(43) Peat or turf in great abundance, generally cheap.

Food

(44) Potatoes and milk, bread occasionally. They rear considerable quantities of geese. They comfort themselves with a roast one at Eves [underlined], washing it down with a little potteen [farmers].

(45) The same, sometimes worse [cottiers].

(46) In summer buttermilk, but in winter nothing but potatoes, a herring now and then [labourers].

Education

(47) Yes, the Protestant part of the community have greatly improved by Sunday Schools.

(48) From 20d to 2s as the masters are fed with the children. About 10 schools.

(49) The Catholics who mostly live in the back part of the country are mostly coarse, rough in their manners but education is beginning to polish them.

Health and Benevolence

(50) Health good as their nerves are braced by hard industry and snuffing [sniffing] the cooler air [underlined].

(51) None that I know of [friendly societies]. The inhabitants practise charity to the poor and needy.

PRODUCTIVE ECONOMY

Improvements and Farmers

(52) Part of Omagh, no other of any consequence [towns].

(53) As the hand of the industrious maketh rich, improvements would be made if the lands would be lowered, but the county cuts are almost intolerable.

(54) Mr Scott of Strachroy, Mr John Scott of Crenynary, Mr Harvey of Crenenagh, Mr John Johnstone of Killy Brack, Mr James Adams of Mayne, Mr Fullen of Mayne, John Chambers Esquire, Mull.

Parish of Cappagh

Linen, Flax and Manufactures

(55) Diminishing [linen manufacture], the prices of cloth being so low.

(56) Only 1 bleach green and I believe 3 flax mills.

(57) Ploughing twice, sometimes potato or barley. Mostly at home as small quantities of seed are sown, very little of the seed saved [flax].

(58) Mostly scutched at home [flax], the quantity being small, usually dried by fire on [?] fences.

(59) Coarse, the spinner can earn from 2d ha'penny to 3d per day, as 10d is got for spinning a spangle which generally is effected in 4 days [warp yarn].

(60) From 20d to 2s, for the most part sent to Armagh, none expected [fine yarn].

(61) Grow a part, purchase the remainder from Strabane, Derry [flax].

(62) If not spun in his own house, he buys it green in the market, and the bleaching the yarn of a web will cost about 2s.

(64) No yarn greens. I don't think they would serve, as weavers wish to handle their yarn.

(65) Of a coarse texture, from 48 to 50 beer, from 10d to 1s 2d [linen], Omagh and Newtownstewart <Newton Stuart> [markets].

Woollen Manufacture

(66) None.

(67) None, as the inhabitants occasionally manufacture cloth for their families [woollen staples].

(68) Coarse, generally on the small wheel.

(69) None except what serves the family [woollen stockings].

(70) A few and well [sheep].

Other Manufactures and Fisheries

No cotton manufactured. No kelp burned. No fisheries except for eel, trout and pike.

Parish of Clogher, County Tyrone

Statistical Memoir by Lieutenant R. Stotherd, 1833-5

NATURAL STATE

Name

Clogher parish, county Tyrone. [Irish letters] Cloch-oir or "golden stone." Cathal Maguire, the coadjutor of the bishop of Clogher, who died in 1498 AD, a very learned man of his time and parson of Iniskeen [Enniskeen] says: that Clogher took its name from a stone said to have been an altar on which sacrifice was offered to Kerman Kellstack after the establishment of a Christian church at Clogher; that this stone inlaid or ornamented with gold was kept in the church at the right side of the altar in his own time; and this idea is prevalent among the inhabitants at the present day, and is supported by the actual existence of a stone said to be the cloch-oir or identical stone which gave name to the town and which now lies close to the church at its south western corner. This stone, which certainly bears marks of great antiquity, is 5 feet long, 2 feet broad and 1 foot 6 inches deep. It is deeply indented on the upper side as if characters had been cut in it. They are of the following form [text drawings]. Its side also appears to have been inlaid with a tablet or plate which has been removed [text drawing, 2 feet high].

In pagan times it was a druidical sanctury, where many arts of divination were practised. Ware, volume 1 p175: "In time of paganism the devil used to pronounce juggling <jugling> answers from this stone like the oracles of Apollo Pythius."

O'Connor, *Annales IV Magistrorum* p105: "Flaherteus, de veterum Hibernorum idolatria scribens, Maguirium (decanum Cloghorensem circa annum 1470) citat dicens 'Ex Hibernorum oraculis celebrabantur prater lapidem fatalem Crom-Cruach et Clogh-oir, i.e. lapis aureus unde Clochorensis sides episcopalis nomen habet in Orgiellia, ubi a lapide aureo idolum responsa dare solebat. Hic lapis, inquit in suis scholiis D. Cathaldus Maguir, asservabatur Clochoriae ad dextram ingredientis ecclesiam, quem gentiles auro obtegebant quia in eo colebant summum partium Aquilonalium idolum Kermand Kelstack dictum." The stone is to this day in the same place here mentioned. It is said that the Kings of Ergal were crowned on this stone and the Deans of Clogher installed on it.

Ledwich's *Antiquities*, p73: "Our Cloghar, which now (O'Brien in voce) signifies a congregation, originally imported a stone about which people met for religious duties, nor can there be any doubt but the natives said they were going to the cloghars as the Scotch to the clachans." [Insert marginal note: O'Connor's *Annales Quatuor Magistrorum* note 1 p119, translated by C. O'Connor from Irish manuscripts in the Stowe Library and printed at the Duke of Buckingham's press at Stowe]. "Clochair, an Irish word signifying 'to collect together."

It has been suggested that the name of Clochoir or "golden stone" originated in the exceeding richness of the land which immediately surrounds the town.

Locality

Clogher is situated at the southern extremity of the county Tyrone and in the barony of Clogher. It is bounded on the north by the parishes of Donacavey and Clogherny, east by Errigal Keerogue and Errigal Trough, all in the county Tyrone; south by Tedavnet in the county Monaghan and west by Aghalurcher and Enniskillen in the county Fermanagh, a small part of the former parish being in the county Tyrone and barony of Clogher. Its form is compact, measuring in extreme length from north to south 12 and a quarter, and in breadth 11 and a half British statute miles.

NATURAL FEATURES

Hills

Few parishes of the same extent can vie with Clogher in natural beauty and advantages. It is enclosed on the north west by the Aghintain mountains, rising to the height of 1,031 feet above the level of the sea, on the south by the range of Slieve Beagh, whose summit level is 1,254 feet above the sea, and on the east by Shantavny and the mountains of Ballygawley with an altitude of 1,037 feet; being traversed and intersected by an intermediate ridge of considerable altitude, in the centre of which stands Knockmany, wooded to its summit by the praiseworthy exertions of the Reverend Francis Gervais. South of this ridge and between the sloping mountain ranges of Slieve Beagh and Aghintain the broad valley of Clogher expands, whose surface is diversified by numerous minor knolls and ridges, beautifying by their variety and

Parish of Clogher

extent this interesting district. North of the Knockmany ridge and comprising a large part of the manor of Cecil, an extent of level ground extends to the verge of the parish, whose general level, however, is considerable, between 400 and 500 feet above the level of the sea.

Lakes

The lakes in this parish are not numerous and lie principally in the valley of the Launy or Clogher river and on the summit of the Slieve Beagh ridge. Of the former, the principal are Round lough, and Lough Faddan in the vicinity of Fivemiletown; Ballagh lough intermediate between that village and Clogher, and Augher lough within the demesne of Augher Castle. Of the mountain loughs, the most extensive and the most numerous lie on the extreme verge of the parish and county. Of these, the principal are Lough-in-Albanagh, Lough Sallagh, Lough Gallnane, Lough-na-Heery, Lough-na-varad, Lough-na-sliggan, Lough-na-blaneybane and Lough McCall. Situated in the gorges of the mountain, their placid and unruffled surfaces tend to soften the bleak and barren aspect of this wild and retired district. The mountain lakes are said to be very deep, but there being no boats thereon I had not an opportunity of sounding them. The lakes at Augher I sounded very carefully and found a depth of 49 and a half feet near its south western edge, being only 42 feet deep in the centre. A list of the lakes within the parish together with the extent of each is given [see Fair Sheets].

Rivers

No river of magnitude or importance traverses any portion of this extensive parish. The Launy river [insert marginal note: Carlisle's *Topographical dictionary*], after receiving the contributions of the numerous minor streams and water courses from the Aghentain and Slieve Baugh ranges, flows from west to east through the valley of Clogher. Passing through the demesne of Favour Royal in Errigal, where it assumes the name of the Blackwater, it turns south east, and forming the south eastern boundary of the county Tyrone, which it separates from Monaghan and Armagh, it falls into Lough Neagh.

The River Launy is formed by the union of 3 smaller streams at a point about half a mile north west of the town of Clogher. The first of these or most northern branch has its source on the mountain boundary between the townlands Ballynass

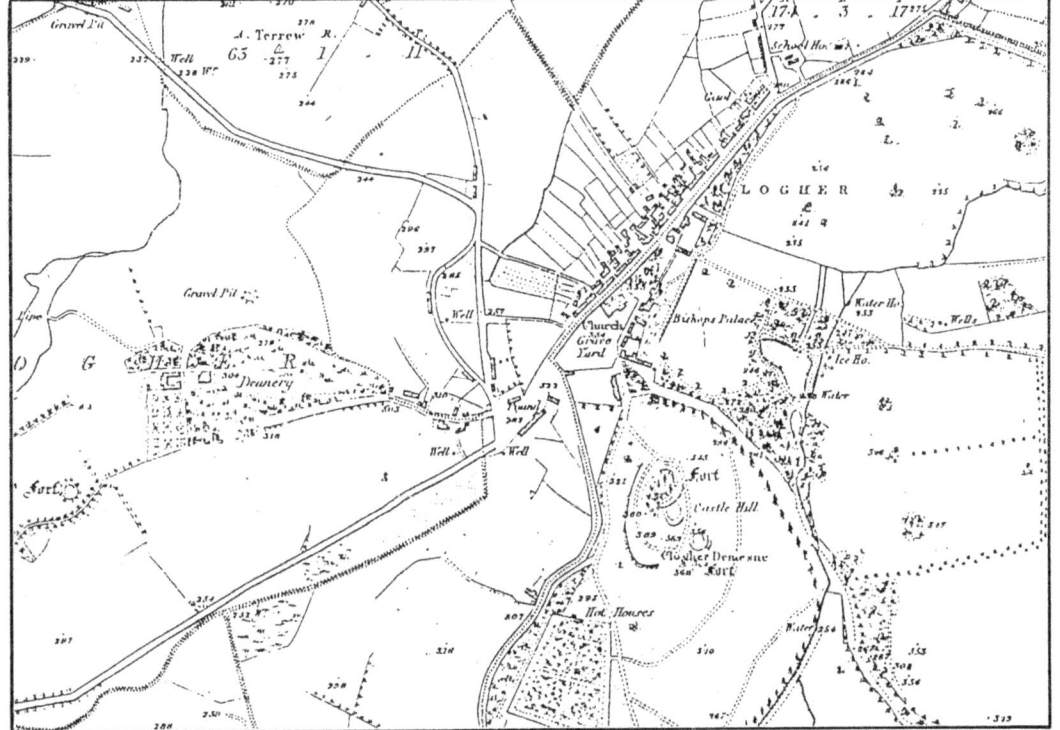

Map of Clogher from the first 6" O.S. maps, 1830s

and Beagh, at an elevation of 839 feet above the sea and close to the trigonometrical station of Aghentain. Flowing east through the Dromores, bounding Kilnahushogue on the south and Mallaberry on the north, it passes through the demesne of Killyfaddy and unites its waters with the 2 streams before mentioned at Ballymagowan. The second or intermediate branch has its source at an elevation of 920 feet in the mountain townland of Cole and about 100 yards south of the trigonometrical station. Flowing south about 2 and a half miles and bounding Cole and Edergole, it turns east, and passing under the old ruin of Aghentain Castle, after various windings it joins the other 2 streams. The course of this branch being much longer than the others, it may be considered as the true source of the Blackwater river. The third stream descends from an elevation of 920 feet in Fardross mountain, flowing north passes through Fardross, and, after bounding the demesmes of Caraclogher and Daisyhill, unites with the first mentioned branches at the meeting of Ratory, Ballymagowan and Terrew townlands.

The Ballylaster, by its union with the Launy at Corick, contributes much to the enlargement of that river. It has its source in Lough Albanagh in the Slieve Beagh mountains and close to the trigonometrical station, and flowing north east it receives in its course the contributions of the numerous little streams from that face of the mountain. Nothing need be said of any other streams in this parish.

Bogs

Independent of the mountain bogs which contain an almost inexhaustible supply of turbary, the flow bogs in the valley are both numerous and extensive. Of these latter, the principal are the chain of bogs lying north of Fivemiletown and extending about 2 miles in length from east to west. The surface of these bogs inclines with the face of the country, dipping from west to east in a gradual slope from Blacklands, where the average level is 380 feet, to Aghenlark near Screeby lough where it is 328 feet above the level of the sea.

The Tully bog, at an average level of 210 feet embracing a portion of several townlands, supplies Augher and its vicinity with turbary. Next in extent is that on the boundary between Lislea and Eskragh at a level of 430 feet above the sea, and numerous small patches scattered through the whole extent of the parish, affording a general but limited supply of turbary to their immediate localities.

Of the mountain bogs, the most important are those of Corboe, Tatnadaveny, Altanaveragh and Kilnakushogue. They embrace a very extensive district of flat bog, lying at an average level of 600 feet, the supply of fuel from which is excellent and although distant from the place of consumption is easy of access.

In the bogs there was formerly a great quantity of both oak and fir, but this supply is now nearly exhausted and the oak is generally of a bad quality. In Tulnavert bog a great number of stags' horns have been found at various periods, but principally about 20 years since. They were probably those of the red deer. The bog in which they were found is now a fine meadow. In Tattyburns <Tallyburns> also a canoe was discovered in 1823, of which see an account under its proper head.

Woods

The only evidences of the existence of natural woods in former times in this parish are to be found in the bogs, in which large quantities of oak and fir timber, as has been before observed, have been discovered. In the bishop's deer park the hazel and thorn bushes are of great antiquity, but it is probable they were originally planted for the use of the deer [insert marginal query].

In Aghendara townland, also in the eastern boundary of the parish, is a considerable extent of scrubby ground which may be considered as the remains of underwood, but no timber trees now remain of the forests which probably in remote ages shaded its glens and valleys.

Climate

No meteorological register kept in the parish. The climate though extremely moist is very salubrious, and the natives, though few particular instances of great longevity occur, are generally healthy and live to a good old age. On the boundary between Aghalurcher and Clogher an old soldier died about 27 years since, who said himself that he was 117 years of age and was at the battle of Culloden. The extreme humidity of the climate may be attributed to the prevalence of the south westerly winds, charged with moisture from the exhalations of Lough Erne, and more remotely from the western ocean. The clouds thus gathering on the summits of the Aughintain and Slieve Beagh ranges of mountains by natural attraction combine and fall in rain over the intermediate valley of Clogher.

Zoology

With regard to the fish a striking difference may be

remarked between the mountain and the lowland lakes, the former abounding in trout only, whereas the latter produce only pike, perch, eels, roach and bream but no trout. In Lough McCall the trouts are not numerous, but they are very large, from 4 to 8 lbs and even larger, in the mountain loughs from half a lb to 2 or 3 lbs. The River Blackwater yields also a good supply of trouts and some salmon, and a few of the former are found in the Ballylaster water.

The Reverend Francis Gervais of Cecil exerted himself very much to introduce pheasant into this neighbourhood. His extensive plantations led him to hope for the greatest success, but although he went to a very great expense he entirely failed. The want of water on the base of Knockmany and the deficiency of large trees for the birds to perch in led them to forsake this for a more congenial locality. Grouse on the mountains, partridge, snipe and woodcocks in the valleys. Wild geese are seen sometimes in great numbers on Slieve Beagh in the winter season, some curlews also. I must not forget to notice the numerous flocks of waterfowl on Augher lough at all seasons of the year. Being protected by Sir James Richardson Bunbury they are very tame, and it would be very curious and interesting to notice the different varieties that appear during a hard winter season. Of these, certainly not the least interesting is the sheldrake.

MODERN TOPOGRAPHY

Towns

Neither of the 3 towns Clogher, Augher or Fivemiletown, from their present circumscribed limits, is deserving of more than the name of village, although the two former before the Union received the right of returning 2 members to parliament and have been otherwise distinguished in history.

Town of Clogher

This little town at a very early age appears to have been a place of some importance, and to have exercised privileges which gave it considerable influence over the surrounding district. It is situated on the River Launy, on an acclivity rising gradually towards the west and terminating on that side rather abruptly. From the commanding position of the church and Bishop's Palace, occupying the highest point of this ridge, the appearance of the town from the west and north is very picturesque. It is 76 and three-quarter Irish miles from Dublin Castle. For interesting details relative to this town, the probable derivation of its name etc., see Ware volume 1 p175, Ledwich's *Antiquities* p73.

ANCIENT TOPOGRAPHY

Church at Clogher

The church is said to have been founded by Saint Patrick in the year 443 [marginal note: Britt. Ecclasiarum Antiq. Ensern, 445]. "Clocherensi ecclesiae praefuisse Sanctum Patricium priusquam Armachiam concessisset, Jocelinus refert, de discipulo ipsius, et in ecclesia illa successore Kertenno ita scribens. Quia Sanctus Patricius talis discipuli diligebat praesentiam, providet illi ecclesiam nec a sede archiepiscopali, quam in Armachia constructurus erat, angelo jubente, nimis [?] remotam, nec eidem metropoli ne forte a secuturis archiepiscopi graveretur, valde vicinum. Sic profecto factum est, ut vir Domini non vexaretur, sedem primum frequentando, et Patricium sanctum visitando ob vice longuiquitatem, nec eius ecclesiae despicabilis videretur, ob nimiam vicinitatem. Expletis aliquantis diebus, praefecit illum Clochereni ecclesia quam ipse Sanctus Patricius tunc regebat. Est autem hic Machartinus ille pro sapia ortus, B. Patricii in Italia et Hibernia comes individuus."

Ware, volume 1 p175: Saint Macartin built a monastery at Clogher at the command of Saint Patrick "in the street before the royal seat of the kings of Ergal." [Insert note: in another account an abbey of Regular canons dedicated to the Virgin is stated to have been founded here in a very early age.

AD 1041: the cathedral was rebuilt and dedicated to the memory of Saint Macartin. AD 1295: Bishop Mathew Macatasaid built a chapel over the sepulchre of Saint Macartin at Clogher and rebuilt his cathedral. Ware volume 1 p177: "AD 1395: the cathedral, episcopal court, 2 chapels, the monastery and 32 houses were consumed by fire. [Insert note: in another account this fire is said to have happened on the 20th April 1396, when the episcopal palace and everything belonging to the church and chapter was consumed. The two first were rebuilt by Arthur McCamoil, bishop. AD 1692: Bishop Tenison repaired and beautified the palace. AD 1720: Bishop Sterne expended 3,000 pounds in building and improvements at Clogher."

The present cathedral was built by him. It is a plain but commodious structure capable of containing 800 persons. It has a handsome organ and a choir maintained by the bishop. The chapter consists of 14 canons. There is a stone built into the churchyard wall on the side of the palace, and about 2 feet under a curiously carved head, hollowed out like a cup. It was supposed that headaches were cured by placing the head in this stone.

There is a similar one in another part of the wall supposed to be equally efficacious in curing warts [text drawing].

The curiously carved head mentioned above appears to be that of a female, of which the following is a rude sketch [text drawing].

Bishop's Palace

The Bishop's Palace although situated close to the town and church has all the advantages of retirement. It is a very handsome and capacious building, the terrace on the south commanding a richly wooded and beautiful landscape, backed by the deer park and the mountains of Slieve Baugh. The left wing of the palace was built in the year 1779, the right wing about 1817. The main building or principal part of the palace was completed by Lord Robert Tottenham, the present bishop, in 1823, having been commenced by his predecessor.

Bishops' Portraits

There are portraits of the following bishops at the palace, namely Miles Magrath translated or promoted AD 1570, the first after the Reformation. George Montgomery, 1605; James Spotiswood, 1621; Henry Jones, 1645; John Leslie, 1661; Robert Leslie, 1671; Roger Boyle, 1672; Richard Tenison, 1690; St George Ashe, 1697; John Sterne, 1717. For some years this country was so disturbed by the rapparees that no bishop was appointed. Robert Clayton, 1745; John Garnett, 1758, by Dr Campbell; John Hothan, 1786; Dr William Foster, 1796; Dr John Porter, 1798, by Sir Thomas Lawrence. [Insert additions: Lord John George Beresford, 1819; Dr Percy Joclyn, 1820; Lord Robert Tottenham, 1822].

Diocesan Library

The diocesan library, consisting of about 500 volumes chiefly theological, was bequeathed to the Bishops of Clogher by Bishop Garnett, who also benefitted his successors by planting most of the trees which now ornament the demesne.

Bishops' Demesne

The demesne was surrounded with a wall by Bishop Clayton. A deer park was added to it and stocked by Bishop Garnett. An hydraulic ram (invented by Montgolfier) was put up here for the supply of water by Lord Robert Tottenham, the present bishop, at the expense of about 300 pounds. It throws water to the height of 110 feet, supplying the town, palace and offices by about 3 hours work of a man per diem, and worked for nearly 12 years before it was materially out of order. This was a great acquisition to the town, before which it was miserably supplied with water, depending principally on wells at a considerable distance. There stood a tree in the demesne within these few years, under which it was said Dean Swift was married to Stella.

Coins

Some labourers digging in what is called the Nuns' hill in the demesne found a small brass coin, a tradesman's token struck during the civil wars of 1641, but except the initial letters of his name, PR, the inscriptions are illegible. He appears to have been a bell-founder, from a bell which appears on one side of the coin, which, however, was in very bad preservation.

2 other coins were dug up in the garden of the Clogher day school by Mr Triggey, the master, both groats of Edward IV, the larger one English, the smaller Irish. The legend on the first (when perfect) was: (obverse) "Edward di gra rex Ang[li] Fr[anciae] Hyb[erniae]"; (reverse) "posui deum adjutorem meum", and in the inner circle "civitas London", denoting the place in which it was coined. The legend on the second is: (obverse) "rex Angli et Franciae" with the arms of England and France quarterly in a shield; (reverse) "Dominus Hiberniae" and 3 crowns in the field denoting the 3 kingdoms. 3 other coins of Henry VIII were found.

Letters from Lieutenant Larcom to Lieutenant Stotherd about Coins

My Dear Mr Stotherd, the coin (Mr Petrie says) is a tradesman's token struck during the civil wars of '41, but except the initial letters of his name, PR, the inscriptions are illegible. He appears to have been a bell-founder. In such bad preservation the coin is of no interest whatever. In haste, Thomas Larcom, 29 January 1835.

My Dear Stotherd, the coins are both groats of Edward IV, the larger one English, the smaller Irish. The legend on the first, when perfect, was: (obverse) "Edward di gra rex Ang[liae] Fr[anciae] dus Hyb[erniae]"; (reverse) "Possui deum adjutorem meum", and in the inner circle, "civitas London", denoting the place in which it was coined. The legend on the second is: (obverse) "Rex Angli et Franciae" with the arms of England and France quarterly in a shield; (reverse) "dominus Hiberniae" and 3 crowns in the field denoting the 3 kingdoms. This is from Mr Petrie. [? Yours faithfully] Thomas A. Larcom, 12 April 1835.

Parish of Clogher

Foundation of the See

In another account, this very ancient episcopal see is said to have been founded by Saint Karteen in 490. Lanigan, AD 506: "Saint Maccarthen of Clogher died in 506 and was succeeded by Saint Tigernach, who fixed his see or residence at Cluaneois (Clunes or Clones), still retaining the government of the church of Clogher, for which reason he was surnamed Ferdachrioch or 'the man of 2 districts." Saint Tigernach founded the church of Clones before he was appointed bishop. About the 11th century the bishopric of Louth was annexed to that of Clogher. AD 1610: in the 7th year of the reign of James I the revenues of the abbey were annexed to the bishopric, and the charter of the manor of Clogher is dated in the same year.

Ancient Entrenchment

Close to the palace on a hill called the Castle hill are the remains of a very ancient entrenchment, occupying a most conspicuous and commanding position. I could find no record or tradition which would in any way give a clue to ascertain its antiquity. The following sketch will give some idea of its extent. There is no appearance of walls about it, and the whole seems originally to have been constructed of earth. The principal fort is planted. [Plan of forts showing planting and ditches]. No other remains of antiquity are visible in the neighbourhood of the town.

MODERN TOPOGRAPHY

Town of Clogher

The town consists of one long street, one side of which is occupied by the demesne wall, the other side only being built upon. By knocking down a portion of the demesne wall equal in extent to the length of the street, from near the market house to its eastern extremity, and substituting a low wall and coping stone surmounted by an iron railing, a charming prospect would be opened to the inhabitants, and the appearance of the town would be greatly improved.

Public Buildings

The cathedral church, situated at the western end of the town on a commanding eminence, is a plain but commodious structure, capable of containing 800 persons. The market house built by the bishop, a sessions court house which has been recently very much improved, a new bridewell, very commodious, well planned and built, and equal to the exigencies of the town and neighbourhood, but in the construction of which the improvement of the appearance of the town has certainly not been considered; the bishop's schoolhouse at the eastern end of the town; the above are all the public buildings within the limits of the town.

There are several miserable inns but no good hotel in the town, but post horses and cars may be obtained at Shepherds's, near the church. An attempt has recently been made to improve the town which was deserving of greater success. In 1830 Joseph Trimble Esquire built at considerable expense a row of 6 new and handsome houses, 3 of which only in 1834 were occupied. The town in general has a neat appearance, is built of stone and slated, although it has but few really good private houses within its precincts. It is neither lighted or paved.

SOCIAL AND PRODUCTIVE ECONOMY

Local Government

Clogher was a charter town before the Union. By whom granted, date, constitution of corporate body etc., see Charter. Manor courts are held every 3 weeks in each of the 6 manors into which the parish is divided, with the exception of Clogher which has ceased to hold courts since the death of the late sovereign Joseph Briney Esquire in 1830-1, the present bishop as Lord of the Manor of Clogher declining to nominate a new seneschal.

Dispensary

In the town is established a dispensary, open at all times but particularly on Friday from 10 till 2, at which hours the surgeon, Dr Richard Twigg M.D., attends. Sometimes the number of patients who attend amount to from 50 to 60 weekly. It is supported by a private subscription of about 80 pounds yearly, to which the county adds 50 pounds. Dr Twigg also occasionally attends patients in their houses: his fee for country visits is 2s 6d.

Loan Fund

There is also a loan fund in the parish, of which the dean is the treasurer [and] the Reverend William Story, his curate, the secretary. It is supported by contributions from the gentry of the parish. From 10s to 40s are lent to the poor and needy on the security of two respectable persons, which loans are repaid by weekly instalments together with the interest. This establishment has been found a very great benefit, relieving the temporary distresses of the honest and industrious poor.

Savings Bank

A savings bank was established in the town in June 1832, since which period up to 26th April 1834 the number of depositors amounted to 88. The total deposits since the opening to the 26th April 1834 amounts to 1,148 pounds. Interest paid on deposits, 3 pounds 6s 8d per cent. Sums received from a shilling to 30 pounds. The depositors are generally in the class of farmers, servants and mechanics.

Fairs

The old fairs of Clogher were 2, held on the 6th May and 26th July. Monthly fairs have been held since the beginning of 1834 by the mutual agreement of the inhabitants on the first Saturday of every month. This arrangement no doubt originated with the spirit dealers of the town, for whose especial benefit they have been established. The 3 market days before Christmas are more than usually numerously attended and are called "margamores" or "great markets." There is a very good supply of meat, both beef, mutton and pork on market days. Butter, eggs and poultry are also not deficient. The yarn market is also very numerously attended. The fairs of Clogher seem to be particularly distinguished for the supply of pigs, cows and a few horses. No tolls or customs are levied.

Post and Conveyances

It is a daily post town. There is no regular public conveyance to Clogher. An effort was made to establish a daily car from Armagh through Clogher to Enniskillen and back, but it failed. It is extraordinary that so extensive an agricultural district should be so entirely without a public conveyance, the nearest coach being at Ballygawley, through which the mail from Derry to Dublin passes.

Schoolhouse

Immediately adjoining the town is the schoolhouse, which has a few acres of land attached for the benefit of the schoolmaster, who receives a salary of 40 pounds per annum from the bishop. The children are instructed in reading, writing and arithmetic, and the girls in needlework. They are all frequently examined in the holy Scriptures. Here any children of the neighbourhood whose parents are very poor may obtain gratuitous instruction, and 12 boys are supplied with comfortable clothing at the bishop's expense, 1 suit annually and 2 pairs of shoes each.

Provision for the Poor

Every Christmas the bishop distributes among the poor 3 beefs <beeves> and a couple of sheep. Some of the poorest receive in addition a small sum of money and each of His Lordship's labourers receive half a crown as a Christmas box. There is also a weekly distribution allowed by the bishop of a sum amounting to nearly 30s to about 20 old and very poor persons. The collection in the church weekly amounts to about [blank]. With these exceptions there are no endowments of a charitable nature, and the poor, the aged and the infirm depend on voluntary subscription and temporary relief.

MODERN TOPOGRAPHY AND SOCIAL ECONOMY

Village of Augher

For information relative to the village of Augher, which before the Union was a corporate town and returned a member to the Irish parliament, see the Charter. [Insert query: 2 members ?]. Proprietors: the town of Augher is the property of Sir J.R. Bunbury Bart and J.C. Moutray Esquire of Favour Royal. It is situated about one and a quarter miles east of Clogher, on a bend of the River Launy, and is 75 and a quarter miles (Irish) from Dublin Castle. The charter was granted to it by King James I, constituting Augher a free borough with a corporate body consisting of 1 burghermaster, 12 free burghers and the commonalty with various chartered rights.

It is now a miserable village. It is a penny post town daily, has a weekly market on Monday, principally for corn. The fairs are held on 28th March, 12th May, 14th August and 12th November, and the 3 last markets held on the 3 market days previous to Christmas are called "margermores" or "great markets" and are very numerously attended. They may be considered as fairs. It is a mean-built miserable town, with very trifling signs of improvement. The houses are thatched and slated indiscriminately. In 1830 a market house was built, having a public room over it in which the petty sessions are holden every fortnight. The magistrates who attend are Sir James Bunbury, J.C. Moutray Esquire, Reverend Francis Gervais, Witney Moutray Esquire, Charles Tottenham Esquire, Robert Waring Maxwell Esquire and Hugh Gore Edwards Esquire.

ANCIENT TOPOGRAPHY

Augher Castle

The wretched appearance of the village, however,

Parish of Clogher

only serves to contrast more strongly with the beautiful little lake and demesne of Augher Castle, the seat of Sir James Richardson Bunbury Bart. [Insert note: "The policy of the English and the turbulence of the times obliged all to whom grants of land were made to erect castles. When this castle was built it is not easy to discover. In 1602 there being a rumour, says Cox, that the Spaniards were again landed in Munster, Sir Henry Dowkra was placed at Augher. Pynnar's survey informs us that in 1600 Lord Ridgway had 315 acres at the Augher, for which he was to build a town, and had then performed thus far of the conditions: he had made 15 houses, whereof 2 were of lime and stone, the rest all cage work and couples. A principal burgess was to inhabit each house and to have 2 acres, besides commons for cattle. The whole number of burgesses to be 20", Grosse's *Antiquities*, 1795. Rising from the edge of the lake the old castle stood, a striking and picturesque ruin until about the year 1827 when he commenced the repair, which he finally completed in 1832 by adding 2 wings and other additions in the castellated style, in keeping with the character of the place and the old buildings.

The old castle appears to have been square with circular towers at the angles, with a dungeon <dongon> or keep in the centre, well flanked [text drawing]. In Carte's *Life of the Duke of Ormond*, Captain Mervyn is said to have been beseiged in the castle of Augher in 1641, at the breaking out of the rebellion. He was relieved by Sir William Stewart and convoyed to Derry. A garrison was left in Augher which being beseiged by Sir Phelim O'Neill <O'Neile> in person, gallantly stood a storm on November the 7th and repulsed the rebels with the loss of 200 men. They, however, soon afterwards quitted it for want of provisions. The ruins of the 4 circular towers with the connecting walls were visible in 1829. Spur Royal is the only name by which the castle is designated in the old family papers and in the charter granted to Augher by James I. Sir James Bunbury can give no reason for the name, but conjectured that it is owing to the shape of the main tower.

MODERN TOPOGRAPHY AND SOCIAL ECONOMY

Fivemiletown

In the patent, the ancient names of Ballynalurgan and Liscallaghan occur, but in that instrument they have been changed to Blessingbourne, by which name the present proprietor, Colonel Montgomery,

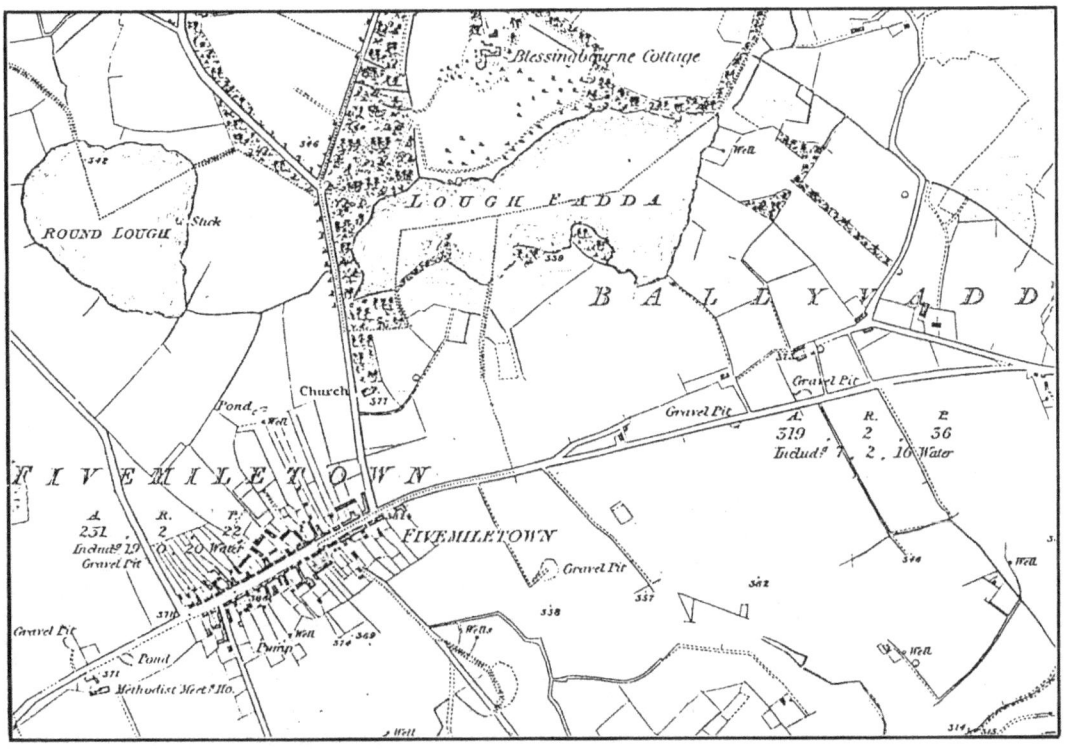

Map of Fivemiletown from the first 6" O.S. maps, 1830s

is anxious the village should be designated. No mention of Fivemiletown in any old document.

Buildings

The village was built in part by Margetson Armar Esquire (grand-uncle to the present proprietor), who purchased the manor of Blessingbourne from the late Lord Ferrard in 1731. All the tenements have been rebuilt since the year 1792. 39 houses have been rebuilt since 1804 and 18 houses built since 1804, the whole of which are slated. The following public buildings have been erected by Colonel Montgomery, the proprietor of the entire village, namely the shambles, the sessions house, the police barracks and a male and female schoolhouse. The following remark has been made by him which is worthy of notice, namely that there are 6 holdings or tenements in the village of Fivemiletown which were leased in perpetuity before he became possessed of the estate, and (strange to say) they are the only ones which are in a state of dilapidation and decay. One would suppose that a permanent interest in the premises would induce the owners to preserve and improve them. He has found notwithstanding that where such property is held by the middling and working classes, the very reverse is the case throughout this part of the country.

SOCIAL AND PRODUCTIVE ECONOMY

Commerce and Local Government

The town is on the whole in a progressive state of improvement, but much still remains to be done. There is a weekly market on Fridays and every alternate Friday a cloth market; 5 patent fairs viz. January 20th, 2nd Saturday in March, Thursday before Whit Sunday, the 3rd Saturday in August and the 20th November.

There is neither dispensary [nor] savings bank in the town, but the inhabitants of this end of the parish may avail themselves of those establishments at Clogher. Petty sessions are held every fortnight in Fivemiletown. The magistrates who attend are Hugh Montgomery, Oliver Bourke and William Patterson Esquires. The people are in general well behaved and the country quiet, the annual number of complaints at petty sessions not exceeding 200 on an average of 3 years. The usual force of police in the town is from 4 to 6. A seneschal is appointed by the Lord of the Manor of Blessingbourne, who holds a court leet monthly which is well administered. Within the precincts of the town are 2 places of worship, a chapel of ease which will contain about 300 persons and a Methodist meeting house.

Table of Trades and Occupations in 1833

[Insert addition: linen merchants 1, cloth merchants 3, grocers 3, publicans 14, ironmongers 3, cartwrights 2, stone masons 2, nailors 3, smiths 4, coopers 2, butchers 3, bakers 3, tailors 6, shoemakers 5, carpenters 3, slaters 1, dyers 1, mantua makers 2, auctioneer 1, flax dressers 2].

Newtown Saville

Newtown Saville is an inconsiderable village in the townland of Tamlaght at the northern end of the parish. It takes its name from Sir George Saville, its founder. 2 fairs are held here in the year, namely on the 1st of May and 1st of November. The church and Glebe House are situated close to the village in the townland Dunbiggan. The former will contain about 200 persons, but 180 conveniently. The house, which is small but comfortable, was built by the Board of First Fruits, and with 15 Irish acres set off as a perpetual cure.

MODERN TOPOGRAPHY

Gentlemen's Seats

The Bishop's Palace and Augher Castle, the seat of Sir James Richardson Bunbury Bart, have been described [earlier].

Cecil, beautifully situated at the foot of Knockmany hill, and the residence of the Reverend Francis Gervais, was built by him in 1829 and 30. It is a very handsome and convenient house in a plain style of architecture. The demesne contains 641 acres 2 roods 35 perches, comprising part of the townlands Knockmany, Ardunshion, Clarmore, Cloneblaugh, Eskermore and Annagarvey, and including 210 acres 1 rood 8 perches of wood, the whole of which together with 63 acres 32 perches in the adjacent townlands of Latbeg, Eskernabrogue, Tullyvernon, Glenhoy and Glenegeera the present enterprising proprietor has himself planted. [Insert addition: the manor of Cecil was created for Sir William Parsons, one of the lords justice, at the breaking out of the rebellion in 1641].

The following striking fact was mentioned to me by Mr Gervais, from which a very curious estimate may be made of the change in the value of money within the last century. About 120 years since the Cecil estate, comprising 39 townlands, was sold by H. Maxwell of Tynan for 6,250 pounds. Mr Gervais gave 95,000 pounds in 1811 for a part of this estate, the remainder having been sold a few years previously for 35,000 pounds, and Clone-

Parish of Clogher

blaugh and Claremore were purchased subsequently for 4,500 each. The improvement in the land did not produce this great change, for Mr Gervais in 1811 when he purchased found it in a wretched state. To his assiduity, care and enterprise are alone to be attributed the great improvements that are now observable in the manor of Cecil.

Killyfaddy House, the seat of Robert Waring Maxwell Esquire, a new house built in 1827 in a very plain style but convenient and commodious. It is surrounded by recent plantations, which the proprietor is constantly enlarging. In 1833 they amounted to 83 and a half statute acres of woods, namely 35 and a half acres in Killyfaddy, 19 and a half in Aghadrummin, 14 acres 16 perches in Lower Killeny, 1 acre 2 roods 16 perches in Upper Killeny, 4 acres 2 roods 16 perches in Carntallmore, 8 acres 16 perches in Mallaberry. At a great expense and much labour he has formed an artificial sheet of ornamental waters on the east side of the house, covering about 8 acres with a small island in the centre which is planted. The house is pleasantly situated at the foot of Mallaberry and the Nab Hill. The house is well supplied with excellent water from a spring at a considerable distance from the house on its north side, and a tank has been formed about 60 feet above it from which the water is conveyed in pipes about one-eighth of a mile.

Half-way between Augher and Clogher is Corick, the residence of the Reverend J.B. Story, chancellor of the diocese, beautifully situated on an insulated eminence at the foot of which runs the Launy river. It commands a charming view of the surrounding country. The house is old, but some additions were made in 1833 by the present proprietor with a view to comfort and convenience.

Close to the town is the Deanery, now occupied by the Honourable and Very Reverend Robert Maude, Dean of Clogher, who has much improved this pleasant and retired residence by opening a new avenue, and converted the old entrance into a very pretty terrace walk.

2 miles west of Clogher is Daisy Hill, the residence of [blank] Webb Esquire. The demesne embraces parts of the 2 townlands of Lisbuie and Findermore.

Fardross House, the ancient residence of the family of Gledstanes, who are large proprietors in its neighbourhood, is situated about 2 miles south west of Clogher, in a very retired spot at the foot of the mountains. The family is non-resident and the house is going into decay.

On the road to Omagh at the northern extremity of the parish is Cork Hill. Hugh Gore Edwards Esquire the proprietor erected the present house in 1832-3. It has little either in situation or appearance to recommend it.

Blessingbourne Cottage, the residence of Colonel Montgomery, was built in 1810. It is about a quarter of a mile north of Fivemiletown on Lough Fadda. It is a very pretty little place in the cottage style and is kept in the nicest order.

About the same distance west of Fivemiletown on the road to Brookeborough is Corcreevy House, the property of the Reverend William Burnside, now leased to and the residence of Colonel Driver.

Communications

No mail coach road or great thoroughfare traverses this parish. The principal roads are from Clogher to Fivemiletown, from Clogher to Fintona, from Clogher to Omagh and from Clogher to Ballygawley and to Aughnacloy. The whole of these are kept in good order at the expense of the county. New roads have been opened from Fivemiletown to Fintona, to Monaghan and to Clones at the expense of the counties Fermanagh and Tyrone. By these new lines the distance from Fintona to Monaghan and Clones will be shortened 3 miles and 8 miles respectively. The distance to Dublin from Fivemiletown is shortened 8 statute miles. The new line of road from Clogher to Fintona is a great improvement and has opened an inexhaustible supply of turbary from the townlands Corboe, Tatnadaveny, Altanaveragh and Kilnahushogue to the town of Clogher. The line of road from Clogher and Augher to Omagh has within a few years been greatly improved.

An attempt was made to bring a coach from Dublin through Aughnacloy and Augher to Omagh. After running for a season it was given up until the line of road should be improved, projects for which were already in agitation in 1833. The direct line from Derry to Dublin by Omagh and Monaghan would pass through Augher, very much reducing the distance. The principal impediments to the adoption of this new line are the bad roads through a very hilly country between Omagh and Augher on the one side; the improvements in this direction are, however, in progress. Between Augher and Monaghan a very dreary mountain line extends without an intermediate town or village. The line of road on this side is capable of great improvement.

ANCIENT TOPOGRAPHY

Antiquities

But very little is known of the general history and

state of this parish in former times. In ancient works of art it presents but little to interest the antiquary. The old castle of Augher, as has been already described, has risen from its ruins, and but little interest is excited in viewing the ruinous old walls of the castle of Aughentain or Ochentane. Of the period of its destruction or any other information with regard to it, I could not obtain any. [2 text drawings: castle walls].

The Reverend Francis Gervais of Cecil possesses several very curious relics which have at different times been discovered on his property in the manor of Cecil. See the accompanying sketches [Ancient Topography]. There is also a druidical altar or cromleck on the summit of Knockmany.

Social Economy

Ecclesiastical Documents

Division of the parish of Clogher into separate districts as to the duties of the several curates. [Transcription in another hand].

Newtown Saville to consist of the manors of Cope and Cecil (excepting the townlands of Roy and Tullyvernan in the manor of Cecil and as much of the manor of Cope which lies on the Clogher side of the circular road leading from Johnstons of the chapel, to Carentall mill, including Mr Maxwell's house and demesne), which shall belong to the Clogher division.

Fivemiletown to consist of the entire manors of Aghentain and Blessingbourne, together with the townlands of Glennoo, Newry, Killycorran, Gunnel, Mossfield, both the Nurchossys (except Milltown which belongs to Fardross) in the manor of Clogher and Balloch and Annagh in the manor of Augher.

District of Clogher to consist of the manors of Clogher and Augher, excepting the townlands above mentioned as added to the district of Fivemiletown, and also of Roy and Tullyvernan in the manor of Cecil, and as much of the manor of Cope as lies on the Clogher side of the road leading from Johnston's of the chapel to Carentall mill, as before mentioned, including Mr Maxwell's house and demesne. This arrangement made at Cecil the 15th May 1823, by the Dean of Clogher, the Reverend Dr Story, chancellor, and Reverend Francis Gervais, in presence of Thomas Birney, curate of Clogher.

Summary: Newtown Saville district: manor of Cecil (except Roy and Tullyvernon), manor of Cope except what lies on the Clogher side of the road from Johnston's of the chapel to Carentall

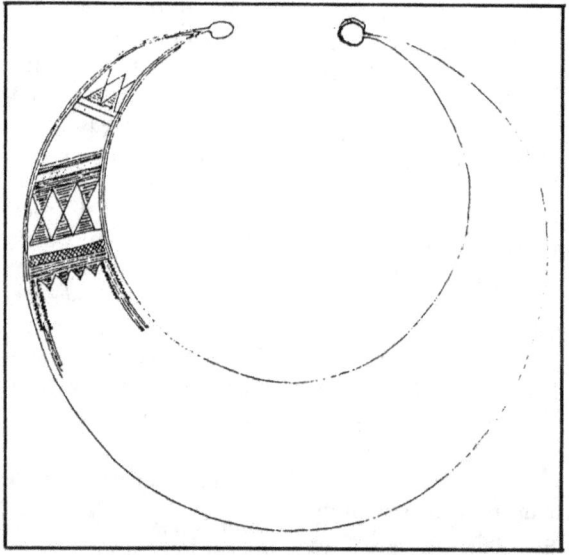

Gold ornament found in Tulnafoile

Parish of Clogher

bridge. Fivemiletown district: manor of Aghentain and Blessingbourne, and townlands of Glennoo, Newry, Killycorran, Gunnel, Mossfield, both Nurchossys in manor of Clogher, and Ballagh and Annagh in manor of Augher. Clogher district: manors of Clogher and Augher (excepting the townlands added as above to the district of Fivemiletown), Roy and Tullyvernan in manor of Cecil, and the part of manor Cope above excepted.

Tithe Applotment in 1831

An applotment of the sum of 850 pounds sterling on the parish of Clogher in the county of Tyrone, being the yearly amount of tithes agreed on under the Tithe Composition Act by and between the said parish and the Honourable and Very Reverend Robert Maude, Dean of Clogher, to be paid him annually for 21 years to be computed from the 1st day of November 1829. Applotted by us the undersigned commissioners legally apppointed by the Honourable and Very Reverend Robert Maude and by the parish of Clogher for that purpose. Dated at Clogher this 14th day of February 1831, signed James Trimble, Edward Beatty, commissioners.

Tithes: Manor of Clogher

[Table gives: name of townland, acres taxed, amount of tithe paid, number of tenants and holdings, amount of tithes, size of farms or holdings].

Ballymagowan, 166 acres 2 roods 23 perches, 31, 9 pounds 7s 1d ha'penny, 1 to 12 acres <each>.

Ballywholan, 1,223 acres 1 rood 20 perches, 33, 9 pounds 13s 6d ha'penny, 1 to 145 acres.

Ballyscally, 254 acres, 27, 3 pounds 9s 11d ha'penny, [blank].

Cloghlin, 47 acres 31 perches, 4, 11s 10d, 7 to 17 acres.

Corleaghan, 524 acres, 3, 1 pound 10s 8d, 131 to 262 acres.

Corcloghy or Corcloghey, 699 acres, 4, 2 pounds 2s 8d ha'penny, 7 to 459 acres.

Clogher, 97 acres 2 roods 37 perches taxed, [blank] tenants or holdings, 7 pounds 4s 1d, size from 0 to 12 acres.

Clogher Demesne, 342 acres, 1, 22 pounds 2s 9d, 0 to 342 acres.

Crossowen, 21 acres 3 roods 8 perches, 6, 1 pound 7s 10d, 2 to 9 acres.

Corick, 134 acres 3 roods 17 perches, 9, 8 pounds 10s 6d ha'penny, 1 to 101 acres.

Carnakinny, 42 acres 3 roods, 3, 2 pounds 5s, 9 to 24 acres.

Drumhirk, 97 acres 1 rood 39 perches, 9, 4 pounds 19s ha'penny, 3 to 28 acres.

Farneetra, 46 acres 21 perches, 14, 2 pounds 14s 7d ha'penny, 1 to 20 acres.

Frughmore, 148 acres 3 roods 4 perches, 16, 7 pounds 10s 2d ha'penny, 1 to 26 acres.

Grange, 681 acres 3 roods 21 perches, 1, 4 pounds 13s 1d, 0 to 681 acres.

Gunnel, 51 acres 2 roods, 2, 3 pounds 4s, 0 to 26 acres.

Killycorran, 65 acres 1 rood 1 perch, 5, 4 pounds 5d, 6 to 26 acres.

Lisnamoghery, 109 acres 1 rood 28 perches, 24, 5 pounds 12s 4d ha'penny, 1 to 10 acres.

Lismore, 83 acres 23 perches, 6, 3 pounds 18s 11d, 7 to 27 acres.

Mulloghatinny, 110 acres 2 roods 32 perches, 20, 5 pounds 14s 11d ha'penny, 1 to 33 acres.

Newry, 98 acres 3 roods 2 perches, 5, 5 pounds 9s 5d, 6 to 39 acres.

Retory, 90 acres 1 rood 21 perches, 13, 4 pounds 5s 8d ha'penny, 1 to 17 acres.

Shanco, 99 acres 3 roods 18 perches, 14, 1 pound 18s 10d ha'penny, 1 to 18 acres.

Tullybroom, 117 acres 7d, 15, 5 pounds 18s 10d, 1 to 10 acres.

Terew, 35 acres 2 roods 14 perches, 5, 2 pounds 7s 3d, 3 to 16 acres.

Total Irish acres in the manor of Clogher taxed: 5,389 acres 1 rood 7 perches at 130 pounds 13s 9d.

Tithes: Manor of Augher

Augher, 141 acres 3 roods 5 perches taxed, 41 tenants and holdings, tithes 9 pounds 6s 8d, size of holding 1 to 5 acres each.

Altnaveagh, 189 acres 3 roods 6 perches, 28, 8 pounds 19s 9d, 1 to 17 acres.

Annaloghan, 174 acres 1 rood 35 perches, 25, 7 pounds 19s 3d, 1 to 32 acres.

Annagh, 58 acres, 2, 3 pounds 10s 10d ha'penny, 10 to 48 acres.

Altnacarney, 104 acres 1 rood 36 perches, 12, 4 pounds 8s 5d, 1 to 48 acres.

Aghamilkin, 119 acres 2 roods 37 perches, 10, 2 pounds 9s 7d, 7 to 11 acres.

Aghindarragh, 166 acres 2 roods 24 perches, 11, 2 pounds 17s ha'penny, 5 to 31 acres.

Ballygreenan, 115 acres 1 rood 39 perches, 13, 6 pounds 14s 7d ha'penny, 3 to 18 acres.

Ballagh, 89 acres 2 roods, 10, 5 pounds 9d, 1 to 35 acres.

Ballymacan, 1,035 acres 3 roods 12 perches, 32, 10 pounds 17s 5d ha'penny, 3 to 143 acres.

Ballynagorragh or Ballynagoragh, 117 acres

1 rood, 21, 7 pounds 4s 1d ha'penny, 1 to 16 acres.

Branter, 32 acres, 4, 1 pound 13s 5d ha'penny, 4 to 15 acres.

Cauldruin, 68 acres 1 rood 10 perches, 13, 4 pounds 3s, 1 to 13 acres.

Car, 98 acres 3 roods 20 perches, 17, 5 pounds 16s 9d, 1 to 24 acres.

Cornamuckla, 120 acres 1 rood 13 perches, 15, 5 pounds 13s 11d ha'penny, 4 to 17 acres.

Cavan, 110 acres 1 rood 24 perches, 7, 2 pounds 7s 11d ha'penny, 9 to 27 acres.

Cargagh, 82 acres 3 roods 10 perches, 13, 2 pounds 7s 7d, 2 to 13 acres.

Cloonycappogue or Cloonacappogue, 123 acres 1d, 12, 2 pounds 10s 5d ha'penny, 6 to 18 acres.

Carrickavoy, 14 acres 3 roods 20 perches, 4, 7s 8d, 1 to 8 acres.

Castlehill Demesne, 135 acres 2 roods 2 perches, 1, 10 pounds 2s 3d ha'penny, 0 to 135 acres.

Derrydrummond, 95 acres 1 rood 2 perches, 6, 1 pound 10s 5d ha'penny, 5 to 27 acres.

Derries, 63 acres 3 roods 5 perches, 7, 2 pounds 5s 11d ha'penny, 4 to 20 acres.

Dernascobe, 86 acres 1 rood 3 perches, 14, 4 pounds 2s 5d ha'penny, 1 to 13 acres.

Kilclay, 127 acres 1 rood 33 perches, 15, 7 pounds 5s 10d, 3 to 33 acres.

Kilrudden, 84 acres 3 roods 1 perch, 2, 3 pounds 2d, 38 to 46 acres.

Lisgorran, 133 acres 1 rood 15 perches, 7, 2 pounds 1s 8d ha'penny, 5 to 30 acres.

Lisbawn or Lisbane, 73 acres 1 rood 29 perches, 4, 1 pound 6s 7d ha'penny, 6 to 51 acres.

Mulloghmore, 162 acres 29 perches, 18, 6 pounds 14s 6d ha'penny, 1 to 33 acres.

Mullans, 87 acres 2 roods 26 perches, 13, 5 pounds 11s 9d ha'penny, 1 to 13 acres.

Springtown, 100 acres 3 roods 22 perches, 10, 4 pounds 8s 8d, 5 to 19 acres.

Slatmore, 242 acres 2 roods 32 perches, 25, 8 pounds 9s 6d ha'penny, 3 to 70 acres.

Slatbeg, 459 acres 2 roods 18 perches, 15, 7 pounds 5s, 7 to 40 acres.

Sessagh, 38 acres 1 rood 25 perches, 11, 2 pounds 6s 9d ha'penny, 1 to 5 acres.

Tavinymore or Tavenamore, 213 acres 3 roods 16 perches, 24, 6 pounds 2s 10d ha'penny, 3 to 18 acres.

Tully, 87 acres 3 roods 39 perches, 12, 3 pounds 6s 2d ha'penny, 1 to 29 acres.

Total Irish acres in the manor of Augher taxed: 5,157 acres 2 roods 29 perches at 170 pounds 7s 6d ha'penny.

Tithes: Manor of Cecil

Cormore, 299 acres 33 perches taxed, 43 tenants or holdings, tithes 12 pounds 15s 8d, 3 to 14 acres size.

Annagarvey or Annagarvy and Divinagh, 103 acres 2 roods 14 perches, 13, 4 pounds 2s 6d, 2 to 33 acres.

Bank, 33 acres 3 roods 34 perches, 4, 1 pound 5s 11d, 3 to 10 acres.

Belnaclogh, 104 acres 32 perches, 7, 4 pounds 15s 5d, 1 to 14 acres.

Beltinny, 288 acres 23 perches, 37, 12 pounds 7s 1d, 1 to 18 acres.

Cecil Demesne, 367 acres 35 perches, 1, 18 pounds 3s, 0 to 367 acres.

Clarmore, 163 acres 1 perch, 22, 7 pounds 7s, 1 to 15 acres.

Clonyblagh, 152 acres 1 rood 38 perches, 24, 6 pounds 9s 6d, 2 to 12 acres.

Dunbiggin, 179 acres 1 rood 24 perches, 18, 7 pounds 9s, 1 to 11 acres.

Eskermore, 217 acres 3 roods 38 perches, 24, 9 pounds 3s 10d, 1 to 25 acres.

Eskernabrogue, 164 acres 6 perches, 19, 5 pounds 10s 3d ha'penny, 1 to 17 acres.

Fernandrum, 324 acres 3 roods 37 perches, 30, 14 pounds 7s 3d, 2 to 19 acres.

Glenageera, 217 acres 3 roods 21 perches, 25, 8 pounds 10s 11d, 1 to 18 acres.

Glenhoyse, 75 acres 2 roods 32 perches, 8, 3 pounds 18s 5d, 4 to 17 acres.

Kilnakeery, 397 acres 2 roods 37 perches, 31, 15 pounds 14s, 1 to 21 acres.

Knockmany, 25 acres 16 perches, 4, 1 pound 2s 9d, 4 to 9 acres.

Latbeg, 145 acres 3 roods 30 perches, 11, 5 pounds 2s 10d, 1 to 71 acres.

Lisnarable, 205 acres 1 rood 11 perches, 17, 8 pounds 3d, 1 to 21 acres.

Longridge, 44 acres 3 roods 34 perches, 7, 1 pound 8s 10d, 2 to 10 acres.

Roy, 38 acres 1 rood 28 perches, 4, 2 pounds 12s 3d, 1 to 17 acres.

Tamlaght, 229 acres 1 rood 19 perches, 33, 9 pounds 17s 5d, 1 to 20 acres.

Tullycorker, 182 acres 9 perches, 21, 7 pounds 17s 1d, 1 to 17 acres.

Tullyvernan, 100 acres 2 roods 38 perches, 11, 5 pounds 4s 1d, 4 to 13 acres.

Tulnafeole, 314 acres 3 roods 7 perches, 28, 11 pounds 1s 10d, 1 to 63 acres.

Techeny, 370 acres 21 perches, 41, 12 pounds 1s 10d, 1 to 27 acres.

Total acres taxed in the manor of Cecil: 4,746

Parish of Clogher

acres 1 rood 18 perches at 196 pounds 7s 11d ha'penny.

Tithes: Manor of Cope

Altanarvey, 338 acres 3 roods 26 perches taxed, 17 tenants or holdings, tithe 8 pounds 13s 11d, 4 to 84 acres size.

Aghendrummond or Aghindrumond, 50 acres 3 roods 24 perches, 4, 2 pounds 12s 5d, 3 to 23 acres.

Ballaghneed, 238 acres 2 roods 34 perches, 18, 8 pounds 8s 2d, 2 to 46 acres.

Corboe, 419 acres 1 rood 28 perches, 22, 11 pounds 15s 4d ha'penny, 3 to 84 acres.

Carntall, 134 acres 3 roods 30 perches, 18, 7 pounds 9s 3d, 1 to 23 acres.

Corkhill, 147 acres 1 rood 34 perches, 14, 7 pounds 1s, 1 to 49 acres.

Dromore, 556 acres 3 roods 11 perches, 21, 12 pounds 18s, 3 to 63 acres.

Esera, 316 acres 1 rood 6 pounds, 25, 12 pounds 6s 6d, 1 to 50 acres.

Fogart, 170 acres 28 perches, 15, 5 pounds 15s 6d, 1 to 17 acres.

Killyfaddy detached, 26 acres 1 rood 10 perches, 3, 1 pound 11s 5d, 10 to 16 acres.

Killyfaddy demesne, 200 acres 2 roods 28 perches, 1, 10 pounds 12s, 0 to 201 acres.

Kilnahushogue or Kilnahushog, 363 acres 8 perches, 33, 10 pounds 19s 1d, 1 to 22 acres.

Lislee, 103 acres 3 roods 2 perches, 5, 3 pounds 11s 8d, 13 to 26 acres.

Largnaglare or Lurgnaglare, 195 acres 15 perches, 18, 7 pounds 8s 8d, 6 to 19 acres.

Mullans, 99 acres 1 rood 34 perches, 12, 3 pounds 19s 2d, 1 to 19 acres.

Tatnadavney or Tatnadavny, 452 acres 2 roods 32 perches, 18, 11 pounds 8s 4d, 11 to 69 acres.

Total acres taxed in the manor of Cope: 3,814 acres 2 roods 30 perches at 126 pounds 10s 5d ha'penny.

Tithes: Manor of Mountstewart

Aghendarragh or Aghendara, 151 acres 1 rood 25 perches taxed, 9 tenants or holdings, tithe 7 pounds 9s 3d, 9 to 22 acres size.

Aghengowly or Aghengowley 130 acres 28 perches, 9, 6 pounds 2s 9d, 4 to 28 acres.

Aghenlork, 151 acres 1 rood 23 perches, 9, 6 pounds 8s 5d, 6 to 32 acres.

Aghentain, 52 acres 1 rood 16 perches, 6, 3 pounds 3s 5d, 1 to 23 acres.

Ballyness, 479 acres 3 roods 25 perches, 18, 7 pounds 19s 6d, 2 to 117 acres.

Bolies, 255 acres 1 rood 30 perches, 15, 6 pounds 6s 5d, 6 to 106 acres.

Carnegat, 276 acres 3 roods 37 perches, 10, 3 pounds 17s 2d, 9 to 74 acres.

Cavanakirk, 247 acres 1 rood 5 perches, 14, 7 pounds 17s 6d, 1 to 50 acres.

Cole, 673 acres 2 perches, 19, 6 pounds 15s, 4 to 102 acres.

Donaghmoyne or Donaghmoyn, 105 acres 2 roods 5 perches, 6, 6 pounds 8s 9d, 9 to 26 acres.

Edergole, 651 acres 1 rood 19 perches, 11, 6 pounds 16s 8d, 5 to 105 acres.

Gurlaw, 107 acres 1 rood 30 perches, 6, 5 pounds 2s 6d, 7 to 40 acres.

Killeny or Killeany, 54 acres 19 perches, 6, 1 pound 18s 8d, 4 to 16 acres.

Killygordon, 366 acres 6 perches, 12, 3 pounds 17s 5d, 8 to 67 acres.

Knocknacarney, 102 acres 1 rood 7 perches, 12, 3 pounds 19s 5d, 4 to 18 acres.

Lislane, 554 acres 1 rood 31 perches, 12, 13 pounds 18s 9d, 3 to 32 acres.

Losset, 112 acres 1 rood 37 perches, 6, 5 pounds 15s 10d, 3 to 36 acres.

Lungs, 129 acres 3 roods 31 perches, 7, 7 pounds 11s 9d, 4 to 54 acres.

Mallybeney, 174 acres 27 perches, 12, 6 pounds 5s 1d, 3 to 28 acres.

Mountstewart, 377 acres 1 rood 8 perches, 19, 8 pounds 1d, 3 to 70 acres.

Prolisque, 145 acres 3 roods 10 perches, 14, 6 pounds 8s 4d ha'penny, 4 to 16 acres.

Rehorrin, 190 acres 36 perches, 12, 8 pounds 12s 6d, 5 to 43 acres.

Rosemealan or Rosemealin, 117 acres 2 roods 5 perches, 7, 5 pounds 13s 8d, 1 to 36 acres.

Scientian, 173 acres 9 perches, 8, 4 pounds 8s 7d, 1 to 43 acres.

Screeby, 142 acres 1 rood 6 perches, 10, 7 pounds 17s 10d, 6 to 20 acres.

Sess, 191 acres 1 rood 11 perches, 19, 6 pounds 11s 1d, 1 to 43 acres.

Shantana, Shantanagh or Shantonagh, 210 acres 33 perches, 6, 3 pounds 18s 7d, 7 to 58 acres.

Skelgagh, 137 acres 1 rood 3 perches, 10, 4 pounds 16s, 2 to 28 acres.

Townagh, 54 acres 1 rood 14 perches, 6, 2 pounds 16s 6d ha'penny, 7 to 11 acres.

Tatnafinnell or Tatnafinnel, 526 acres 3 roods 25 perches, 13, 7 pounds 11s 3d ha'penny, 3 to 207 acres.

Total acres taxed in manor of Mountstewart: 7,042 acres 3 perches at 184 pounds 8s 9d ha'penny.

Manor of Blessingbourne

Annagh, 73 acres 2 roods 3 perches taxed, 7

tenants or holdings, tithe 7 pounds 15s 8d ha'penny, 3 to 40 acres size.

Ballyvadden, 183 acres 3 roods 22 perches, 28, 8 pounds 13s 5d ha'penny, 1 to 13 acres.

Blessingbourne Cottage demesne, 64 acres 2 roods 34 perches, 1, 3 pounds 7s 8d, 0 to 64 acres.

Blacklands, 65 acres 3 roods 12 perches, 3, 19s 11d, 16 to 29 acres.

Corcreevy Barnside, 191 acres 1 rood 27 perches, 22, 9 pounds 18s 4d, 1 to 87 acres.

Fivemiletown, 120 acres 1 rood 3 perches, 32, 8 pounds 3s 4d, 1 to 6 acres.

Gortmore Birney and others, 129 acres 22 perches, 15, 5 pounds 2s 7d ha'penny, 1 to 27 acres [bracketed together with Corcreevy with note "perpetuity"].

Ranenly, 71 acres, 9, 3 pounds 10s 5d ha'penny, 3 to 26 acres.

Total acres taxed in the manor of Blessingbourne: 899 acres 3 roods 3 perches at 41 pounds 11s 6d.

Notes on Tithe Applotment

[Different hand] Parish of Clogher, Irish acres titheable.

Manor of Cecil contains 4,746 acres 1 rood 18 perches at 196 pounds 7s 11d ha'penny.

Mountstewart contains 7,042 acres 3 perches at 184 pounds 8s 9d ha'penny.

Augher contains 5,157 acres 2 roods 29 perches at 170 pounds 7s 6d ha'penny.

Clogher contains 5,389 acres 1 rood 7 perches at 130 pounds 13s 9d.

Cope contains 3,814 acres 2 roods 30 perches at 126 pounds 10s 5d ha'penny.

Blessingbourne <Blessingburne> contains 899 acres 3 roods 3 perches at 41 pounds 11s 6d.

Total Irish acres taxed 27,049 3 roods 10 perches at 850 pounds, roads, rivers and canals excluded. Also in the manor of Clogher 8 townlands being abbey lands. For 21 years from the 1st November 1829. Lisbuie, Findermore, 2 Nurchosys, Aughnaglough, Tulnavert, Fardross, Glennoo, [all] abbey lands and tithe free.

ANCIENT TOPOGRAPHY

Urns

2 urns of this size and one larger, see accompanying sketches [drawings of decorated urn]. 3 small urns containing bones which were so small that it was doubted whether they were human. Found in townland Ardunshion, parish of Clogher in the spring of 1826, by people who were setting potatoes.

Golden Ornament for the Neck

Golden ornament for the neck (query). Found in Tulnafoile townland, parish of Clogher, in making a road in a small quantity of gravel in the centre of a bog, weight about 2 oz. The Reverend F. Gervais, the possessor, gave 4 pounds 4s for it, was offered 8 pounds. It is very thin but very pure gold. Sketched full size by R. Stotherd, Lieutenant Royal Engineers, March 1833. [Drawing of lunula with detail of end clasps].

Note on Historical Source

Aughinleck man[uscript] library. *Memoir of the life of Dr Spotiswood* written by himself, extracted from the above manuscript library. Very interesting as giving a great deal of information relative to Augher and Clogher.

Earthen Vase

An earthen vase found in the autumn of 1826 with some human bones, some teeth and a part of a skull <scull>. All the bones found in the vase are still present in it. It was found enclosed within 4 flagstones, with a flag at bottom and another at top, about 3 feet beneath the surface. Sketched by Lieutenant Stotherd in May 1833, the full size. The vase is in the possession of the Reverend Francis Gervais of Cecil, parish of Clogher, on whose property it was found, in townland Ardunshion.

Brass Pot and Quern

A large brass pot was also found on Knockmany, full of deer's tallow or butter. It was 1 foot 6 inches high and would hold about 8 or 9 gallons. A quern or hand millstone was found near Eskragh chapel.

Watch

Mr Gervais has a watch found in the county Fermanagh, date 1603, Giles Smith (maker), of very rude construction, of silver, oval. Size [outline drawing in text]. [It] was purchased by Thomas Young Esquire from a country man in the neighbourhood of Gardenhill.

Patent of Killyfaddy Manor

Richard Cope Esquire, patent of Killyfaddy manor, 15th of Charles I, December 21st. Rent 32 pounds 6s 3d, and again 22 pounds 10s 9d to keep 8 pikemen with 8 muskets. Tithes of the estate granted to Richard Cope Esquire, but no proof of being demanded. Could not grant more than 40 years or 3 lives to real native Irish.

Parish of Clogher

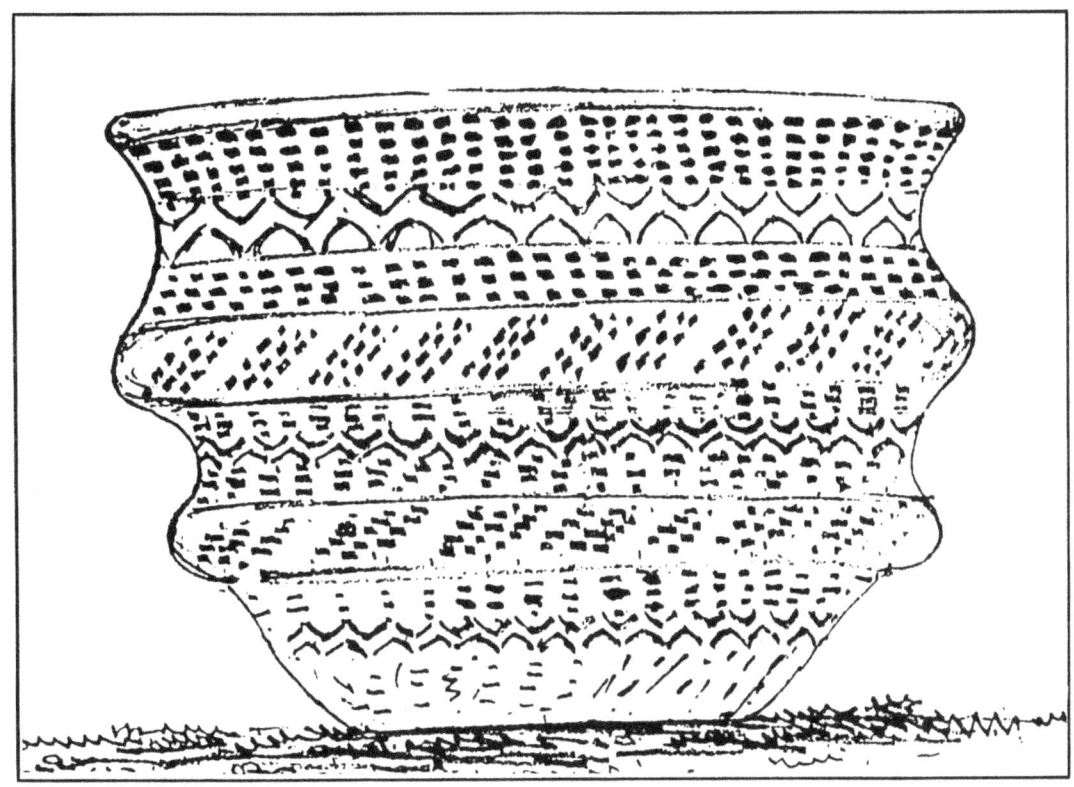

Earthen vase from Ardunshion

Brass Object

The Bishop of Clogher has two similar ornaments found with a large snaffle bit in the county Clare in a large Danish rath on the western coast. Found on Knockmany, year unknown, near the druid's altar on the summit, either brass or copper. Now in the possession of Reverend F. Gervais of Cecil, the proprietor of Knockmany. [Drawing] sketched full size by R. Stotherd, Lieutenant Royal Engineers, March 10th 1833.

SOCIAL ECONOMY

Tithe-free Townlands

The following townlands in the parish of Clogher are tithe free. The glebe lands are marked thus (X). Glebe lands: the dean's demesne, Carraclogher, Lisbeg, part of Drumhirk, Bigh, Tulliquin. Abbey lands: Lisbuoy, Aughnaglough, Tulnavert, Findermore, Fardross, Nurchosy (Scotch) settled by natives of Scotland, Nurchosy (Irish) settled by natives of Ireland, Glennoo.

MODERN TOPOGRAPHY

Places of Worship

In the parish there are 3 churches, namely the cathedral and 2 chapels of ease. 3 churches: the cathedral which holds 800 persons, Fivemiletown church which holds 300 persons, Newtown Saville church which holds 200 persons. 1 Presbyterian meeting house at Killyfaddy, holds 400 persons. 2 Seceding meeting houses: 1 Seceding meeting house at Tullyhun, holds 150 persons, 1 Seceding meeting house in Longridge, holds 150 persons. 3 Roman Catholic chapels: 1 at Eskragh holds 600 persons, 1 at Aughadrummin holds 800 persons, 1 in the manor of Aughintain holds 500 persons. At Ballynagoragh Fort there is a regular Roman Catholic congregation in the open air. Subscriptions are now collecting to build a chapel on the spot. The congregation here is large. The see of Clogher consists of one bishop, one dean, one archdeacon, one chancellor and one precentor.

ANCIENT TOPOGRAPHY

Canoe and Crannog

In Tullybroom a canoe was found in 1823 in a bog, from which it would appear that in former times the extensive flat in which it was found was covered with water, although there is no lake in that neighbourhood and there is no tradition of its having been so. The canoe was found about 1 mile from the river. At the point where it was found there were appearances of a framework of oak in the bog, like an island, and a number of stones have recently been moved from the edge of the bog which have the appearance of a wharf.

SOCIAL ECONOMY

Printed Table of Subscriptions to Widows' Fund

Subscriptions for the benefit of the widows of the diocese of Clogher for the year 1827. [Table contains the following headings: benefices, subscribers, subscription for 1827 and arrears paid].

The Lord Bishop of Clogher 40 pounds; the vicar-general, Dr Hamilton, 3 pounds 3s.

Aghabog: the Very Reverend Dean Hood 1 pound 15s, the Reverend W. Row 10s 6d, arrears 1 pound 10s. Aghalurcher: Reverend Dr Russell 3 pounds, Reverend A. Hurst 10s 6d, Reverend J. Wilson [blank]. Aghavea, Mr Stewart 1 pound 15s, Mr Hare 10s 6d. Aghnamullen: Very Reverend Dean Roper 3 pounds, arrears 41 pounds 10s 9d farthing, Reverend William Roper 10s 6d.

Ballibay: Mr Langrishe, 1 pound 10s. Belleek: James Tuthill [blank]. Bohoe: Thomas Johnston 1 pound 10s, Mr Moore 10s 6d.

Carrickmacross: Reverend Dr Robinson 3 pounds, Mr Whitaker 10s 6d. Cleenish: Mr Sweeny 2 pounds 10s 9d farthing, Mr Porteus [blank], Mr Clarke [blank], Mr James Achinleck 10s 6d. Clogher: Honourable and Very Reverend B. Maude 3 pounds, Reverend T. Birney 10s 6d, J.B. Story 10s 6d, H.A. Burke 10s 6d, Very Reverend Dean Roper 3 pounds. Clones: Reverend Mr Taylor 10s 6d, Mr Ball 10s 6d, Mr Collins 10s 6d. Clontibret: Venerable Archdeacon Dean Russell [blank]. Currin: Reverend William Moffat 2 pounds 10s, arrears 2 pounds 10s, Andrew Foster 10s 6d.

Derrybrusk: George Harris 15s. Derryvolan: Dr Miller 3 pounds, Mr Rogers [blank], Mr James Irwin [blank]. Devenish: Hugh Lawder [blank], Andrew Young [blank]. Donagh: Mr Pratt 1 pound 10s. Donaghmoyne: J.G. Porter 2 pounds 15s 4d ha'penny, Mr Devereux 10s 6d. Dromore: Honourable and Reverend Mr Plunket 3 pounds, Mr Marshall 10s 6d, Mr Leahy 10s 6d. Drumkeeran: Mr Richardson [blank], Francis Hurst 10s 6d. Drumsnat: Allen Mitchell 15s. Drumully: Mr Hewitt 1 pound 10s, Mr E. Simpson 10s 6d.

Ematris: Reverend Mr Annesley 1 pound 10s. Enniskillen: Honourable Reverend I.C. Maude 2 pounds 5s, Reverend Mr Laird 10s 6d. Errigle: B. Hobart [blank].

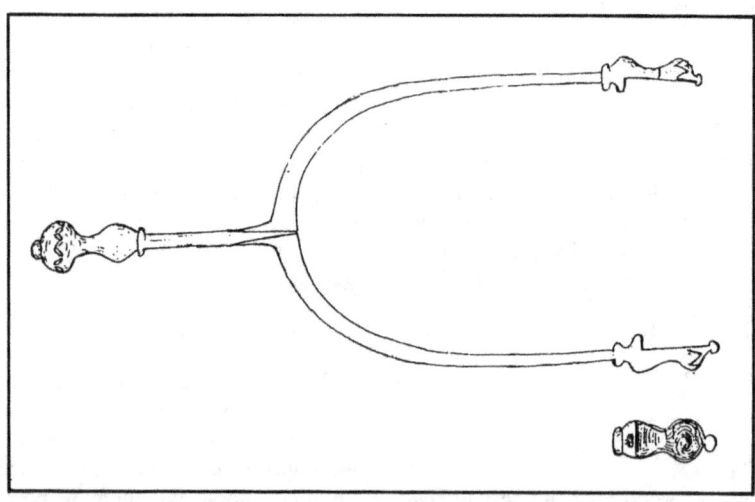

Brass ornament found on Knockmany

Parish of Clogher

Fintona: William Atthill 2 pounds 15s, William Tomes [blank].

Galloon: Dr Story 2 pounds, J.M. Graydon [blank].

Innis McSaint [Inishmacsaint]: Mr H. Hamilton 2 pounds 5s, Mr Dunbar 10s 6d, Charles Gayer [blank], Mr Read 10s 6d. Inniskeen: Reverend J.B. Sterling [blank].

Killanny: Sir H. Lees Bart 2 pounds 15s, Mr Handcock [blank]. Kilmore: Mr Schomberg 1 pound 15s, Mr Witstone [blank]. Kilskeery: J.G. Porter 2 pounds 15s 4d ha'penny, Arthur Irvine 10s 6d. Killeevan: John Wright [blank].

Magheracloone: Patrick Cumming 1 pound 10s. Magheracross: John Erwin 1 pound 15s. Magheraculmony: William Atthill 2 pounds 5s, Mr Clifford [blank]. Monaghan: Charles Evatt 2 pounds 10s, Mr Maffet [blank]. Mucknoe: Mr Hacket 1 pound 15s, Mr Sneyd [blank].

Rossory: Mr Auchinleck [blank], John Auchinleck [blank].

Tydavnet [Tedavnet]: H.L. St George [blank], Mr Potterton 10s 6d. Tyhollan [Tehallan]: H.C. Crookshank 2 pounds. Templecarne: Mr Jacob [blank], Mr Ingram 10s 6d. Trory: Mr Young [blank]. Tullycorbet: Mr Jellett [blank].

Tubrid chaplain: Mr Stack [blank]. The preacher: I.R. Tarleton [blank]. Diocesan schoolmaster: Mr Mooney [blank]. Carrick schoolmaster: Mr Twiss Palmer 10s 6d. Total 125 pounds 6d farthing.

[Names of widows, each paid 13 pounds 17s] Mrs Stanley, Mrs Stack, Mrs Caulfield, Mrs Hurst, Mrs Weir, Mrs Cochrane, Mrs Ryan, Mrs Tuthill, Mrs Ovens, Mrs O'Flagherty, Mrs Foster, Mrs Bagwell, Mrs Brandon. 14th widow Mrs Annesley.

Expenditure: Balance due last year 17 pounds 6d 11d ha'penny, subscription 1827, 125 pounds 6d farthing, arrears for 1827 46 pounds 13s 3d farthing; year's interest for October 1827, 57 pounds 17s 4d.

Per contra: 13 widows 180 pounds 1s, printing 1 pound 1s, postage and stationery 19s, error Rev. H. Hamilton 5s, balance to be funded, if this year 1828 will pay the 14 widows, 64 pounds 12s 1d.

[Handwritten addition: 14 widows 193 pounds 16s; average annual subscription: 125 pounds [difference] 68 pounds 18s].

Balance in both cases 246 pounds 18s 1d, signed I.B. Story, treasurer.

Education

[Table contains the following headings: name of townland where situated, religion and sex of pupils, remarks as to how supported, when established].

Fivemiletown male school, 40 Protestants, 14 Roman Catholics, 54 total pupils; Scriptures are read.

Fivemiletown female school, 33 Protestants, 13 Roman Catholics, 46 total pupils; Scriptures are not read.

Tullyhone day school, 35 Protestants, 1 Roman Catholic, 22 males, 14 females, 36 total pupils; Scriptures are read.

Ballagh day school, 18 Protestants, 4 Roman Catholics, 14 males, 8 females, 22 total pupils; Scriptures are read.

Fardross day school, 34 Protestants, 4 Roman Catholics, 26 males, 12 females, 38 total pupils; Scriptures are read constantly.

Scientien day school, 7 Protestants, 45 Roman Catholics, 32 males, 20 females, 52 total pupils; Scriptures are not read.

Morrily, 29 Protestants, 18 Roman Catholics, 26 males, 21 females, 47 total pupils; Scriptures seldom read.

Nurchassy, 16 Protestants, 12 Roman Catholics, 19 males, 9 females, 28 total pupils; Scriptures seldom read.

Aghnaglough, 19 Protestants, 27 Roman Catholics, 27 males, 19 females, 46 total pupils; the master has no objection but they are not read in common.

Aghenlark, 15 Protestants, 6 males, 9 females, 15 total pupils; Scriptures are not read.

Prolisk, 38 Protestants, 18 males, 20 females, 38 total pupils; Scriptures are read.

Eskregh national school, 12 Protestants, 70 Roman Catholics, 48 males, 34 females, 82 total pupils; no bibles but a few testaments in the school.

Beltany male school, 43 pupils, all Protestant; Scriptures are read.

Beltany female school, 42 Protestants, 7 Roman Catholics, 49 total pupils; Scriptures are read.

Tullyvernan male school, 34 Protestants, 7 Roman Catholics, 41 total pupils; Scriptures are read.

Tullyvernan female school, 42 Protestants, 7 Roman Catholics, 49 total pupils; Scriptures are read.

Chapel day school, 2 Protestants, 50 Roman Catholics, 30 males, 22 females, 52 total pupils; Scriptures are not read.

Ranenly day school, 21 Protestants, 12 Roman Catholics, 21 males, 12 females, 33 total pupils; Scriptures not read constantly.

Clogher male school, 28 Protestants, 10 Roman Catholics, 38 total pupils; Scriptures are read.

Clogher female school, 24 Protestants, 4 Roman Catholics, 28 total pupils; Scriptures are read.

Lisgorran day school, 18 males, 12 females, 30 total pupils, all Roman Catholics.

Aughendara, 2 Protestants, 33 Roman Catholics, 19 males, 16 females, 35 total pupils.

Ballynagoragh, 2 Protestants, 35 Roman Catholics, 28 males, 9 females, 37 total pupils; [Lisgorran, Aughendara and Ballynagoragh all bracketed together: Scriptures not admitted into the school]. Lislee, 39 Protestants, 13 Roman Catholics, 34 males, 18 females, 52 total pupils; Scriptures are read.

Eskeratrool, 11 males, 6 females, 17 total pupils, all Protestant; Scriptures are read.

Kilnahushogue, 17 males, 15 females, 32 total pupils, all Roman Catholics; Scriptures not admitted.

Ballyscally, 40 Protestants, 40 Roman Catholics, 40 males, 40 females, 80 total pupils; Scriptures read occasionally.

Miss Gervais' <Jervais's> male school, 24 Protestants, 4 Roman Catholics, 28 total pupils; Scriptures are read.

Miss Gervais' female school, 33 Protestants, 8 Roman Catholics, 41 total pupils; Scriptures are read.

Augher day school, 32 Protestants, 31 Roman Catholics, 31 males, 32 females, 63 total pupils; Scriptures seldom read.

Augher female school, 3 Protestants, 14 Roman Catholics, 2 males, 15 females, 17 total pupils; Scriptures seldom read.

Genegan day school, 18 males, 14 females, 32 total pupils, all Roman Catholics; Scriptures not read.

Fivemiletown day school, 37 Protestants, 15 Roman Catholics, 30 males, 22 females, 52 total pupils; Scriptures are read.

Fivemiletown: Table of Schools

[Table] Fivemiletown, 44 Protestants, 20 Roman Catholics, 64 total pupils, all males; subscriptions and scholars' fees aided by the Board of National Education, established 1832.

Fivemiletown, 28 Protestants, 19 Roman Catholics, 47 total pupils, all females; subscription and scholars' fees aided by the Board of National Education, established 1833.

Fivemiletown, 39 Protestants, 18 Roman Catholics, 32 males, 25 females, 57 total; [supported] by scholars' fees, established 1832.

Ranenly, 28 Protestants, 13 Roman Catholics, 27 males, 14 females, 41 total; [supported] scholars' fees, established 1818. NB In 1832 2 schoolmasters died who had kept schools attended by children of all persuasions for several years.

Schools

[Table] The number of scholars in the parish of Clogher, both male and female.

Fivemiletown day school, Established Church boys 22, Presbyterian boys 18, Roman Catholic boys 14; Scriptures read.

Fivemiletown female school, 14 Established Church, 19 Presbyterians, 13 Roman Catholics; Scriptures are not read.

Tullyhane day school, 8 Established Church boys, 13 Presbyterian boys, 1 Roman Catholic boy, 14 Presbyterian girls; Scriptures are read.

Ballanogh day school, 6 Established Church boys, 6 Presbyterian boys, 2 Roman Catholic boys, 6 Presbyterian girls, 2 Roman Catholic girls; Scriptures are read.

Fordross day school, 18 Established Church boys, 6 Presbyterian boys, 2 Roman Catholic boys, 10 Established Church girls, 2 Roman Catholic girls; Scriptures are read constantly.

Sientian day school, 3 Established Church boys, 29 Roman Catholic boys, 4 Established Church girls, 16 Roman Catholics girls; Scriptures are not read.

Morrily day school, 8 Established Church boys, 7 Presbyterian boys, 11 Roman Catholic boys, 6 Established Church girls, 8 Presbyterian girls, 7 Roman Catholic girls; Scripture but seldom read.

Nurchasy day school, 10 Established Church boys, 1 Presbyterian boy, 8 Roman Catholic boys, 5 Established Church girls, 4 Roman Catholic girls; Scriptures not read but seldom.

Aughnaglnugh day school, 10 Established Church boys, 3 Presbyterian boys, 14 Roman Catholic boys, 6 Established Church girls, 13 Roman Catholic girls; the master has no objection to the Scriptures but they are not read in common.

Analaik day school, 6 Established Church boys, 2 Established Church girls, 7 Presbyterian girls, Scriptures are not read.

Prollisk day school, 18 Presbyterian boys, 2 Established Church girls, 18 Presbyterian girls; Scriptures are read.

Eskard national school, 2 Established Church boys, 3 Presbyterian boys, 43 Roman Catholic boys, 3 Established Church girls, 4 Presbyterian girls, 27 Roman Catholic girls; no bibles but a New Testament in the school.

Beltiny day school, 24 Established Church boys, 19 Presbyterian boys; Scriptures are read constantly.

Parish of Clogher

Beltiny female school, 18 Established Church, 24 Presbyterian, 7 Roman Catholic; Scriptures are read every day.

Tullyvernon day school, 22 Established Church boys, 12 Presbyterian boys, 7 Roman Catholic boys; Scriptures are read.

Tullyvernon female school, 22 Established Church, 20 Presbyterian, 7 Roman Catholic; Scriptures are read.

Chapel day school, 30 Roman Catholic boys, 2 Established Church girls, 20 Roman Catholic girls; Scriptures are not read.

Renenly day school, 8 Established Church boys, 4 Presbyterian boys, 9 Roman Catholic boys, 6 Established Church girls, 3 Presbyterian girls, 3 Roman Catholic girls; Scriptures not read constantly.

Clogher <Clougher> day school, 38 Established Church boys, 10 Roman Catholic boys; Scriptures are read.

Clogher female school, 24 Established Church, 4 Roman Catholics; Scriptures read.

Lisgarrin day school, 18 Roman Catholic boys, 12 Roman Catholic girls; Scriptures not admitted into the school.

Aughendarragh day school, 1 Established Church boy, 18 Roman Catholic boys, 1 Established Church girl, 15 Roman Catholic girls.

Bellinagunaugh day school, 2 Established Church boys, 26 Roman Catholic boys, 9 Roman Catholic girls; Scriptures not admitted.

Lislee day school, 9 Established Church boys, 17 Presbyterian boys, 18 Roman Catholic boys, 8 Established Church girls, 5 Presbyterian girls, 5 Roman Catholic girls; Scriptures are read.

Eskerschool [Eskeratrool] day school, 9 Established Church boys, 2 Presbyterian boys, 4 Established Church girls, 2 Presbyterian girls; Scriptures read.

Fivemiletown boys' school, 18 Established Church boys, 3 Presbyterian boys, 9 Roman Catholic boys, 15 Established Church girls, 1 Presbyterian girl, 6 Roman Catholic girls; Scriptures read.

Killenalurchey day school, 17 Roman Catholic boys, 15 Roman Catholic girls; Scriptures not admitted.

Ballyshally day school, 10 Established Church boys, 10 Presbyterian boys, 20 Roman Catholic boys, 10 Established Church girls, 10 Presbyterian girls, 20 Roman Catholic girls; Scriptures are read occasionally.

Miss Gervais' male school, 18 Established Church, 6 Presbyterians, 4 Roman Catholics; Scriptures read.

Miss Gervais' female school, 20 Established Church, 13 Presbyterians, 8 Roman Catholics; Scriptures read.

Augher boys' school, 18 Estalished Church boys, 13 Roman Catholic boys, 14 Established Church girls, 18 Roman Catholic girls; Scriptures but seldom read.

Augher female school, 2 Roman Catholic boys, 3 Established Church girls, 12 Roman Catholic girls; Scriptures but seldom read.

Genagan day school, 18 Roman Catholic boys, 14 Roman Catholic girls; Scriptures not read.

[Totals]: 254 Established Church boys, 171 Presbyterian boys, 334 Roman Catholic boys, 208 Established Church girls, 153 Presbyterian girls, 258 Roman Catholic girls. [Overall totals]: 592 Roman Catholics, 424 Presbyterians, 463 Protestants, total 1,379.

Names of Teachers

Walker, Dougherty, Hamilton, Triggey, Stocks, Gillespie Senior, Gillespie Junior, Richey Senior, Richey Junior, Kelly Senior, Kelly Junior, Strode, Camble, Hawes, [?] Melloy, [? Freeman or Truman], Irvine, McSurly Senior, McSurly Junior, McCorlenton, Boay, Boar, Palmer, Gallagher.

Female teachers: Miss Thompson, Miss Bullick, Miss Coe, Miss Niely, Misses Walker, Miss Geary, Widow Finnighan, Miss Finnighan, Miss Triggey.

Townland Statistics

PRODUCTIVE ECONOMY

Mr Maxwell's Property

Mr Maxwell's property of Killyfaddy: Carntoll, Aughandrumman, Fogart, Mullins, Ballaghneed, Corbaud, Leslie, shown by Thomas Rogers bailiff. Averages 20s the arable land, from 10 to 20 acres the general size of farms. Produce: potatoes, oats and flax. Some farms, the land too light for flax. It is seldom that an acre of wheat is seen in this property; have seen but one field of wheat on this property in 11 years.

Hugh Montgomery's property, manor of Blessingbourne: Ballyvadden, proprietor Hugh Montgomery Esquire, soil light limestone, gravel, adapted to grazing and tillage. Produce: barley, wheat, oats, potatoes and flax. Leased in portions varying from 3 acres to 20, in 3 lives or 31 years. Turbary abundant, limestone, gravel and sand abundant.

Ranenley, manor as above. Proprietor idem, soil idem, produce idem, wheat excepted. Leased in 1 lot for 3 lives or 31 years, turbary none, but in the adjoining lands, limestone as above.

Anagh, manor as above. Proprietor idem, soil light gravelly loam adapted for grazing and tillage, produce as above, leases none. Turbary abundant, limestone quarry 1, brick clay abundant, appearances of chalybate <calybeate> springs.

Fivemiletown, manor as above. Proprietor ditto, soil limestone, gravel and clay, produce as before. Leased some part in town fields for 3 lives or 31 years and some parts at will. Turbary abundant, limestone, sand and gravel abundant.

Gortmore, manor as before. Proprietor as before, soil as before, produce as before, leased for ever, turbary abundant, limestone gravel and sand abundant.

Corcreevy, manor as before. Proprietor as before [marginal note in different hand: Mathew Burnside Esquire]. Soil as before, fine sheepwalk, produce as before. Leased for ever, turbary abundant, limestone and gravel abundant.

TOWNLAND DIVISIONS

Mount Stewart and Lower Dromore

The townland of Mount Stewart is an extensive townland stretching westward at the back of the Aughentain ridge of mountains into the parish Donacavey, by which it is almost surrounded. Its surface is hilly and is covered by extensive tracts of mountain heath, turf bog and rough pasture lands. The soil is poor and gravelly, but capable of great improvement.

Lower Dromore: it contains extensive tracts of mountain heath, turf bog and rough pasture land.

Tatnadaveny and Lislee

Tatnadaveny is an extensive mountain townland extending from north east to south west about [blank] miles. It is intersected by the new road to Fintona, opening a communication with the very extensive and valuable bog from which, at the adjacent island of Kilnahushogue, the town of Clogher is principally supplied with turf. It is sold in cars or cages drawn by small mountain ponies at from 1s 1d to 2s per car, according to the season. The centre and south west of this townland is principally bog and heathery waste, but the inhabitants are numerous over the cultivated portions.

Lislee, see townland name book.

Altanaveragh and Lurganaglare

Altanaveragh is traversed by the new road from Clogher to Fintona, opening a communication with the very extensive heathy bog, which, with the numerous smaller patches of bogland scattered over the surface, occupies about the half of the townland.

Lurganaglare: towards the south western extremity there are extensive turf bogs. The remainder of the townland is under tillage. In the centre of the townland is a fir plantation of about [blank] acres.

Corkhill Demesne

Raveagh Lodge, the seat of Hugh Gore Edwards Esquire, is situated in this townland. The house is unfinished, but it is pleasantly situated on a gentle eminence, and will be a great improvement to this part of the country when completed. A long but narrow skirting plantation surrounds the house and there is a small fir planting towards the western extremity of the townland. There is also a bog on its northern boundary. The whole of the demesne is in the hands of the proprietor.

Lisnarable

Lisnarable, a long townland stretching north west and south east about 1 and a quarter miles, its average breadth being little more than a quarter of a mile. A large tract of bog and marshland stretches along its western boundary, and it contains extensive bogs both at its northern and southern extremities. The principal road from Augher to Clogher to Omagh traverses in its whole extent, which road is now undergoing improvement with a view of running a coach from Monaghan to Augher on this line to Omagh. A Roman Catholic chapel is situated at its southern end on the east side of the road. It contains two ancient forts or mounds.

Fernandrum and Kilnaheery

Fernandrum, a townland of [blank] acres, having an extensive bog at its eastern extremity. A good crossroad leading from the Omagh road by Newtown Saville to Ballygawley passes through the townland, and several minor roads branch off north and south communicating with the farmhouses and with the mills in Kilnaheery.

Kilnaheery, a townland of [blank] acres. A line of bogs extends through the centre of the townland, from which the inhabitants are well supplied with fuel. A corn mill at the western end of the townland on the river. It is well intersected by cross and car roads in every direction. There is an ancient fort or mound in this townland.

Parish of Clogher

Tulnafoile and Tychany

Tulnafoile, a long townland of [blank] acres, stretches north west and south east nearly 2 miles, its average breadth being about half a mile. Extensive bogs occur both at its northern and southern ends. A small lake on its western boundary containing 1 acre 1 rood 14 perches.

Tychany, a townland of [blank] acres. Extensive tracts of heath and bogland cover its northern extremity. Its southern end is all under cultivation. An oval plantation of firs crowns one of its highest points. There are 3 old forts or mounds in the townland.

Eskragh

Eskragh, a townland of [blank] acres. It extends from north to south about 1 and three-quarter miles, having a mean breadth of about half a mile. Large bogs cover its south western end. It is traversed by the 2 roads from Augher and Clogher to Omagh, and a new and improved line connecting the two have recently been opened between them. A chain of gravelly eskraghs stretch through the townland, from which it is supped to have derived its name and which are crowned by fir plantations by Hugh Gore Edwards Esquire, the proprietor.

Dunbiggan

Dunbiggan, a townland of [blank] acres. It contains a sufficiency of boglands to supply fuel to its inhabitants. Townlands have been sold off at the northern end of the parish for a perpetual cure, the church and Glebe House for which are built in this townland. The new coach road to Omagh passes through it, from which a lateral branch runs off north east communicating with Newtown Saville. The church is small and plain; the Glebe House is also small but convenient.

Tamlaght

Tamlaght, a townland of [blank] acres. This townland contains a sufficiency of bogland for the supply of its inhabitants with fuel. The village of Newtown Saville is situated in the north of this townland, through which the road from Ballygawley to Omagh runs. The mail coach road also passes within 1 and a half miles of the village, from which there is a direct road across to the mail coach road. This townland has several small patches of bogland scattered over its surface, sufficient for the supply of its inhabitants with fuel. There is a large ancient fort or mound, through the centre of which the road runs close to the village.

Beltany and Cormore

Beltany, a townland of [blank] acres. There is a good deal of bogland on its eastern and southern boundaries, and a small bog in the centre of the townland. [There is] a schoolhouse at its north western extremity. The road from Ballygawley to Newtown Saville bounds it on the east for the span of 1 mile, and a crossroad from Augher to the same village traverses it from south to north. This schoolhouse was founded and it is supported by the funds arising from the property left by Sir Erasmus [Smith].

Cormore, a townland of [blank] acres, extending from north west to south east more than 1 and a half miles, mean breadth about half a mile. The new coach road by Augher to Omagh passes through this town. There are two small ancient forts or mounds in the townland.

Glenegeera and Belnaclough

Glenegeera, a townland of [blank] acres extending north west and south east 2 miles, its mean breadth being about a quarter of a mile. There is an extensive fir plantation at its eastern end and much rough pasture land scattered through the townland, [and] a small fort in this townland.

Belnaclough, a townland of [blank] acres, extending north west and south east about 1 and a quarter miles, its mean breadth being about a quarter of a mile. Seceding meeting house at its eastern extremity.

Longridge, Annaloughan and Bank

Longridge, a townland of [blank] acres. A great part of this townland is composed of rough pasture land. There is an ancient fort on its eastern boundary.

Annaloughan, a townland of [blank] acres. An extensive turf bog extends along its western boundary.

Bank, a small townland of [blank] acres, about [blank] of which are turf bog. The remainder is held in 3 small farms.

Glenhoy

Glenhoy, a townland of [blank] acres, the whole of which is under cultivation, with the exception of about [blank] acres of planting and [blank] acres of bog and boggy pasture land. It is a long and narrow townland extending north west and south east 1 and a quarter miles, its mean breadth being less than a quarter of a mile.

Eskermore

Eskermore, a townland of [blank] acres, extending north west and south east about 1 and three-quarter miles, varying in breadth from a quarter to half a mile. A ridge of hills branching off east north east from Knockmany stretches away towards Glenhoy, Belnaclough and Glenegeeragh. Up the steep face of this hill Eskermore extends, its steepest part being planted by the Reverend F. Gervais, the proprerietor. A deep gulley intervenes between it and Knockmany; this is also planted and there are 2 other plantations at the southern end of the townland, the whole covering about [blank] acres of land. There are about [blank] acres of bog at the south of the townland and [blank] acres of rough pasture laid at the north. The remainder is all under cultivation. There is a schoolhouse at the northern extremity of the townland.

Diviniagh and Annagarvey

Diviniagh, a townland of [blank] acres, of which [blank] are in bog, the remainder are cultivated.

Annagarvey, a small townland of [blank] acres, containing about [blank] acres of bog and [blank] acres of plantation. The Reverend Francis Gervais, the proprietor, has erected in the townland a corn mill.

Ardunsheon and Knockmany

Ardunsheon, a townland of [blank] acres, the entire of which north of the road to Omagh has been taken into his demesne by the Reverend Francis Gervais of Cecil. Its eastern end is low and tolerably level with some bogs and boggy land in the centre. Towards the west it is considerably elevated, a steep hill rising to the height of [blank] feet above the sea, the sides of which are covered with plantations, with which also the entire townland is skirted This townland being in the hands of its active proprietor exhibits an air of improvement unhappily but rarely met with.

Knockmany, a townland of [blank] acres. The entire of this townland, with the exception of [blank] acres at its northern extremity, has been taken into the demesne of the Reverend Francis Gervais of Cecil.

Acreages of Townlands

Cloneblaugh townland: 95 acres 2 roods 16 perches of Cloneblaugh is included in Cecil demesne. The lake on boundary between Cloneblaugh and Ardunshion contains 3 acres 3 roods 24 perches. Townland Ardunshion: the whole townland is now included in Cecil demesne, 163 acres 3 roods 14 perches. Clarmore: 3 acres 2 roods 16 perches of Clarmore is included in Cecil demesne. Annagarvey: 40 acres 2 roods of Annagarvey are now included in Cecil demesne. Eskermore: 24 acres 32 perches of Eskermore are now included in Cecil demesne, and 9 acres 2 roods 32 perches of Eskermore at first shown as part of Knockmany. Cecil demesne is very extensive, comprising parts of the townlands Knockmany, Ardunshion, Clarmore, Cloneblough, Eskermore and Annagarvey, and contains 641 acres 2 roods 38 perches. [It] contains a lake, 3 acres 3 roods 24 perches, which abounds in eels. Lislain and Donaghmoyne: on the boundary between them is a small lake of 2 acres 8 perches. Killyfaddy demesne comprises parts of the following townlands, namely Killyfaddy, Achadrummin, Carntullmore, Mallaberry, Upper and Lower Killeny. It contains an artificial sheet of water formed at great labour and expense on the boundary between Achadrummin and Killyfaddy, containing 9 acres 2 roods 32 perches.

Findermore

In Findermore, and forming part of Daisy Hill demesne, is a small lake or pond of water of 2 roods 16 perches. This demesne is composed of parts of the 2 townlands Lisbuie and Findermore, and contains about 136 acres 38 perches.

Fair Sheets by J.R. Ward, received 30 November 1835

NATURAL FEATURES

Hills

The parish of Clogher is traversed by 2 high ridges of ground running pretty nearly in a parallel direction from west to east. The southern ridge is the highest, being at one point 1,250 feet above the level of the sea. The northern ridge attains within the parish boundary the height of 950 feet. The lowest ground in the valley between these 2 ridges is about 150 feet above the sea. Though the rise of the ground towards the south is the most considerable, its slope presents a less abrupt appearance than that of the northern and lower ridge. This latter is also rendered more remarkable to the eye by being broken up into more distinctly marked features, with occasionally a sharp cut or ravine

Parish of Clogher

down which some small streams come to discharge themselves into that branch of the Blackwater river which runs past the town of Clogher from west to east.

Lakes

[Table gives name, locality, altitude, extent and depth, if known]

Glenoo lough, townland of Glenoo, altitude 517 feet, contains 4 acres 1 rood, depth not known.

Lough Sallagh, townland of Ballymacan, altitude 1,206 feet, contains 2 acres, depth not known.

Round lough, townland of Fivemiletown, altitude 342 feet, 12 acres, depth not known.

Lough Fadda, townland of Annagh Demesne, altitude 339 feet, 19 acres 2 roods, depth not known.

Screeby lough, townland of Screeby, altitude 320 feet, 11 acres 3 roods, depth not known.

Ballagh lough, townland of Ballagh, altitude 320 feet, 12 acres, depth not known.

Ballymacan lake, townland of Ballagh, altitude 460 feet, 4 acres 3 roods 30 perches, depth not known.

Lough McCall, townland of Ballyscally, altitude 560 feet, 5 acres 2 roods, depth not known.

Lough-na-Sliggan, townland of Grange Mountain Bar, altitude 790 feet, 3 acres 1 rood, depth not known.

Lough Esbrick, townland of Grange Mountain Bar, altitude 1,080 feet, 3 roods, depth not known.

Lough-in-Albanagh, townland of Grange Mountain Bar, altitude 1,164 feet, 14 acres 2 roods, depth not known.

Glenboar lough, townlands of Corleaghan and Corloughy, altitude 1,070 feet, 4 acres 1 rood, depth not known.

Lough Navarad, townlands of Corloughy and Ballywholan, altitude 1,030 feet, 12 acres, depth not known.

Lough Galluane, townlands of Corloughy and part of the next county, 4 acres, depth not known.

Loughnabeery, townland of Corloughy and part of the next county, altitude 980 feet, 10 acres, depth not known.

Loughanoid, townland of Ballywholan, altitude 535 feet, 3 acres, depth not known.

Loughnablaneybane, townlands of Cavan and Cullamore, altitude 599 feet, 19 acres, adjacent to parish.

Carrickavoy lough, townland of Carrickavoy and Aghindarrah, altitude 546 feet, 5 acres.

Rivers

A shallow branch of the Blackwater river runs through the parish of Clogher very close to the town of the same name. Its course is very serpentine, its bed for the most part shallow and pebbly, and its banks, which in this part are never overflowed, are green and fertile. The river contains a few trout and pike. Numberless tributary streams run into and in fact produce this river from the high ground north and south of this parish. Some of them have very deep rocky holes and steep banks, and occasionally form very bold ravines.

Bogs

The tops of the mountain in the south of the parish are mostly flow bog. There are likewise several good banks for fuel. North of Augher there is a very extensive tract, the height above the sea is from 207 to 223 feet and from 27 to 40 feet above the River Blackwater. Timber occurs in almost every part of it, principally oak, fir and birch. The stumps have the appearance as if the trunks were broken off or burnt. The depth of the bank is from 6 to 14 feet. [There is] a tract of bogs consisting of upwards of 120 acres situated in the townlands of Aghinlark, Gortmore and Ballyvadden, the height above the sea is from 350 to 340 feet. There is very little timber in it. A few trunks and branches of birch only are to be met with, the depth of the bank is from 5 to 11 feet. There are several patches of bog near the western boundary. Their average altitude is 350 feet. Birch roots and branches are thinly scattered over them. The banks average from 3 to 10 feet in depth.

Woods

No natural woods in the parish, but there are considerable plantations and a great quantity of growing timber around the several gentlemen's seats and residences.

Climate

This parish is considered subject to continual rains from its proximity to the 2 lakes, Lough Erne and Lough Neagh, which the inhabitants suppose to have the property of attracting the showers.

PRODUCTIVE ECONOMY

Crops

The crops are wheat, oats, barley, potatoes and flax. Wheat is sown in October and November and reaped in August and September. Oats are sown in March and cut in September. Barley is sown in March and cut in September. Potatoes are planted in April and May and dug in November for winter stock. Flax is sown in April and May and pulled in August. There is very little difference between the mountains and plains.

MODERN TOPOGRAPHY

Public Buildings

Besides those mentioned in the towns, there are: a Roman Catholic chapel situated in Aghintain townland. It is a plain whitewashed building 50 feet long and 25 feet broad. It was built in 1805 and cost 400 pounds, which was defrayed by the congregation. It holds 900 persons.

A Roman Catholic chapel situated in the townland of Aghindrumman. It is a plain whitewashed building 60 feet long and 30 broad. It was built in 1795 and cost 600 pounds, which was defrayed by the congregation. It accommodates 1,200 persons.

A Roman Catholic chapel situated in the town of Lisnorable. It is a neat whitewashed building 60 feet long and 30 broad. It was built in 1795 and cost 500 pounds, which was paid by subscriptions and the congregation. It holds 1,000 persons.

A Presbyterian meeting house situated in the townland Carntallmore. It is a plain stone building [blank] feet long and [blank] broad. It was built in [blank] and cost [blank], which was paid by [blank]. It accommodates [blank] persons.

A meeting house situated in Ballaghneed townland.

A Presbyterian meeting house in Longridge townland, a plain white building 50 feet long and 24 broad; it will accommodate 320 persons.

Gentlemen's Seats

Corcreevy, the property of Mr William Smith Burnside of Newry, is at present tenanted by Colonel Dixon. It is situated in the townland of the same name [and] was built in 1810. It is a neat stone building consisting of 2-storeys. The demesne is 134 acres 36 perches in extent and is tastefully ornamented with trees. There is a small garden and an orchard in it.

Blessingbourne Cottage, the residence of Colonel Montgomery, is situated in the townland of Annagh Demesne. It is a very neat building built in a cottage style, the demesne consisting of 121 acres 27 perches, including part of a lake in front of the cottage.

Kilfaddy, the residence of Captain Maxwell, is situated in Kilfaddy demesne [and] is a plain stone building. The demesne consisting of about 200 acres is very tastefully wooded.

Tracing of Manor of Cecil

Parish of Clogher

The Deanery is situated in Carryclogher townland. It is whitewashed stone building of 2-storeys.

The Bishop's Palace, situated in Clogher Demesne, is a fine freestone building erected in 1820. The office houses are commodious and extensive. The demesne consists of 566 acres 3 roods 22 perches. There is a great quantity of planting and some large trees on it, which add much to the scenery in the neighbourhood. There is a deer park in the south west corner in which deer are constantly kept. The garden is small but contains a great plenty of food, which the gardener disposes of to the inhabitants of Clogher and its neighbourhood.

Fardross, the seat of Ambus Upton Gledstone Esquire, is situated in Fardross Demesne. It is a small house very plain in appearance. The demesne consists of 175 acres, part of it is prettily wooded.

Cecil, the residence of Reverend Francis Gervais <Jervis> Esquire, is situated in Cecil demesne. It is a new and handsome stone building consisting of 3-storeys. The extent of the demesne is about 300 acres, including the wooded hill of Knockmany. The planting of the demesne is about 14 years growth and already adds much to the beauty of the neighbourhood.

Corick, the residence of Dr Story, is situated in Corrick demesne. It is a plain white building consisting of 8-storeys. The demesne consists of about 150 acres. The trees are very fine.

Augher Castle, the seat of Sir James Bunbury, is situated near the town of Augher. It is a new handsome building. The demesne consists of 149 acres 1 rood 32 perches, including the large lake in front of the castle which is 21 acres 2 roods 8 perches. The demesne is tastefully wooded.

Corn Mills

[Table] Corcreevy, corn mill and kiln, wheel 16 feet by 4 feet, fall of water 14, breast wheel.

Nurchossy Scotch, corn mill and kiln, 12 feet 6 inches by 2 feet, fall 10 feet, breast wheel.

Aghintain, [blank].

Annagarvey, corn mill, wheel 16 feet by 4 feet, breast wheel.

Augher tenements, [blank].

Carntallbeg, corn mill, wheel 10 feet 6 inches by 1 foot 8 inches, breast wheel.

Terrew, [blank].

Communications

The parish is well intersected with roads. The principal is the main road between Aughnacloy and Enniskillen. It enters the parish about 2 miles east of Augher and traverses south west. There are 13 miles in the parish. It is well laid out and kept in excellent order. The average breadth is 28 feet.

The main road from Ballygawley joins the above road at Augher. It is in very bad condition, but a new cut is in progress. There are 2 and a quarter miles in the parish and the average breadth is 28 feet.

The main road from Omagh to Augher, of which there are 7 and a quarter miles in the parish, is a tolerable good road and kept in good repair. The average breadth is 26 feet.

The main road between Clogher through Fintona to Omagh.

The new main road from Fivemiletown to Fintona traverses nearly north and south. This is a good and well laid out road. There are about 5 miles of it in the parish. Its average breadth is 27 feet.

The main road between Augher and Monaghan, traversing from the north to south for 4 miles in the parish, is a hilly road but kept in good repair. The breadth is about 26 feet.

Beside the above there are a great number of crossroads which are very useful. They are in good repair and are kept so at the expense of the barony. The main roads were made at the expense of the county and are kept in good repair by the county and barony.

General Appearance and Scenery

The parish of Clogher contains a greater variety of ground than is generally met with in the same extent. The centre of the parish, in which are the towns of Clogher and Augher, is a rich and fertile valley bounded on the north and south by high ridges of mountain, which, covered with the dark heath peculiar to some parts of this country, give it an air of seclusion and almost of confinement. Immediately about the towns of Clogher and Augher the ground is very beautifully varied, and being tastefully planted with luxuriant trees has an air of cultivation and fertility very pleasing to the eye. Some of the hills on the mountain ridges have also been covered with plantations by the resident gentry, which contributes to the general richness of appearance. A great number of small streams intersect and beautify the valley, almost all of which flow towards Lough Neagh. Looking down from Knockmany, a high point on the northern ridge nearly opposite the town of Clogher, the view embraces the beautiful park and demesne of the Bishop of Clogher, Sir James Bunbury's, Mr Gervais' <Jarvis's> and others, all remarkable for their beauty. There are also a great many small lakes dispersed through the parish, which is thus very prettily studded with wood and water. From Knockmany it is possible to distinguish Dungannon on a clear day.

Social Economy

Obstructions to Improvement

Want of encouragement and longer leases.

Local Government

There are 8 magistrates residing in the parish, none of them stipendiary. They are within convenient distances, firm and respected by the people. The police force stationed in the parish is 1 officer, 3 sergeants and 12 men. Petty sessions are held in Augher and in Fivemiletown and road sessions in Clogher. The normal number of magistrates attending is 2 or 3. Outrages are on the decrease, which is occasioned by the vigilance of the police. Illicit distillation is not carried on in the parish, nor is there any smuggling. Insurances of property: in general there are a few instances of houses [being insured]. They can be easily effected. The West of England seems to be the favourite office. There is no cause to distrust any of the offices.

Dispensary

The poor have found considerable benefit since the establishment of a dispensary in the town of Clogher in 1812. The house in which it is held was not built for the present purpose. It is taken at rent of 4 pounds 8s per annum. The attending surgeon receives 170 pounds per annum, which is defrayed by various means: the county gives 50 pounds, the bishop gives 100 pounds and other subscriptions amount to about 25 pounds per annum. Out of this sum between about 50 pounds and 60 pounds per annum goes to purchase medicine.

Schools

The introduction of schools is of great utility. The people are anxious for their children to attend them, but they complain of not being able to pay the small sum charged, which very seldom exceeds 2s 6d per quarter. The table will serve to show the particulars.

Poor

There is a society (called the Penny Week Society from the generality of subscribers paying at the rate of 1d per week) the object of which is to assist the poor of the parish in giving them clothing and implements of industry. The treasurer of this society is Mrs Story of Corrick. The Bishop of Clogher distributes clothing, blankets and food to the poor every Christmas and to some he gives money.

Religion

The greater part of the people are Prostestants or Protestant Dissenters. The proportions are Episcopalians, Presbyterians, Methodists, Roman Catholics [blank]. The clergy of the Episcopalians are supported by churchlands and tithes, the Presbyterian by the regium donum and tax on the sittings, the Methodist and Roman Catholics by voluntary contributions from their several congregations.

Habits of the People

The cottages in the parish are chiefly of stone, but some built of mud only are to be met with. They are mostly all thatched, have glass windows and consist of but 1-storey, which is sometimes divided into 2 apartments. The people seem to pay very little regard to comfort or cleanliness, either in their person or habitations. Their food is potatoes and oaten bread, sometimes varied with stirabout or flummery. They seldom get fresh meat, but salt beef and pork dried are used on particular occasions of festivity. The fuel is turf at all times, but in some parts it is rather scarce. The dress of the people is, except on Sundays and holidays, very slovenly. No one kind is very remarkable. There are no remarkable instances of longevity, the usual number in a family is 5, early marriages are not common. They have very little amusement or recreation. Dancing used to be in great repute but it has now gone out of fashion.

Emigration

Emigration prevails to a small extent.

Table of Schools

[Table contains the following headings: name of townland where situated, religion and sex of pupils, remarks as to how supported, when established].

[2 schools bracketed together]. Fivemiletown, 13 Protestants, 28 Roman Catholics, 91 males, Fivemiletown, 31 Protestants, 17 Roman Catholics, 48 females, total 139 pupils; the National Board contributed 18 pounds per annum; the average donations from pupils is 24 pounds and Colonel Montgomery makes up the salary to 60 pounds

Parish of Clogher

between the master and the mistress; established December 1834.

Aghinlark, 30 Protestants, 5 Roman Catholics, 15 males, 21 females, 35 total; [supported] by pupils paying from 1s to 2s per quarter, established April 1834.

Fardross Demesne, 45 Protestants, 11 Roman Catholics, 16 males, 40 females, 56 total; supported by 10 pounds per quarter each from Captain Moutray and Mr Gledstane and by 9d per quarter from each pupil, not known when established.

Ballyscally, 69 Protestants, 64 Roman Catholics, 68 males, 65 females, 133 total; supported by subscription from children who pay from 1s 8d to 3s 4d per quarter, not known when established.

Ballynagurragh, 95 Roman Catholics, 65 males, 30 females, 95 total; children pay from 1s 6d to 2s per quarter, established 1821.

Clogher, 24 Protestants, 18 males, 6 females, 24 total; not known when established.

Augher, 37 Protestants, 21 males, 16 females, 37 total, established 1829.

Tullyveran, 75 Protestants, 5 Roman Catholics, 40 males, 40 females, 80 total; not known when established.

Tatnadaverny, 34 Protestants, 20 males, 14 females, 34 total; children pay from 1s to 2s 6d per quarter, established 1830.

Skelgah, 44 Protestants, 8 Roman Catholics, 34 males, 18 females, 52 total; children pay from 1s to 1s 6d per quarter, not known when established.

Murley, 15 males, 25 females, 40 total pupils; children pay 4 pounds per annum, established 1831.

MODERN TOPOGRAPHY AND SOCIAL ECONOMY

Fivemiletown

Fivemiletown is said to derive its name from its distance from Clogher, which is about 5 Irish miles. It is 78 Irish or 99 and three-quarter English miles from Dublin by the mail road, and its latitude is 54 degrees 20 minutes north and longitude 7 degrees 16 west. It is in the diocese of Clogher, province of Ulster, county Tyrone and parish Clogher. The main road from Armagh to Enniskillen passes through it, and like the generality of small towns it consists of but one street, about a fifth of a mile in length. The surrounding country is fertile and well cultivated, and from the quantity of planting has a picturesque appearance.

Public Buildings

There is a church on the north east of the town which was built in [blank], a plain stone building with a tower and short spire. It is in length 60 feet and in breadth <breath> 30 feet. It will accommodate 500 persons, the general attendance is about 160. The income of the curate is [blank] pounds per annum.

[There is] a small Methodist meeting house at the west end of the town, a plain building 48 feet long and 24 broad. It was built in 1820 and cost 140 pounds, which was defrayed by public subscription. It will accommodate 200 persons, though attendance is about 150. The session house is a common kind of building situate in the centre of the town.

Streets

As before said the town consists of but one street, regular and clean. There are about 25 houses of 1-storey, 90 of 2-storey and 10 of 3-storey. They are all built of stone [and] are generally clean in appearance, and about two-thirds are slated, the remainder are thatched. Colonel Montgomery has built a comfortable schoolhouse and a residence for a master and mistress.

People

Petty sessions are held once each month. The magistrates are Colonel Montgomery, residence Blessingbourne Cottage, Mr Burke resides in the town and Mr Patterson at Gortmore. They are respected by the inhabitants. Markets are held every Friday and there are 8 fairs in the year: in August one, in November one, December three, January one, in March one, May one and in June one. There are no tolls or customs levied. Cattle, pigs, sheep and soft goods are the principal traffic. There is a mail car which runs to Enniskillen and a caravan which runs between Armagh and Enniskillen passes though the town. There is a national school, for particulars see table [of schools]. There is no provision for the poor. The people have very little amusement except attending the fairs.

Occupations

[Table] Publicans 15, grocers 9, bakers 1, drapers 2, hardware dealers 1, surgeons 1, whitesmiths 1, hucksters 3, lodging houses 7, carpenters 1, smiths 1. The police force stationed here is 1 sergeant and 3 men.

Town of Clogher

Clogher is situated about 6 and a half miles east of Fivemiletown, is 102 miles from Dublin and is in the same diocese, province and so on as the latter. The main road between Armagh and Enniskillen passes through it. There is but one street and there are no houses with the exception of the market house on the south side of it. Its length is a quarter of a mile. The appearance of the town as viewed from either end is rather picturesque. It is sometimes called the half-city of Clogher.

Buildings

There is a cathedral, a court or session house and a market house. The cathedral is a strong building with a square tower without a spire. Its form and dimensions are: [ground plan, main dimensions 114 by 52 feet]. It was built in 1717, the cost not known. It will accommodate about 500 persons, the general attendance is about 200. The court house is a plain stone building erected in 1805 at an expense of [blank] pounds, which was defrayed by the county. Bishop Porter gave the ground free for the purpose. It is in length 70 feet and breadth 50 feet. It is only used for quarter sessions, held here twice each year, and for road sessions. The market house is an open stone building erected in [blank], the cost not known.

Streets

There is not a comfortable hotel in the town, and in general the houses have a very bad appearance. There are about 18 of 1-storey, 22 of 2-storey and 6 of 3-storey. They are all built of stone and the greater part are slated. The last six mentioned are new and are built of stone. They are situated at east end of the town. The Bishop's Palace, situated at the back of the cathedral, is a fine stone building, but is scarcely seen from the town. See Gentlemen's Seats.

Fairs in Clogher

Clogher was formerly a borough for 2 members, but it was deprived of its charter at the Union. Most of the inhabitants are employed in retail dealing or labouring. There is a savings bank which was established in 18[remaining figures blank]. Saturday is market day throughout the year. The principal commodities are potatoes and oatmeal. There are a few pigs and sheep and some soft goods sold. Fairs are held on every third Saturday and on the 6th May and 26th July. The traffic is the same as on the market days. The last mentioned is called a "spolien" fair, and people amuse themselves on that day by stuffing themselves with mutton and mutton broth.

People

Insurances are not common, nor do any combinations exist. There is a caravan which passes through the town on to Enniskillen. It leaves Armagh at 6 a.m. and arrives in Clogher at 12 noon, leaves again for Enniskillen at 1 p.m. and arrives at about 6.30 every day. It returns between the above towns at much the same hour. The fares are from Clogher to Armagh 2s 9d and from Clogher to Enniskillen [blank].

There is a dispensary which is supported by [blank]. It has added much to the comfort of the poorer classes; for diseases see table. Hired cars are to be had. The inhabitants are civil but little hospitality is to be met with among them.

Trades and Occupations

Surgeons 2, grocers 2, publicans 9, general dealers 1, smiths 1, shoemakers 1, butchers 1, bakers 3, saddlers 1, lodging houses 5, tailors 1. The police force is an officer, a sergeant, and 6 men, one of whom is a mounted man.

Town of Augher

Augher is situated 2 miles north east of Clogher. It consists of one street besides a few hovels on the road to the latter. Its length is about quarter of a mile. The court house with a market place underneath is a plain building 40 feet long and 20 broad. It was erected in 1807. Petty sessions are held once a fortnight. The houses have a dirty appearance. There are about 81 of 1-storey, 29 of 2- and 2 of 3-storeys. They are all built of stone. About one-tenth of these are slated, the remainder are thatched.

Commerce and Occupations

Monday is market day. The commodities are potatoes and meal principally. Fairs are held on the 12th May, 12th August, 12th November, 22nd, 23rd and 24th December, the 3 Mondays preceding Christmas and the 12th February. The traffic is cattle, horses, sheep and pigs.

[Table gives trade or occupation and number] grocers 5, spirit dealers 8, hucksters 2, carpenters 2, wheelwrights 1, smiths 2, lodging houses 3, butchers 1. The police force is a sergeant and 3 men.

Answers to Queries of the North West of Ireland Society [1820s]

SOCIAL AND PRODUCTIVE ECONOMY

Barony of Clogher

[Each query numbered].

Parish of Clogher

1st. Tyrone, 2nd. Barony of Clogher. 3rd. The barony contains 3 parishes: 1st, the parish of Errigal <Errigle> Keerogue or Ballinasaggart, rector the Reverend Mr Graham, non-resident. The presentation to this living is in the gift of Mr Moutray. 2nd, the parish of Clogher in the diocese of Clogher, rector the Reverend Dean Bagwell, resident. The presentation is in the gift of the Crown. 3rd, the parish of Fintona in the diocese of Clogher and in the gift of the Bishop of Clogher. Rector the Reverend William Atthill, non-resident. Besides these three, the barony contains a small wing of the parish of Errigal Trough and a small wing of the parish of Aghalurcher.

Townlands: Manor of Clogher

[Table gives townland, acres arable and mountain acres, proprietor's name].

Bishop's demesne, 340 acres arable.
Farnortragh, 60 acres arable,
Lisnamaughry, 93 acres arable.
Mullaghtinny, 100 acres arable, 240 acres mountain.
Ballyscalley, 134 acres arable, 150 acres mountain.
Shanco, 53 acres arable, 90 acres mountain.
Lismore, 72 acres arable, 150 acres mountain.
Fardross, 436 acres arable.
Freighmore, 146 acres arable.
Fendermore, 100 acres arable.
Murchossy, 181 acres arable.
Kilcurren and Gunnel, 100 acres arable.
Newry, 84 acres arable.
Tulnavert, 128 acres arable.
Aughnaglough, 127 acres arable.
Rectory Keerogue, 72 acres arable, see of Clogher.
Glebe, 118 acres arable, Dean of Clogher.
Terew, 36 acres arable.
Ballymagowan, 145 acres arable.
Coreek 133 acres arable, see of Clogher.
Drumherk Walker, 54 acres arable, Dean of Clogher.
Drumherk Alcan, 74 acres arable.
Tullybroom, 99 acres arable.
Glenoo, 160 acres arable, 1,080 mountain.
Kiltarrnan, 70 acres arable.
Lisbury, 127 acres arable.
Carnahenny, 36 acres arable.
Millpark Murchossy, 4 acres arable.
Ballywhollan, 150 acres arable, 1,100 acres mountain.
Curcloughin Lismore, 20 acres arable, 100 acres mountain.
Curcloughin Freighmore, 20 acres arable, 100 acres mountain.
Cloughin Tullybroom, 7 acres arable, 80 acres mountain.
Crossowen, 20 acres arable, see of Clogher.

Townlands: Manor of Aughin

Annagh, J.C. Moutray. Aughadanagh, the heirs of the late J. Richardson Esquire, non-resident. Altnaveagh, J.M. Richardson. Aughermelkin, Altnakenny, heirs of J. Richardson. Annaloghin, N.M. Montgomery, non-resident. Ballagh, J.C. Moutray Esquire. Ballymachan, Aylmer Gledstone Esquire, a minor and non-resident. Ballingorragh, Mr Nevin, non-resident. Ballyreenan, N.M. Montgomery Esquire. Carnamuclagh, J.M. Richardson Esquire. Cargragh, and Cavan, heirs of J. Richardson. Caldrum, Atcheson Moore Esquire, non-resident. Carr, J.N. Richardson. Dernascoby and Banter, heirs of J. Richardson. Derrydrummond, R.G. Gresson, non-resident. Derrys and Lisgoran, heirs of J. Richardson. Mullaghmore, J. Berney Esquire, resident. Mullins and Sassaigh, J.M. Richardson Esquire. Killclay, Reverend G. Griffin. Kill, Mrs Moran, non-resident. Kilrudden, A. Gledstone Esquire, a minor. Slatbeg, J.C. Moutray Esquire. Tatty, J.M. Richardson Esquire. Tavannamore, A. Gledstone Esquire.

Townlands: Manor of Killyfaddy

Aughendrummon, Altnariver, Carntall, Carnben, R.W. Maxwell Esquire, resident. Corkhill, Captain Edwards. Dromore, R.W. Maxwell Esquire. Eskeragh, Captain Edwards. Fogart, Graycoil, Killeney, R.W. Maxwell Esquire. Killnahushog, Mrs Cairnes, non-resident. Lislee, R.W. Maxwell Esquire. Larnaglan, Captain Edwards. Mullins and Tatnadaveragh, R.W. Maxwell Esquire.

Townlands: Manor of Cecil

Ardunchin, Anagarvey, Bank, Beltinny, Betnaglogh, Cormore, Cloneyblagh, Reverend Mr Gervais. Clanmore, Mr Thompson, non-resident. Dunbiggen, Eskernabrogue, Eskermore, Fannahendron, Glenhoyse, Glenogira, Knockmany, Kilnaheny, Longridge, Latbeg, Lisnarable, Roy, Tullycorken, Tulnafevel, Tainlot, Teaheny, Tullyvernan, Reverend Mr Gervais.

Townlands: Manor of Mountstewart

Cess J.C. Moutray Esquire. Aughinlack, Gillygordan, Edergacal, Lattyneel, Cole, Carnagat, Ballyness, Bolags, Lislane, Lincension, Shanterragh, Cavencork, Skelgaph, Prutasque, Girlaw, Screbeagh, Mountstewart, Earl of Blessington, non-resident. Rose-malland, J.C. Moutray Esquire. Molly-Barney, Earl of Blessington. Beagh and Tullyhern, Dean of Clogher. Annaghs, Ballyvadden, Corcrievy, Gortmore, H. Montgomery Esquire, resident.

Enumerator

If the rest of this survey be approved of, the return of the parish of Clogher will be rendered more complete when the enumerator completes his census of the parish of Clogher. He expects to finish it in about 3 weeks.

PRODUCTIVE ECONOMY RURAL

Farms

5th. The general size of the farms in the barony is from 10 to 20 acres, farms are seldom found to contain 40 or 50 acres. The produce of all the small farms is expended on the family, very little comparatively is exposed to sale, but a very large proportion of the crops of the large farms is brought to market. Hence it is a natural question how are rents paid, and how is clothing and other necessaries procured? By the produce of the spinning wheel and loom. When cloth and yarn are a good price, the small farmer feels himself independent and comfortable. Those farms are generally enclosed by thorn fences. Sometimes there is very little enclosure, particularly in the parish of Fintona and on the skirts of the mountains. This circumstance is exceedingly to be regretted. A careless fence of sods, or a shallow ditch without any kind of thorn or other shrub is often thought sufficient to repell the inroads of the cattle from the cornfields, and hence every person almost is obliged to keep herds for their cattle. Plough tillage is almost universally the mode of culture in use preparatory to oats and barley. Potatoes are set in the lazy bed fashion, except in a few instances when they are put in with the plough. I have observed Mr Grayton of Fivemiletown putting down the potatoes with the plough in long rains.

Crops

The principal crops of this district are barley, oats, potatoes and flax. Wheat is rarely sown: the soil is generally too light and the climate too humid for a good crop of wheat. If a piece of ground be required to be reclaimed, potatoes are first planted. Flax or barley succeeds if the ground is sufficiently rich, if not, a crop of oats is sown. Potatoes are the first crop. Flax or barley the next, to which oats succeed as long as the ground will bring a crop. Sometimes it is the practice to break up the lea and sow a crop of oats, after which potatoes are planted and then oats as long as the ground is in a condition to bear a crop. The land in this district, particularly in the parish of Fintona, was capable of great improvement, to which nothing would more contribute than large ditches, good fences and deep drains. The most cursory observers must see the great deficiency of this district in these respects.

Pasture

6th. The pasture lands are generally situated on the sides of the mountains or on the sides and tops of the highest hills. Young cattle are often sent to the mountain to be grazed. There is very seldom to be found any large extent of pasturage, except on the sides of mountains, to which no kind of improvement can be directed that would in any manner compensate for the expense and trouble. Besides the mountains, all land is immediately thrown into pasture when it is no longer capable of bearing a crop, in which state it is suffered to lie until there is some prospect of a profitable return in breaking it up. The lands in this district are not suited to the fattening of black cattle, except in the richer soils of Clogher, as for instance on Mr Moutray's grounds, in the bishop's demesne at Clogher and Corrick, the residence of Dr Story, and at Castle Hill, the residence of Mr Richardson.

NATURAL FEATURES

Hills

7th. This barony is bounded on the south by a long ridge of hills called the Slieve Bay mountains, which separate the county of Tyrone from the county of Monaghan and abound in an excellent kind of freestone. Besides these, another ridge of hills runs through the barony from east to west, which has no particular denomination but is named from the neighbouring townland to which it is attached. From the hill called the Many Bowls in the parish of Errigal Keerogue to Scregagh mountain in the parish of Fintona is one range of hills, which is interrupted and broken at many places. To this range belongs Knockmanny and Mullabanny in the parish of Clogher. There is an extraordinary kind of hills in this barony called eskers, which run in a very continued and regular range. They are shaped like the roof of an house, are not very high and in some places run for 2 or 3 miles. These hills are principally found in the northern part of the parish of Clogher and in the parish of Fintona.

Parish of Clogher

Bogs

8th. This barony is abundantly supplied with turf. Except some parts of the parish of Clogher, every townland almost has a portion of bog attached to it. Therefore to enumerate them all would be almost impracticable. There is a very large bog called the Star bog, in the parish of Errigal Keerogue, which is the largest bog in this barony. There is another called the Rathkeeranbane in the parish of Fintona. The mountains are of course not estimated or included in this account, the summits of all of which are covered with bog to the depth of 3 or 4 feet. The turf cut in the mountain is of the best description. There are two kinds of timber chiefly found in the bogs, oak and fir. The former is of very little use, being fit almost for nothing but ground joists, but the latter is an excellent kind of timber and equal in every respect to foreign deal. It is supposed that the turpentine contained in the fir preserved it from rotting. Timber is generally found on the verge of the bogs, rarely in the centre, and usually it is 5 to 10 feet deep.

Woods

9th. Woods and plantations are very thinly scattered through this district. In the parish of Fintona scarcely a single plantation is to be found, except around the Glebe House and in Mr Eccles' demesne. However, in the parish of Clogher there are some extensive and valuable plantations. Mr Gervais, whose estate lies in the latter parish, is showing a spirited example. His plantations are very judiciously placed. They sweep round the sides of the highest hills in all varieties of curves. Knockmanny and Longford's glen are now tastefully decorated with every species of forest trees, and Sir John Stewart has lately planted 6 or 8 acres of ground in the parish of Errigal Keerogue. Besides these new plantations there are some extensive woods around Mr Moutray's residence. Corrack, the residence of Dr Story, has some very thriving plantations; the same may be observed of Castle Hill, the residence of Mr Richardson, and the Bishop of Clogher's demesne is very well planted both with old and young timber. Besides these, there is scarcely any other planting in this barony that deserves the least notice, indeed there is not a greater desideratum in the whole district than planting. Orchards there are none unless you give that name to a few apple and pear trees planted in gentlemen's gardens. It is very much to be regretted that some encouragement is not given by landlords for planting. Nothing would tend to ornament the country so much, nothing would produce so valuable and certain a return.

10th. Various kinds of trees are planted, ash, oak, elm, firs of various kinds, beech, birch and larch, but larch seems to have the preference, if we may judge from this circumstance, that a greater quantity of it is planted than of any other. It is more rapid in its growth and serves for more farming purposes than any other, ash and oak only excepted. Alder is found to thrive very well in moory ground and is a great favourite for such situations.

PRODUCTIVE ECONOMY

Rents

11th. The highest acreable rent in the parishes of Clogher and Errigal Keerogue is as follows: for the best land 2 pounds 5s, for middling land 1 pound 10s, for inferior land 15s. In the parish of Fintona the land in general is not so good and may be estimated as follows: for the best 1 pound 14s 1d ha'penny, middling one pound, inferior from 10s to 15s. The mountainous parts of this barony are not included in the above valuations. Either a quantity of the mountain is thrown into the farms in the adjoining lowlands, or a large extent is let for a certain sum without any measurement.

Turbary

12th. This district is very well circumstanced in respect of bogs. In the parish of Fintona portions of bog are allotted to every farm without any rent whatever. In the parishes of Clogher and Errigal Keerogue turf is more scarce, and the tenants in some places pay for their bogs at the rate of 2s to 4s per acre.

Improvements

13th. There is a slow but gradual improvement in tillage in the barony. After a lapse of 20 years a very considerable improvement may be observed in the mode of culture. It is asserted, and a great probability, that double the quantity of corn and potatoes is produced in this district at present than was produced 20 or 30 years ago. I say with great probability because rents have been nearly doubled in that space of time, yet the produce of the ground is as cheap at present, as well as all kinds of stock, as they were 30 years ago, and this can be accounted for on no other grounds but that the lands are made to produce more, that is are better tilled than at the former period. The farmers understand better the mode of preparing and mixing manure with lime and mud. The lands are better drained and enclosed, and much ground has been reclaimed, both mountain and bog, that was never before under cultivation. Farming implements have also been greatly improved within the above mentioned period. The rude cars commonly known by the name of slide cars and panniers on horses' backs have given place to cars with log wheels, and these latter to cars with spoke wheels and to farming carts. Spades, ploughs and harrows have also received much improvement. Thus though much remains to be done yet it is gratifying to see that any advance is made in the several departments of cultivation.

Nurseries

14th. Fences of whitethorn are now in general use. Beech fences might be used to great advantage when shelter for cattle is required, inasmuch as the leaves remain on the trees during the winter. Holly fences also, if they were not so difficult to rear, would be both useful and grateful to the eye; the bright green of the holly skirting our roads would be a cheerful sight during the devastation of winter. But there is one grand obstacle to the forming of fences and to planting in general, which is that there is not a single nursery to be found where trees and thorn quicks are to be procured nearer than 20 miles. Everyone must see what an impediment this is to all kinds of improvement in planting. The quicks that are brought to market are withered and greatly injured before they are planted, thus the farmer is discouraged when he sees his fences declining and all his labour lost. What a pity that some spirited person does not establish a nursery somewhere in or convenient to this barony.

Employment

15th. Employment is becoming more abundant now than in latter years. Whether this arises from the paucity of labourers, in consequence of the great emigration to America, or from the increase from tillage cannot be said. It is thought that the population is diminished by emigration. In spring and harvest the demand for labourers here, as everywhere else, is much greater than in any other season of the year. During the depth of winter and the middle of summer there is nothing comparatively to be done. It is very difficult to say what is most likely to give general employment. A better mode of culture than at present exists would certainly increase employment if encouragement were given to improvements in agriculture; particularly if spade tillage were adopted there would be a greater demand for labourers. Add to this if some woollen manufacturer were established in our neighbouhood, employment would become more general and all the spare hands including the children would find abundance of work.

Wages

16th. Servants' wages are rather on the advance. There is a rise from a guinea to 30s in the year for wages. The following is accurate return of the present rate of wages. Boys: best from 2 pounds 5s 6d to 3 pounds, inferior from 1 pound 10s to 1 pound 14s 1d ha'penny in the half-year. Girls: best 1 pound 10s, inferior 1 pound in the half-year. Herd boys get from 11s 4d ha'penny to 16s in the half-year. Labourers when they are not fed earn from 1s to 1s 3d a day. However, this is not the practice with the farmers and is only adopted by the gentlemen. The more common practice is to feed the labourers, in which case they receive from 8d to 10d a day in spring and harvest, and in other seasons of the year from 5d to 6d. Work by the piece is not much practised in this neighbourhood. However, when it is adopted the following may be considered a tolerably accurate statement of the prices: for mowing from 4s 2d to 5s an acre, for ditching from 1s 6d to 1s 8d the perch, for reaping 11s 4d ha'penny the acre, for cutting and saving turf 1 pound 10s the 120 gauges (a gauge contains a cubic yard), for quarrying stones 3d the load of 6 cwt.

Green Crops

17th. Green crops are very little cultivated in this barony. Clover and vetches are the only green crops known. Clover is coming into more general use every year as the farmer begins to experience the advantages of that crop. Ten persons cultivate clover now for one that cultivated it 5 or 6 years ago. Vetches are scarcely known except by a few gentlemen who cultivate small patches for their horses.

Grasses

18th. There is a prejudice against artificial grasses in this country. The farmer says they impoverish the ground and are as deteriorating as a crop of barley or oats. Here they are seldom sown. Indeed the land is run let out for years until it is no longer capable of bearing a crop, in which state it is suffered to lie until, by degrees, it assumes a green surface. The only artificial grasses that are sown are feather grass (stipa pennata) and rye grass

Parish of Clogher

(lolium perenni). All our meadows are low bottoms of natural grass. There are few or no upland meadows in this country.

Drainage

19th. Both surface and underdraining are practised in this district. There are 2 kinds of drains that have been observed by the reporter. One is commonly known by the name of French drains, where a quantity of small stones are thrown into a drain, in the bottom of which a narrow passage for the water is previously covered by some of the broader and flatter stones. The hole is then filled up with earth and made level with the surface of the ground. Another is where a narrow drain is cut and covered with grassy sods, a foot below the surface of the ground, which is afterwards levelled in the manner of French drains. This a more expeditious method and sometimes answers very well, especially in meadows that do not require to be broken up, but it is certainly not so durable as the former. It is, however, to be regretted that draining of all kinds is too little practised in this district.

Manure

20th. The most usual type of manure made use of in this barony is a compost of bog stuff on the cleaning of ditches and drains intermixed with stable dung and lime. This is found to be the best manure for heavy clay grounds, and uplands in general. The moory bog mud opens and dries the ground. Bogs are generally manured with vegetable earth mixed with stable dung and lime. Clay and soil and subsoil are very often burned for manure in this district. The method is, to construct a circular kiln of sods. In this are placed 2 flues at the bottom for the admission of air, constructed also of sods running in the direction of the diameter and crossing at right angles. Turf or sticks of any kind are drawn in and set on fire, clay is then continually heaped on as long as the fire lasts, which sometimes continues burning for several days. But the more common method is to put up small heaps of clay and put a few turf in the centre, upon which more clay or sods are heaped until the entire mass is consumed. The ashes that proceed from these fires are generally used as manure for potatoes. In the month of May the moory parts of the whole country is involved in smoke from these small fires, if the season proves favourable, and the farmer looks forward to a scanty or abundant crop of potatoes according as the month of May proves favourable or unfavourable for burning.

Irrigation

21st. Irrigation is practised everywhere that it can be adopted with little trouble, but the farmers will go to no expense in irrigating. The Reverend Mr Gervais seems to be the only person who practises irrigation on an extensive scale in this barony.

Dairies and Oxen

22nd. There are no public dairies whatever in this barony.

23rd. No persons makes use of oxen in husbandry in this district except the Reverend Dr Story.

Tillage

24th. Plough tillage is in universal practice in this district. Spade tillage is totally unknown, except in bogs, which being unable to bear the weight of horses, the farmer is obliged to put in the seed with spades, over which a light harrow is drawn, often by the labour of men, to cover the seed more perfectly and to give an even surface.

Grain

25th. The kinds of grain cultivated in this district are oats, barley and rye. Wheat is not found to answer, and is very seldom sown owing it is believed to the lightness of the soil. The prices of grain and provisions this year are as follows: oats from 8d to 1s the stone, barley and rye from 9d to 1s 1d the stone, potatoes from 1d ha'penny to 2d ha'penny the stone, oatmeal from 13s to 10s the cwt, beef from 3d ha'penny to 5d per lb, mutton from 4d to 5d per lb, butter from 8d to 10d per lb.

Land Measurement

26th. Mr Eccles' estate in the parish of Fintona is measured by the Scotch acre or Cunningham measure, Mr Verner's estate in the parish of Errigal Keerogue by the English acre. All the land of this barony is computed by the Irish acre.

Cattle

27th. The old Irish breed is almost the only kind of black cattle found in this district. None of the English breeds are known: you will never meet with an Ayrshire, Devon or Teeswater cow, except perhaps a solitary instance in a gentleman's demesne.

28th. Sheep and young cattle are the only kinds of stock that are kept in this barony, as properly speaking there are no large stock farms in the whole district. The soil does not seem adapted to the fattening of black cattle.

Sheep

29th. There are 2 descriptions of sheep to be found in this district, the English and the Irish breeds. The English breed known by their low broad shape and the freedom of their heads and feet for wool, as well as the superior fineness of the wool, are coming into general use and gives a higher price. The soil seems peculiarly well suited to the fattening of sheep. Every farmer has a few and some have large flocks, which they find to be more profitable than any other kind of stock.

Horses

30th. In the lowlands the old Irish breed of horses are used, which are very well fitted for the culture of the soil. Many farmers take great pleasure in having good horses, some of which are half-bred. In the mountains the horse generally used is the Rathlin or Raghery breed, which is a low strong kind of pony, very well suited to the mountain districts, as well for the ease with which they are fed as for their great strength in proportion to their size.

Pigs

31st. The tall long-legged and long-sided breed of swine are most in demand. The low short legged English breed is not in general use. The farmers, however, seem to gradually be advancing into the latter breed.

Stock

32nd. It is impossible to give anything like a correct return of the quantity of stock. In each parish any enumeration given would be quite wide of the truth. One thing may be said, that stock of all kinds has greatly increased within the last 2 years.

33rd. It is difficult to say what improvements have been made in the different kinds of stocks. The farmers in general take delight in good horses, and the breed in use is very well suited to the country. Some of them are half-bred. There are none of the English breeds. On the whole there appears to be little advancement made in this department. The breed of swine also appear to be stationary. Within the last 20 years in this country no improvement has been made. Not so with respect to sheep: there has been a great improvement in this kind of stock. A very good breed of sheep prevails in this country. For beauty of shape and fineness of wool they are scarcely to be exceeded by any of the native breeds. The breed of black cattle has received no sensible improvement. None of the English breeds have been introduced. It is hoped that the establishment of the North West Society will have a considerable effect in exciting a spirit of improvement in all the different breeds.

NATURAL FEATURES

Lakes and Rivers

34th. The grounds in this barony must be among the highest in the north of Ireland, some of the largest rivers having their rise therein. The Foyle rises to the west of Scregagh mountain. It receives several tributary streams on the south east side of the mountain as it advances towards Fintona. This stream is joined before it reaches Omagh by a river which has its origin from several little currents that spring on the south west side of the same mountain. The Blackwater has its rise in several little streams that spring on the north east side of the same mountain. This current is met before it reaches Clogher by another stream that flows from the north west side of the same mountain; leaving Clogher it proceeds by Aughnacloy <Aughernacloy>, Caledon and Portadown, until it is lost in Lough Neagh. The principal loughs in this barony are Ballagh lough, Castlehill lough and Lough McCall in the parish of Clogher, and Martrey lake in the parish of Errigal Keerogue. All these lakes are comparatively very small.

Gemstones

A very handsome species of chalcedony <calcedony> has been found among the gravel in the streams of the parish of Fintona. It is beautifully veined and figured and very hard. Cornelians and moss agates are also very abundant. Several beautiful specimens of all these stones are in the possession of the reporter.

Metals

35th. No metallic mines whatever have been discovered in this district, although from the presence of chalybeate springs more or less impregnated, iron ore must be abundant in every part of this barony.

Stone

36th. Slieve Bay mountain which bounds the south of this barony has numerous quarries of freestone

Parish of Clogher

that furnish excellent millstones and scythe stones. The same quarries supply stones for window stools, flagging and building. The Bishop of Clogher is at present building his palace with stones quarried in this mountain, which are of a very fine, close grit and therefore are hard to be worked. Quarries of common flat or flinty rock are everywhere to be found all over the barony.

37th. There is not a single quarry of limestone in the entire parish of Fintona, which is a very great inconvenience to the inhabitants of the parish. They are obliged to send to Clabay, which is 5 or 6 miles distant, for limestone, and pay 5d a load. However, limestone is very plentiful in the parishes of Clogher and Errigal Keerogue, insomuch that the roads of Clogher are often repaired therewith. It is generally of a bluish grey colour and of an excellent kind. Limestone is universally burned in this barony with turf. Consequently the expense of burning varies as the expense of the turf.

Coal and Springs

38th. No coal of any kind has ever been discovered in this barony.

39th. There are no mineral springs in this district, if we except numerous chalybate springs that everywhere abound, slightly impregnated, and to which no medicinal virtue has ever been attached. There is, however, an excellent sulphureous spring on the very confines of this barony in the barony of Dungannon, townland of Garvey, much celebrated and much frequented.

Marl

40th. Marl is found in various places in this district, among which we may reckon Ranees and Tullyrush in the parish of Fintona, in Ballyvardon in the parish of Clogher and on the borders of Marlany lake in the parish of Errigal Keerogue. The only kind of marl that has come before the reporter's notice is argillaceous. The value of marl is very little known in this district. It is seldom used when it is found, and never in any other way than to cover meadows.

SOCIAL ECONOMY

Occupations

43rd. The lower orders of inhabitants in this barony have very little concern for domestic comforts. If they can procure plenty of meal and potatoes with a little milk they care for almost nothing else. Even the more wealthy farmer has no knowledge or taste for the comforts and conveniences of life. There is notwithstanding a general disposition to industry in the inhabitants, and the poor prefer in general any kind of work rather than begging. There are 3 ways in which the poor can earn money: by the loom, by the spinning wheel and by labour. The first is by far the best, being constant and tolerably productive. A journeyman weaver can earn from 5s to 6s every fortnight besides his food. The second is very unproductive, 3d a day without food being the utmost a spinner can earn. The last is very profitable as long as it lasts. A labourer gets from 5d to 10d a day besides his food, but labouring work is very inconstant, the whole of the winter and a great part of the summer furnishing little or no employment for the labourer. Hence the labourer is scantily fed and poorly clothed, all the money they can earn being unequal to procure the necessaries of life.

Habits of the People

42nd. There is very little order, cleanliness or neatness in general to be found either in the houses of the more wealthy farmers or in the cottages of the poor. The turf stack often approaches within a few yards of the door and thus intersects the view and stops the currency of the air. The yard in front of the house is full of the odour of the cow house and stable, for they are often built in the very front and sometime adjoining the dwelling house. The lanes and approaches to the house are narrow, rough and filthy in the extreme. Within no order is visible: you may see pigs and fowls eating in the kitchen and everything dirty and confused, the furniture a few pots and noggins, a stool or a broken chair. The potatoes at meals are thrown out in a basket and so laid on the table or on a stool, and the whole family gather round, master, mistress, children and servants in a mass, and eat out of the basket without knife, fork or any other appendage at meals. A man who can give his daughter in marriage 50 pounds or 100 pounds will live in this manner. But this is not universally the case: sometimes everything is seen comfortable, neat and clean, both within and without the farmhouse, the furniture good and decent, the kitchen neatly tiled, the outside of the house well whitewashed and thatched, the yard and lanes about the house in good repair and clean. It is, however, to be regretted that very few instances occur where this order and decency is observed.

Fuel

43rd. Turf, the only fuel, is plentiful in the parish

of Fintona. Every farm has a portion of bog attached to it for which no rent is paid. When turf is sold in the town of Fintona the cost has been for the last 2 years from 10d to 15d the crate. In the neighbourhood and town of Clogher turf is more scarce and dear. The inhabitants are obliged to go to the mountains that lie on either side for fuel, which is sold at from 20d to 2s 6d the crate. In the town and neighbourhood of Ballygawley turf is equally scarce and dear, the inhabitants in general being obliged to go to the neighbouring mountains for fuel or pay at the same rate as at Clogher.

Food

44th. Potatoes and milk is the general food of the farmers of this barony, for breakfast, dinner and supper during 9 months of the year. This is sometimes varied by a bit of bacon for dinner, sometimes butter and oaten bread or eggs are added to the potatoes for dinner. In 3 of the summer months when potatoes begin to fail, stirabout or flummery is substituted for potatoes, for breakfast or supper.

45th. The same report will serve for the manufacturing class or tradespeople.

46th. Potatoes and milk, or when milk grows scarce potatoes and herrings, or potatoes and salt is almost the only food of the poor inhabitants during the entire year. Occasionally a little stirabout is added for supper or breakfast in the summer months.

Education

47th. There is certainly a general desire of instruction in all classes of the people, both Protestants and Roman Catholics. The poor are anxious to teach their children reading, writing and arithmetic, and although the facilities for the education of the Roman Catholics is not so great as for the Protestants, being hindered by their priests from attending Sunday and other schools, yet there is certainly a great desire in the minds even of the Roman Catholics for the education of their children.

48th. The children of the poor pay for their education according to the following rates: for spelling and reading, for writing, for arithmetic, for book-keeping [blank].

49th. It is believed that there is at least an improvement in the morals and cleanliness of children attending Sunday schools. They are not permitted to attend unless they are clean and they are expelled if any gross immorality be committed. It is also hoped that there is in the inhabitants in general a greater respect for the laws, fewer quarrels and less fighting than formerly.

Health

50th. This barony is a very healthy place. The lands are high and the air is wholesome and pure, besides there are no stagnant marshes and lakes. Hence there are few prevalent diseases: fevers and pleurisies are the most common.

Poor

51st. There is no association in this district for improving the condition of the poor that deserves the name of society. The poor are rather assisted by individuals than by societies; indeed the ladies of Clogher have a small association which supplies flannel to several poor women. If we include dispensaries for distributing gratuitous medicines to the poor among societies for improving their condition, there are several in this barony very well conducted: one at Clogher, one at Ballygawley, one at Fivemiletown and one at Fintona. Add to this that there are several Sunday school associations in this barony, than which none are found to have a better effect in bettering the condition of the poor. From these they learn cleanliness, morality and industry.

Towns

52nd. The towns in this barony are Ballygawley, Augher, Clogher, Fivemiletown and Fintona, all of which are post towns except Augher, and all are market towns.

Improvements

53rd. A turn for improvements seems to be increasing, there is more neatness in the culture of the farms and they are better enclosed and drained than formerly, and there is more attention paid to the breed of the several kinds of stocks than in former times. Still there is a lamentable deficiency of planting in all this barony, which makes the country look miserably wild and naked especially in winter. Perhaps premiums for the most approved kinds of stock, for the best cultivated and neatest farms and for the most approved farming utensils might have a beneficial effect. However, if landlords will not give their best assistance, it is in vain to expect that much beneficial results shall arise. If they gave encouragement to improvements among their tenantry, the good effects would soon appear. Planting and good fences is the grand desideratum in all this district.

54th. The greatest improver in this barony is the

Parish of Clogher

Reverend Mr Gervais of Saville Lodge, Clogher. Next to him may be placed Sir John Stewart of Ballygawley, J.C. Moutray of Favour Royal, Esquire, Aughnacloy, Reverend Dr Story of Carrick [Corick], Clogher, R.W. Maxwell of Killyfaddy Esquire. These persons are the most intelligent and most likely to be useful correspondents with the North West Society.

Productive Economy

Linen

55th. The linen manufacture is certainly on the increase in this part of the country, which is quite evident from the circumstance that there has been no decrease in the quantity of linen cloth sold in the Fintona market, although the markets for the sale of linen cloth have been established in Omagh and Ballygawley, to which markets, especially the former, many of the weavers of this part of the country bring their cloth to be sold. The market at Fintona, notwithstanding, continues to thrive as well as at any former period.

56th. There are no mill works of any kind for the bleaching of linen in this barony.

Flax

57th. Flax generally succeeds a crop of potatoes, sometimes a crop of barley or oats, but very seldom. The ground is universally prepared by a light digging with spades, over which a harrow is drawn to level the surface, afterwards the seed is sown. The flax is almost universally consumed in home manufacture, the seed is never saved. When seed has sometimes been saved, the crop produced has been very short and unproductive. This has deterred the growers from adopting the practice.

58th. Flax is generally dressed by the hand and not by mills, although since the establishment of a scutch mill by Mr Gervais the people in his neighbourhood find it their convenience to resort thither to have their flax scutched. It is, however, not a very popular practice. The women say that there is a much greater loss in scutching at a mill than at home. The mill breaks the flax too much and cuts it short, whereas the flax which proceeds from the hands of the women is generally longer and better dressed. Flax dressed at home always brings a higher price. Flax is universally dried over a fire before it is scutched.

Yarn

59th. The grist to which yarn is usually spun in this place is from 2 to 3 hanks in the lb. Warps are spun generally to 2 hanks, and 2 hanks and 4 cuts, weft to 3 hanks in the lb. The spinner generally spins a hank in a day, for which she is paid 3d.

60th. The price of yarn has been last year at the Fintona market, which is the cheap market for yard in the barony, as follows, flax yarn: warps at from 2s to 2s 6d per spangle, weft at from 1s 3d to 1s 8d per spangle, tow yarn at from 1s 8d to 2s 4d per spangle. The flax yarn is almost universally consumed at home, but the tow yarn is bought up by dealers, who carry it to Armagh where it is wrought into coarse cloth.

Spinning

61st. Many of the spinners are too poor to grow their own flax, and therefore are obliged to buy it by the stone undressed or by the pound hackled. Hundreds of poor women subsist entirely by spinning flax or tow, which they purchase in the market. All who are able, of course, sow a little flax seed and pay at the rate of 10s for the ground of a peck. The farmer is not included in the above statement; he sows from 1 to 4 bushels of flax seed every year.

62nd. The double spinning wheel with both hands has not as yet been introduced into this neighbourhood.

Weaving and Yarn Greens

63rd. The weaver generally buys his yarn in the market. In the farmers' houses sometimes the resident weaver is supplied with warps by the spinners of the house, but this is rarely the case. After the yarn is bought the weaver is obliged himself to prepare it for the loom by boiling and bleaching. The expense for ashes, tallow and dressing is about 3s 1d.

64th. There are no yarn greens whatever in all the country and it is not probable that any very considerable benefit would result from the establishment of such greens, the boiling and bleaching which yarn requires preparatory to weaving, being neither very tedious nor troublesome.

Productive Economy

Other Manufactures

There is no woollen manufacturing in this district. Mr Scott of Fivemiletown is building at present a mill at said town for the manufacture of woollen goods. It is, however, only on a very limited [scale ?]. There is no cotton manufacturing in this barony. That no kelp is manufactured and that there are no fisheries need not be mentioned. (Signed) Omichron [in Greek letters].

Parish of Donacavey, County Tyrone

Draft Memoir, received 30 November 1835

NATURAL FEATURES

Hills

The highest part of Donacavey parish is the hill of Tattymoyle, which is situated in the southern part of it and rises to the elevation of 1,031 feet above the level of the sea and 750 feet above the level of the adjoining country. It has a wild appearance and is mostly covered with heather. The slopes of it are broad and gentle, and it forms the highest point of a ridge which extends to the mountain of Shantavney in the parish of Errigal Keerogue and which is the northern boundary of the traditional "Valley" or "Race of the Black Pig" as it is commonly called even to this day among the peasantry, and in which are situated the towns of Aughnacloy, Ballygawley, Augher, Clogher and Fivemiletown. None of this valley, however, is in Donacavey parish.

In the east of this parish there is a projection from the above mentioned ridge and which runs in a north westerly direction, terminating about a mile to the south east of the town of Fintona. Its highest point is 735 feet above the level of the sea. The lowest part of the parish is 280 feet above the sea.

Rivers

In this parish there are 2 small rivers. The first is the Carnalea which rises in the parish of Clogher, runs in a northern direction through the centre of the parish and passes by the town of Fintona. Its length in the parish is 5 miles. Its breadth varies from 15 to 30 feet and its depth from 1 foot to 4. There are no falls nor are there any rapids nor is there any drainage carried on and there are only 2 insignificant corn mills on it. It is not subject to floods. Its bed is rocky. The character and scenery of the banks very dull and uninteresting. The parish is abundantly supplied with water from rivulets and springs.

The second river is called the Twiggery. It rises in the parish of Errigal Keerogue and runs in a north westerly direction and forms the boundary of the northern part of the parish for 4 and a half miles. Its breadth varies from 15 to 25 feet and its depth from 2 to 6 feet. It has no falls, nor rapids. There is no drainage carried on on the banks, but it is subject to floods after heavy rains during all seasons, which subside very soon and are rather injurious than otherwise. In some parts the bed is gravelly, especially in the higher parts, but in the flat land it is muddy, the character and scenery of the banks uninteresting.

There is a chalybeate well in the townland of Belnagarnan, near the town of Fintona. It is situated in a bog.

Lakes and Bogs

Lakes: there are none in the parish.

There is a great quantity of bog in this parish. In the lowlands it is scattered up and down in small patches, but the principal quantity is in the elevated and southern part of the parish. There is hardly any timber found in the bog. The little that is found is generally the trunks of fir trees lying horizontally. The depth of the bog varies from 6 to 20 feet and is in many cases unknown. Insular hills and patches of good land often rise out of the bog.

Woods

There are no natural woods in the parish, nor are there any evidences of woods having formerly existed, but a large number of trees have been planted during the last few years by Charles Eccles and Samuel Vesey Esquires, but principally fir trees.

MODERN TOPOGRAPHY

Town of Fintona

The town of Fintona is situated nearly in the centre of Donacavey and although built on a slight hill on the banks of the Carnalea stream, is still low in its position when compared with the surrounding lands. It contains [blank] houses, of which [blank] are 3-storeys in height, [blank] are 2-storeys and the remaining [blank] are cabins. The public buildings are the church, the Presbyterian meeting house and the Methodist meeting house. There is also a Roman Catholic chapel situated half a mile to the south of the town.

Fintona is 680 yards in length or from one end of the principal street to the other and is 440 yards in breadth, that is, from the extreme north to the extreme south point. The principal street is rather narrow, varying from 45 to 60 feet in breadth, is rather curved and is irregularly built. The houses are generally built partly of stone and partly of brick and are slated when they are above the rank of cabins.

Parish of Donacavey

Productive and Social Economy

Markets and Fairs

There are 15 fairs held during the year in this town: videlicet one on the 22nd of every month and the remaining three which are termed "old fairs" are held on the 1st January, the 4th May and the 30th October.

A market is held every week (on Friday). The commodities disposed of at the fairs and markets are linen, yarn, cows, pigs, sheep, hardwares and a quantity of apples in autumn.

Petty Sessions

Petty sessions are held every alternate Tuesday. The sitting magistrates are Samuel Vesey and Richard Burgess Esquires, who are firm and respected by the people. They are not stipendiary. The latter resides at Seskinore and the former at Derrybard, both of which places are within convenient distances.

Libraries and Debating Society

There are no libraries, reading rooms nor societies in Fintona, if we may except a meeting of shopkeepers who assemble sometimes at each other's houses and who style themselves a debating society. They choose some subject such as historical facts or personages and talk over the pros and cons of the matter amongst themselves. It does not appear to be a very flourishing concern.

General Remarks

The town of Fintona is certainly improving, though very slowly. There is generally some new building struggling into light by tedious efforts. There is no bank nor branch bank in the town. No newspapers are published. The town is well supplied with butcher's meat. The police barrack and one other house only are insured from fire.

Table of Occupations in Fintona

Grocers 22, spirit shops 28, saddlers 2, shoemakers 20, tailors 11, smiths 8, carpenters 7, cloth shops 8, milliners 2, inns 2, lodging houses 18, bakers 7, butchers 4, hatters 2, surgeons 7, general dealers 5, hardware shops 4, watch makers 2, leather cutters 2, tin shops 1.

Modern Topography

Public Buildings

The church of England is situated at the north east

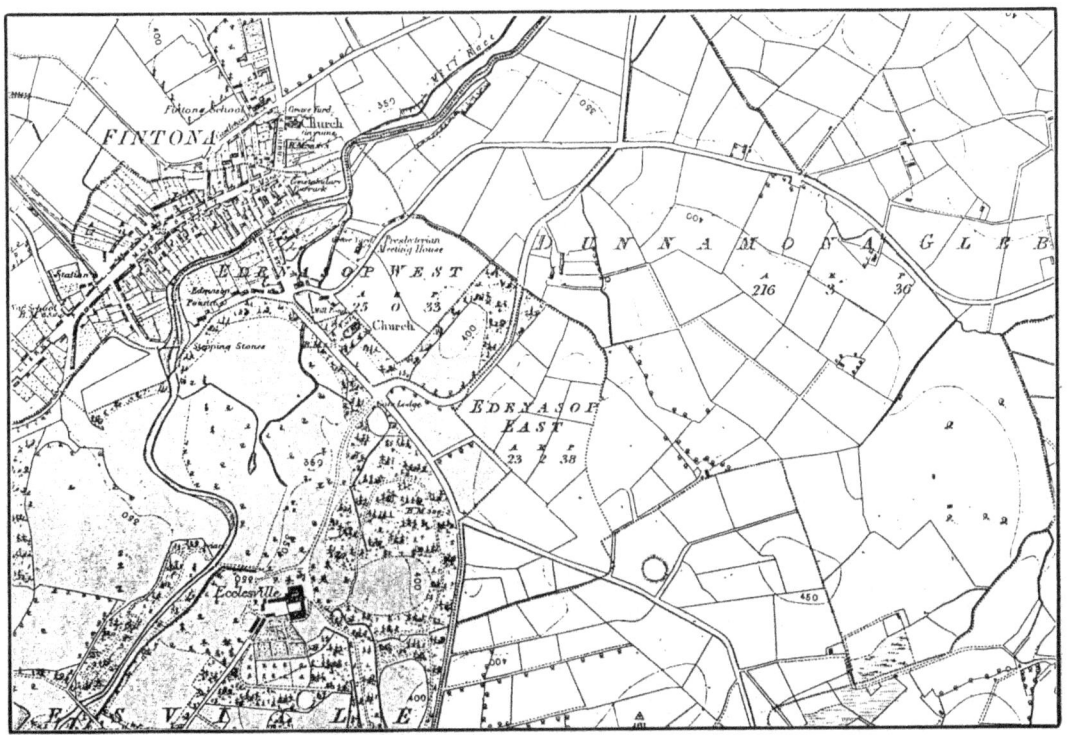

Map of Fintona from the first 6" O.S. maps, 1830s

end of the town on the most elevated point of the slope the latter occupies. It is a rectangular building of small dimensions, with a square steeple but no spire. It was built in [blank] and its cost is [blank]. It will accommodate 800 persons. It is too small for the comfort of the congregation and a new one is being talked of.

A Roman Catholic chapel in the townland of Ecclesville was built in 1780. It is a slated building without spire or steeple.

A meeting house, situated in Cavan townland, built in 1821 at the cost of 165 pounds which was defrayed by subscription; it accommodates 150 persons, the attendance is from 100 to 150. Service is held in it once a fortnight. It is a plain rectangle.

Gentlemen's Seats

Ecclesville, the residence of Charles Eccles Esquire, is situated close to the town of Fintona and built in the usual style of architecture for such buildings, that is if four stone walls and a slated roof can be termed architecture. It is well surrounded with trees and the extent of the demesne is 229 acres and 4 perches. The house is situated rather low: [insert note: Ecclesville is a very handsome stone building of large dimensions and solid appearance].

Derrybard, the residence of Samuel Vesey Esquire, was built in the year 1832 in much the same style as Ecclesville [underlined] by the present resident. [Insert footnote: This house has a convex bow containing 3 windows above and below on the south face. It has also a double porch of masonry, a cut stone cornice of very handsome appearance running round 3 sides of the outer wall, and the spacious offices contiguous form a quadrangle which is entered by a lofty gateway over which there is a belfry and clock]. Its appearance is as good as could be expected considering that the trees about it are all newly planted.

Roads

The main roads from Fintona are those to Omagh, Enniskillen, Fivemiletown and Clogher.

The main road to Omagh is [blank] feet broad and runs for 2 miles in the parish and is in good order and judiciously laid out.

The road to Enniskillen is 30 feet broad and runs for 3 miles in the parish, is kept in good order and judiciously laid out.

The road to Fivemiletown is 30 feet broad and runs for 3 miles in the parish, is kept in good order, as is also the road to Clogher which is 27 feet broad and runs for 2 and a half miles in the parish.

The road to Ballygawley runs for 2 and three-quarter miles in the parish, is 30 feet broad and well laid out.

These roads are all kept in repair by the barony. The cross and by-roads are in many cases unnecessarily numerous.

Bridges

The bridge over the Carnalea stream, at the town of Fintona on the Fivemiletown road, is 27 feet broad and 120 feet long and has but 1 arch which is 40 feet span. It was built in the year [blank]. It is not a good bridge.

Draughton bridge on the Clogher road is a very handsome bridge, considering the rivulet over which it runs. It was built in 1833 of rough hewn stone, has one small but very high arch and cost [blank]. It is 24 feet broad, 120 feet long.

Letfern bridge, on the crossroad from Seskinore village to Clogher, is 20 feet broad and 80 feet long, was built in 1824 and runs over the Twiggery river.

Seskinore bridge also runs over the Twiggery and is on the road to Ballygawley. It is 21 feet broad and 280 feet long and is a very old bridge.

Syonfin bridge on the road to Fivemiletown runs over the Carnalea stream. It was built in the year 1829, is 20 feet broad and 160 feet long and is a good plain strong bridge and has one arch.

Table of Corn Mills

There are no bleach greens in Donacavey.

Lackagh, 1 foot 6 inches breadth, 14 feet diameter, belongs to C. Eccles, breast wheel.

Garvallagh, 4 feet 6 inches breadth, 16 feet diameter, belongs to Samuel Vesey, breast wheel.

Belnagarnan, 2 feet 4 inches breadth, 13 feet diameter, breast wheel.

Tonnaghmore, 2 feet breadth, 13 feet diameter, breast wheel.

Edenasop West, [no further details].

PRODUCTIVE ECONOMY

Crops

Barley is sown in March and April and reaped in Setember; oats the same. Potatoes are set in May and dug in November. Flax is sown in April and pulled in August. The crops are on a par with the surrounding parishes.

SOCIAL ECONOMY

Dispensary

An answer to queries of the Fintona dispensary.

Parish of Donacavey

When established: 12th April 1819. How supported: by subscription and presentments. Average number of patients per annum about 700. Most prevalent complaints: fevers. Whether the sickness is less frequent in the parish since the dispensary has been established: less frequent, as the poor have it in their power to apply for medical aid at the commencement of their illness.

Table of Schools

[Table contains the following headings: name of master or mistress and townland where situated, number of pupils subdivided by religion and sex, remarks as to how supported, when established].

Thomas Buchanan, Fintona, 13 Protestants, 1 Catholic, 14 males, 14 total, privately supported, 1834.

Matthew Robinson, Fintona, 34 Protestants, 6 Catholics, 38 males, 2 females, 40 total.

Francis Walker, Fintona, 33 Protestants, 2 Catholics, 28 males, 7 females, 35 total, privately supported, 16 December 1833.

Patrick Carroll, Fintona, 6 Protestants, 60 Catholics, 38 males, 28 females, 66 total, supported by the Board of Education, 1816.

Alicia Flinter, Fintona, 25 Protestants, 5 Catholics, 6 males, 24 females, 30 total, privately supported, 183[3 ?].

James Donnelly, Fintona, 2 Protestants, 33 Catholics, 22 males, 13 females, 35 total, privately supported, 1811.

James McWilliams of Blackfort, 13 Protestants, 66 Catholics, 50 males, 29 females, 79 total, supported by the Board of Education, 1814.

William Job of Leggatiggle, 55 Protestants, 5 Catholics, 36 males, 24 females, 60 total, under the Hibernian Society, 1831.

Thomas Dunbar of Lianfin, 29 Protestants, 1 Catholic, 17 males, 13 females, 30 total, privately supported, 1833.

Henry Ternan of Garvola, 31 Protestants, 20 males, 11 females, 31 total, under the Hibernian Society, 13th August 1833.

Matthew Blakely of Tonnagh, 27 Protestants, 3 Catholics, 12 males, 18 females, 30 total, supported by the Kildare Place Society, 1829.

Robert McCauley of Lisnacrieve, 25 Protestants, 5 Catholics, 20 males, 10 females, 30 total, supported by the Kildare Place Society, 1827.

James Campbell of Tatymoyle, 10 Protestants, 35 Catholics, 26 males, 19 females, 45 total, supported by the Board of Education, 1828.

James Mullin of Mullisclegagh, 7 Protestants, 31 Catholics, 28 males, 10 females, 38 total, supported privately, December 1829.

Thomas Owens of Cumber, 61 Protestants, 18 Catholics, 55 males, 24 females, 79 total, supported by the Kildare Place Society, 1829.

Mrs Robinson of Lisnagardy, 42 Protestants, 8 Catholics, 50 females, 50 total, supported by Kildare Place Society, 1827.

James Donnelly of Tullyrusk, 24 Protestants, 7 Catholics, 22 males, 9 females, 31 total, privately supported, 1829.

Francis Coletor of Mullawinny, 52 Protestants, 35 Catholics, 48 males, 29 females, 77 total, supported by the Board of Education, 1821.

James Tierney of Carryglass, 12 Protestants, 47 Catholics, 41 males, 18 females, 59 total, supported by the Board of Education, 1834.

Patrick McGinn of Mullanboy, 14 Protestants, 7 Catholics, 21 males, 7 females, 28 total, supported privately.

D. Smith of Drafton, 15 Protestants, 25 Catholics, 20 males, 20 females, 40 total, supported privately.

Owen McSorley of Attaghmore, 24 Protestants, 21 Catholics, 30 males, 15 females, 45 total, supported by the Board of Education, 1833.

10th October 1834, I certify the above return to be as near the truth as we could make it, [signed] William Atthill Junior, assistant curate of Donacavey.

Improvements

The exertions of Samuel Vesey Esquire, in building a new and fine house and in planting to a great extent around it has been a decided improvement to this parish within the last few years.

Local Government

For <petit> petty sessions, see head "Town of Fintona."

Poor

There are no establishments for the relief of the poor in this parish.

Religion

The Roman Catholic religion predominates in this parish to a considerable extent, i.e. 700 Roman Catholics to 500 Protestants, including in the latter amount all the different sects of Presbyterians who occasionally attend church.

Emigration

Emigration prevails in the summer and autumn.

Several families leave the parish every year, principally for New South Wales, a few for America.

Schools

[Table contains the following headings: name, situation and description, when established, income and expenditure, physical, intellectual and moral education, number of pupils subdivided by age, sex and religion, name and religious persuasion of master or mistress. No physical education].

Kildare Street Society, townland of Lisnacreeve, the room an oblong square well fitted up with desks, established in the year 1827; income: from Charles Eccles Esquire and Reverend Joseph McCormick 4 pounds annually, nothing from any society, from pupils 1d per week; expenditure: none on salaries, 10s per annum for repair; intellectual and moral education: the *Dublin reading book*, testaments and spelling book, arithmetic and grammar but none belonging to the Board of Education, and public examination in the church catechism by the Reverend Joseph McCormick; number of pupils: males, 11 under 10 years of age, 5 from 10 to 15, 1 above 15, 17 total males; females, 11 under 10 years of age, 9 from 10 to 15, 20 total females; 37 total number of pupils, 13 Protestants, 9 Presbyterians, 15 Roman Catholics; master Robert McCauley, Episcopalian.

Private school, Draughton, a cabin, established 1828; income: nothing from public societies or benevolent individuals, from pupils 1d per a week; expenditure none; intellectual education: *Universal spelling book* or any the scholars choose to bring; moral education none; number of pupils: 27 males, 9 females, 36 total pupils, 7 Protestants, 3 Presbyterians, 26 Roman Catholics; master Daniel Smith, Episcopalian.

Hibernian Society, Legatiggle, established 1831; income: receives 5 pounds per annum from the Hibernian Society, from pupils 1d a week; expenditure none; intellectual education: spelling, writing, book-keeping and arithmetic taught; moral education none; number of pupils: males, 16 under 10 years of age, 20 from 10 to 15, 36 total males; females, 18 under 10 years of age, 6 from 10 to 15, 24 total females; 60 total number of pupils, 47 Protestants, 10 Presbyterians, 3 Roman Catholics; master William Jebb, Episcopalian.

National school, Carriglass, established 1834; income: receives 8 pounds per annum from the National Board, from pupils 1s 6d per quarter; expenditure none; number of pupils: 46 males, 23 females, 69 total pupils, 14 Protestants, 55 Roman Catholics; master James Tierney.

Statistical Memoir by Lieutenant R. Stotherd, 26 June to 5 July 1835

GEOGRAPHY OR NATURAL STATE

Name

From the various modes in which the name of this parish is found spelt in modern authors, it is difficult to come to a satisfactory conclusion as to its most correct orthography. The customary mode of spelling is that which I have adopted, for which I have also the authority of a parish applotment dated 4th July 1774, McEvoy's *Statistical survey*, the Grand Jury Map of the Barony of Clogher, McCrea and Knox's county map and the Reverend William Tomes, the curate of the parish. It is probable, however, that at an earlier period it was known by the name of Donagh-cavey, as spelt in Beaufort's Map of Ireland, the House of Commons' *Report on the population of Ireland*, also in McEvoy's *Statistical survey* and by the Reverend William Atthill, rector of the parish. In Clogher cathedral, in the stall annexed to this prebend it is marked Donacavy and in Carlisle's Topographical Dictionary, Donagheavy. The name of Donagh-Cavey appears to be derived from Donagh, a church, and Cavey, the name probably of a patron saint. In the *Irish ecclesiastical register*, dated 30th April 1824, it is called Findonagh, a rectory and vicarage or more modernly Fintona. The village of this name which is situated about the centre of the parish is called in Irish manuscripts [Irish letters] Fionn-tonach, Fionn-tonach, pronounced Fintonagh, i.e. "the white mount or rampier", and it is not impossible that this was the original name of the parish. In Carlisle's *Topographical dictionary* we find Donaghcavy and Findonagh mentioned as two separate parishes. This is evidently a mistake, there being no parish of the latter name in the barony of Monaghan, county Monaghan. It is pronounced Don-a-cav[stress]-ey.

Locality

It is 94 Irish miles from Dublin and is situated in the south west of the county Tyrone, adjacent to the county Fermanagh, 73 townlands being in the barony of Clogher and 16 in that of Omagh. It is bounded on the north by the parishes Drumrath and Clogherney, on the east by Clogher, on the south by Clogher and Enniskillen and on the west by Kilskeery and Dromore. Its form is compact, its length from north to south being 8 statute miles, its breadth from east to west being 7, extreme length from north east to south west 9 miles. It contains

Parish of Donacavey

23,052 acres 2 roods 1 perch, of which 18,342 acres 1 rood 8 perches are in the barony of Clogher and 4,710 acres 33 perches in 2 divisions in the barony of Omagh. There are about 16,916 acres under cultivation, about 3,020 acres mountain heather, about 2,790 acres bog, about 141 acres planting, about 155 acres rough pasture lands and about 22 acres marshland, and about 6 acres water.

NATURAL FEATURES

Hills

This parish partakes in the general character for variety of surface which pervades the whole county. On its southern boundary a lofty range of hills branching from the Aghintain mountains stretch from east to west, the ramifications and underfeatures of which extend far into the parish, approaching the town of Fintona. Undulating hills occupy its remaining extent, separated from each other by flat or flow bogs towards the north west or by glens and ravines on the north east. At its northern extremity, in the townland Donamona occurs one of those singular gravelly ridges called eskraghs which have so long occupied the attention of the curious, similar to those in the adjacent parish of Clogher. It runs north east and south west and is composed of the same material, namely rounded pebbles of mica slate, quartz and micaceous sandstone. From the extent and singularity of these eskraghs, they are worthy of a very careful investigation and the subject will be duly considered when treated of in the Memoir of the adjacent parish of Clogher, where they are more extensively developed.

The greatest altitude in the parish is Tattymoyle, 1,031 feet above the level of the sea, subsidiary to which the following are the principal heights, namely: Stranisk, Scregagh 919.6 feet, Legamaghery, Gargrim 708.9 feet, Raneese 735.5 feet, Aughafad 706.4 feet, Derrybard, ground at Fintona church, 361.1 feet, Rathwarren 461.7 feet, Castletown 433.2 feet, Drafton 616.8 feet, Lisnacrieve 653.8 feet, Lisnagardy 460.6 feet, Dundiven 471.6 feet, Bedlam hill, Carriglass 758 feet, Barrack hill, Lisconrea, 592.9 feet, Edinatoodry 684.1 feet, Killyliss Fort 463.6 feet, Fallagheran 400.7 feet, Rathfragan Fort 349.1 feet, Glennan Fort 385.4 feet, Baronagh 372.9 feet, Middle Tattymoyle 928.5 feet, Gulladoo 506.5 feet, Screen 394.4 feet, Black Fort 344.9 feet, Mullaselega 566.9 feet.

Lakes and Rivers

Few parishes of equal content are so perfectly devoid of any expanse of water to vary the aspect of the scene. A small subsidence or hollow in Carriglass bog is covered by about an acre of water in which is an island, of the retired situation of which the illicit distiller is said formerly to have availed himself for the purpose of carrying on his unlawful practices.

On the boundary of the townland of Cavan is a marshy swamp, which when dammed up in winter to form a mill pond covers many acres of good meadow land.

Innumerable small streams have their sources in the hills on the southern boundary of the parish. These flowing northward swell into the 3 small rivulets of Fintona, Seskinore and Dromore, the former of which flows through the town of Fintona and centre of the parish, the latter is on its western boundary; that of Seskinore flowing from the parish of Clogher forms the north eastern boundary of Donacavey for about 5 miles. These rivers from their size are of little importance. Flowing through flat holmes in the north where largest, their water power is not great, but towards their sources where the fall increases it seems capable of greater extension and application. The waters of this parish subsequent to their union in the Drumragh river fall through the channels of the Strule and the Mourne rivers into the Foyle.

Bogs

The flow or flat bogs are very extensive, covering not less than 2,790 statute acres, very equably distributed in small patches through the whole parish. These patches enlarge towards the west and north west, but with very few exceptions every townland has a proportion of turbary within its precincts. The mountain heather covers an extent of 3,042 acres. Beneath its surface lies an almost inexhaustible supply of turf of the very best quality, of difficult access but to which the new line of road to Fivemiletown has opened a communication. These bogs contain embedded some trees of fir and oak, but they are not numerous, and from the dry quality of the soil and the general appearance of the country [insert note: there not being in any part of this extensive district any vestige of the remains of natural wood or underwood] I am induced to believe that it was never very thickly wooded.

Climate

The climate like that of other parts of Ulster is very variable but mild, wet and moisture predominating in the winter months over frost and cold. Even in the summer months a continued succession of fine weather with sunshine need scarcely be looked for, westerly and south westerly winds blowing almost continually charged with rain and vapour. The seasons for ripening the crops are in consequence late, barley ripening in August, oats about a fortnight later, potatoes from the end of August to October. No meteorological register has been kept within the parish.

NATURAL HISTORY

Botany

Same as the rest of Ulster.

Zoology

The usual wild animals and birds are to be found in the fields and bogs and the mountains. [Insert addition: In the deep waters of the river bounding the townlands Freighmore, Raneese and Garvola, several otters have been killed. I saw in 1833 a very large one, which had been killed in the river close above Mr Vesey's mills. Partridges are rare, snipes and woodcocks are more abundant, the green and grey plover are very numerous and the common grouse would be sufficiently plentiful to repay the invigorating toil of the sportsman if well preserved in the heather of Dundiven, Scregagh, Stranisk, Tatemoyle and Carriglass. The goshawk and other birds of prey no doubt help keep down their numbers, but the principal enemy to the grouse are the numerous cur dogs which follow the herds through the heather in the breeding season. Keepers may be appointed, but in vain will the sportsman look for game until the fatal edict has gone forth that "all dogs found in the mountains during the 6 summer months will be shot!" In the waters a few trouts are to be found but scarcely enough to repay the labours of the water whippers. [Insert note: The practice of steeping flax in the small streams is very destructive to the fish].

MODERN TOPOGRAPHY AND HISTORY

Town of Fintona

The situation of the town of Fintona <Fintonagh> is central with regard to the parish, of which it is the market town. It is agreeably situated in a gentle eminence on the circuit road from Enniskillen to Omagh, 15 Irish miles from the former and 7 from the latter town. Extraordinary as it may appear, one of the principal obstructions to the improvement of the town is the circumstance that all the tenements are held off the proprietor, Charles Eccles Esquire, on leases for ever [underlined]. I have observed that whenever a town is in the hands of the lord of the soil, daily improvements are visible, the contrary being the case almost universally whenever the occupying tenant is under no control, as in this case. The town is nearly a third of a mile in length with some lateral streets, yet there are but very few respectable houses. Some effort has indeed been made within the last 3 to 4 years but the progress of improvement is scarcely visible. The houses are principally built of brick and slated and very many of them consist but of one floor. In this respect, however, something has been done lately. The inn has been raised from the ground and should be now tolerably commodious.

General History of Fintona

Of the early history of this town and district, I can obtain little or no information. It is mentioned in an old Irish manuscript as the residence of a branch of the O'Neills. In Pynnar's survey I find "2,000 acres called Fentonagh allotted to John Leigh Esquire, Sir Francis Willoughby being the first patentee." "A bawne of lyme and stone, with 2 flankers and a good large stone house within it in which he dwelleth" is mentioned, and "near unto this bawne there is a small village consisting of 8 houses." This village is the present town of Fintona, and immediately above it on a hill called Castle hill, are the remains of the old bawn, of which some walls only are standing. By letters patent dated 13th August in the 4th year of the reign of King Charles II, the manor of Fentonagh was granted to Praefato Johanni Leigh. By similar letters dated "sexto die augusti, anno regni nostri septimo, Carolus II", a court was constituted and established for the manor of Castleleigh, to be held in the town of Fintona every 3 weeks for the recovery of small debts amounting to 2 pounds Irish. This court is called a court baron, and annually a court called a court leet is held for the purpose of making laws and regulations for the said manor. The court consists of the lord of the manor, the seneschal and 12 jurors for the court baron, and 23 jurors for the court leet. By no act of this court can the person be touched for debt, but the goods can be seized.

Public Buildings

At the north eastern extremity of the town stands the church in a very bad state of repair. It will hold 600 persons, and notwithstanding the overflowing congregations which attend the admirable discourses of the Reverend Atthill, the rector, and the Reverend William Tomes, his curate, the church is suffered to remain in a most disgraceful state. Many of the pews are not even floored and in other respects it is wanting in every necessary comfort. There being a sum of 480 pounds in the hands of Charles Eccles Esquire, raised by assessments off the parish towards the building of a new church, it is to be hoped that something will shortly be done towards this very desirable object.

The Roman Catholic chapel, situated in Ecclesville demesne and about half a mile from the town, will hold about 1,500 persons. [Insert note: The Roman Catholic chapel is numerously attended. The house is in a dilapidated state but collections are making to erect a new one].

There are also one Presbyterian and one Wesleyan Methodist meeting house, the former holding about 400 persons, the latter 250. [Insert note: Service is performed in the Presbyterian meeting house only every other Sunday, the people of that persuasion not being very numerous].

The town can boast neither a court house, market house, nor any other public buildings. Nothing has been done for the encouragement of the useful arts or for the improvement of the intellectual and moral character of the people. There is neither library, reading room, benefit society or savings bank.

It is a post town, communicating by horse with Omagh, and 2 covered cars or caravans each drawn by a pair of horses pass through every day en route from Omagh to Enniskillen about 8 a.m., returning the same day and leaving the latter town at 3 p.m.

PRODUCTIVE ECONOMY

Fairs and Markets

By the patent of Charles, 4 fairs were granted to be held on the 1st January, 4th May, 2nd June and 29th October in each year. A new patent of George III grants 12 new fairs to be held on the 11th of each month, but in consequence of the fair of Enniskillen being held on the 10th, that of Fintona is deferred to the 22nd, so that not less than 15 fairs are now held annually. They are principally for the sale of cows, black cattle and pigs, and are very numerously attended by the neighbouring farmers. The following are the scale of customs paid to Charles Eccles Esquire, lord of the manor. Table of customs: cow 4d, 2 year old cow 3d, 1 year old cow 2d, sheep 2d, pig 2d, goat 2d, lamb 1d, butter per cask 2d, hides 2d, shoemakers 4d, hatters 4d. The above are the only customs now charged.

A market is held on Friday in each week and is celebrated for the quantity of oatmeal sold, being the principal market for that commodity within a very considerable distance. Every alternate Friday is also a large brown linen market, principally nine hundredths, ten hundredths and eleven hundredths and seven-eighths in width. It is perhaps the third linen market in Ireland for quantity and is attended by buyers from the bleach greens of counties Derry and Antrim. On the whole it is a cheap and abundant market.

MODERN TOPOGRAPHY

Gentlemen's seats

Ecclesville, the residence of Charles Eccles Esquire, is situated on the Fintona river to the south and close to the town. It is a handsome and commodious modern mansion, having been very much improved by the late John Dixon Eccles Esquire about 10 years since. It is supposed to have been originally built by Charles Eccles Esquire about 80 years ago and was improved by Daniel Eccles Esquire, about 40 years since. The demesne contains 229 acres, of which 34 were planted by the late proprietor, J.D. Eccles Esquire, whose memory will be long cherished by his numerous tenantry for his active benevolence and kind attention to their interests during a long and constant residence among them.

A new and elegant modern mansion has been built within the last 5 years by Samuel Vesey Esquire. It is called Derrybard House, from the name of the townland in which it is situated and promises from the judicious and extensive improvements of its present worthy and hospitable proprietor to be a valuable addition and ornament to the country, and particularly when contrasted with the following description given of it in Pynnar's *Survey of Ulster* in 1619. Extract: "Sir William Cope Knight hath 2,000 acres called Derribard. Sir Anthony Cope was the first patentee. Upon this there is a bawne of clay and stone pointed with lyme, being 80 feet square with two flankers and a little house within it uncovered, all lying waste and not any one English man at all dwelling on the land, but all inhabited with Irish." No remains of this bawn are now perceptible.

Mills and Manufactories

The parish contains 8 corn and flax water mills and 1 hammer mill used in the manufacture of spades and shovels. Of the former, the corn mill of Samuel Vesey Esquire of Garvola is the most extensive and valuable, the remainder are small and for local use. The hammer mill at Belnagarnon is a very useful and interesting construction, and is used for the rough formation of spades and shovels, which are perfected and prepared for sale at the forges in the town.

Communications

The circuit road from Enniskillen to Omagh is a new and excellent road, traversing the parish from south west to north east and passing through the town of Fintona.

The new road at Clogher is also very well laid out, avoiding the old and hilly line, without increasing the distance, and after a gradual but long ascent bearing along the upper levels until within a few miles of Clogher.

A new road is just completed over the Aghintain mountains to Fivemiletown. Independent of the great utility of this road as a local communication, in connection with the new lines now in progress from Fivemiletown to Monaghan and Clones, it will very materially shorten the distance to both these latter towns, [insert note: opening also a communication between the east of the parish and the limestone at Clabby].

The roads in general in the parish are improving, but some of the old lines which are still open are very hilly. The materials for their formation and improvement are everywhere at hand and of good quality. There is no water communication of any description.

ANCIENT TOPOGRAPHY

Ecclesiastical Antiquities

In objects of antiquarian interest, this parish is very deficient. The old church of Donacavey dates its foundation from the time of Saint Patrick, according to many of the older inhabitants. It is a perfect ruin, the 4 walls only standing, and is not used now unless its yard by the Roman Catholic population of the parish for the burial of their dead. It is situated in the townland of Donacavey about 1 and a half miles north of Fintona. Close to the church is a fragment of an ancient stone cross, which an old dame living close to the church stated that she remembered entire. It is not remarkable either for size or beauty of sculpture.

Pagan Antiquities

About one mile from Fintona near the bridge on the old road to Omagh is a more interesting object of attention. It is a collection of huge blocks of trap or greenstone, having very much the appearance of a druidical remain. The stones of which it is composed are placed on end in the form of a parallelogram; but it does not on enquiry appear to have excited any particular attention, no person knowing anything about it or even appearing to have observed it. It must, however, be remarked that its position is exactly in line with a trap dyke which occurs on either side of it at a very short distance, and from which the materials of which it is composed have at least been supplied, if it is not actually a continuation of the dyke itself.

Forts

Numerous old circular rounds or forts are scattered over the surface of the parish, none of which are particularly interesting either for their size or situation, if we except that of Baronagh which is rather larger than usual.

MODERN TOPOGRAPHY

General Appearance and Scenery

To the hand of man this district is but little indebted for improvement in its general appearance, and I have already observed that no natural woods arise to add their sylvan charms to the scenery. If we except the demesnes of Ecclesville and Derrabard [Derrybard], scarcely a tree appears to diversify the scene. It has, however, great capabilities for improvement in this respect in its undulating surface, backed in the distance by the lofty hills which bound it on the south. How much may be done by planting has been proved by the spirited proprietor of Derrabard House, Samuel Vesey Esquire, whose bleak and almost barren hills have assumed all the charms of woodland scenery within a very few years. The whole parish is thickly studded with good farmhouses, which give it an air of comfort and independence.

SOCIAL ECONOMY

Early Improvements

In Pynnar's survey dated 1619, we find that in the plantation of Ulster in the reign of James I the precinct or barony of Clogher was allotted to English undertakers. To the Earl of Castlehaven were allotted 2,000 acres called Fentonagh; this portion is supposed now to be the manor of Touchet. To Sir Francis Willoughby were allotted 2,000 acres called also Fentonagh, which portion at the time of the survey, 1619, was held by John Leigh Esquire, and is now called the manor of Castleleigh. To Sir Anthony Cope also were allotted 2,000 acres called Derribard; this portion is 1619 was held by Sir William Cope Knight, and is now called the manor of Cope or Killyfaddy, of which the largest part is in the parish Clogher.

John Leigh Esquire, appears alone to have complied with the terms and objects of the plantation. At this early period, 1619, he had built a small village consisting of 8 houses near unto his own "good large stone house in which he himself dwelt." He had planted and estated upon his land of British <Brittish> tenants: freeholders 8, viz. 3 having 120 acres le piece, 2 having 60 acres, 2 having 45 acres, 1 having 66 acres. Lessees for years, 12, viz. 4 having 100 acres le piece, 2 having 66 acres, 1 having 120 acres, 3 having 66 acres, 2 having 40 acres. Cottagers 21, each having a house and garden plot and most of them 2 acres besides commons for cattle, making a total of 41 families.

Of Derribard, Pynnar states that there was "not any one Englishman at all dwelling in the land but all inhabited with Irish" as was also the portion allotted to the Earl of Castlehaven. The early attention to the objects of the colonization of Ulster before referred to is in its effects observable at the present day, through the whole parish generally and in the manor of Castleleigh in particular. The lands are in general held by a very respectable Protestant tenantry, whose interests have at all times been attended to by a resident landlord. There are about 700 Protestant families in the parish of the Established Church and the Presbyterian denomination. The prevailing names are Crauford, Johnston, Noble, Buchanan.

From the opening of the new circuit road from Enniskillen through Fintona to Omagh may be dated an evident improvement. Its beneficial effects on the trade of the town, by opening good markets for the produce of the parish, are very apparent and it has probably tended materially to the improvements in building and the increase in population which have lately taken place. The portion of this road between Fintona and Enniskillen was begun in the year 1825 and completed in 1829. That from Fintona to Omagh was made a few years before.

Local Government and Civil Unrest

The petty sessions are held every fortnight in the town of Fintona, at which generally 3 magistrates attend. Those resident are Charles Eccles Esquire, of Ecclesville and Samuel Vesey Esquire, of Derrybard House. The police force consists of a sergeant and 8 subconstables, stationed part in the town of Fintona and part about 2 miles distant in the north east of the parish. An additional sergeant and 3 subconstables are stationed in the Bar about 4 miles from the town in the south west of the parish. The people are in general quiet and orderly, but, in the autumn and winter of 1832 the spirit of opposition to landlords which manifested itself throughout the barony of Clogher with the view of forcing a reduction of rent, partially extended itself to this hitherto peaceable parish. This spirit has now entirely subsided and it is but justice to the tenantry of the Ecclesville estate that during this disturbed period they remained perfectly quiet and were supposed in no way to have participated in the illegal assemblages which took place. In consequence, however, a subaltern detachment of infantry and a sergeant of cavalry and 8 men were stationed at Fintona until September 1833 the following year. It is to be hoped that the good sense of the people and the just consideration for the interests of their tenantry by resident landlords will prevent the recurrence of similar manifestations.

Manor courts are held as before stated at Fintona for the manor of Castleleigh and at Ballymahatty in the parish Drumragh for the manor of Touchet. There are no revenue police stationed in the parish, the force from Omagh being sufficient to repress illicit distillation, which is now rarely practised.

Dispensary

There is a dispensary in the town supported by voluntary subscriptions and a county grant. The medical attendant states the average number of patients in the year to be near 5,000, and that he cannot state with precision the number of deaths or recoveries as no regular register is kept, and that most cases are those of dyspepsia; but the number of patients mentioned is a sufficient guarantee for its extensive utility. [Table] average number of patients 5,000, rheumatism 30, consumption 4, 4 died, typhus 50, 30 cured, 20 died, cholera 39, 30 cured, 9 died, liver complaints 40; cholera has quite disappeared. Supported by voluntary contributions and county grant.

Schools

[Copy of table of schools in Draft Memoir, q.v.]. Total number of pupils: 561 Protestants, 411 Catholics, 592 males, 380 females, 972 total. NB In addition to the 22 in the above table there is also a school in Donamona, of which no return could be procured, the master having left. Also a few small hedge schools of a very fluctuating character. [Insert note: in many of the national schools the rates paid by the children are 1s per quarter reading, 1s 6d per quarter reading and writing, moderate enough]. The numbers in the preceding table render unnecessary any remarks on the subject of education: we find a peaceable and quiet parish in which the children of Protestants and Roman Catholics are educated in the same schools to the number of near 1,000. Were but the same liberal principle followed throughout the land and the accursed system of agitation put a stop to, this country, instead of being the constant scene of discord and commotion, the never failing prey of the demagogue, would soon evince signs of those permanent improvements in the condition of its people of which it is so capable.

Poor

There is a rent charge of 5 pounds late Irish currency on the townland of Aghafad, left by an ancestor of the Ecclesville family for the benefit of the poor. The rector gives 5 pounds at Easter and a sum of from 15 pounds to 20 pounds is annually subscribed to provide blankets. With these exceptions and the collections in the church which are appropriated to the use of the poor, there is no state provision for the indigent and infirm.

Religion

See return of commissioners. Protestants of the Established and Presbyterian Churches and Roman Catholics are to each other in the above order as 3, 2 and 7 nearly. The glebes of the Established Church are Donamona and Dundiven. On the latter townland is a small Glebe House in tolerable repair, the scene of a very spirited defence by the rector, the Reverend James Johnston, in 1797, when attacked by a body of United Irishmen who were beaten off with considerable loss, although the reverend incumbent was only assisted by a trusty man and young lad to load for him. For an account of this affair, see supplementary letter [Ancient Topography].

Habits of the People

With regard to this head, nothing peculiar to the people of this locality can be said. The Beal [tinne] fire blazes on St John's Eve, but even this ancient custom is gradually dying away. The numerous saints days are regularly kept by the Roman Catholics and the idle and dissipated are never in want of an excuse for quitting their work.

15 [underlined] fairs in the year at Fintona and the weekly market but too frequently offer a temptation to the idler, of which he is ever ready to avail himself, and the town overflows on those occasions with persons who have no business whatever to transact. The number of fair days indeed could very advantageously be curtailed, as tending only to riot and disturbance and being profitable only to the spirit dealer and distiller, but what is the positive loss on these occasions? Look at the crowds of idlers who frequent the fairs throughout Ireland with no object but amusement. How much valuable time is lost? The Irish, I have frequently heard it said, are willing to work. I say that they are most unwilling: when at work they will do double the quantity of work of another man in the same time, with the view of having an idle day afterwards; and poaching, fishing, tracing hares in the snow and such amusements seem to be the great objects of most young people. Steady habits of industry and application are rarely attained by them.

The houses are generally of stone and brick and those of the more respectable class of farmers are tolerably comfortable and generally have an upper storey with glass windows and are thatched. The new houses recently built and building in Fintona are slated. The district is considered very healthy: many persons attain to a considerable age, some to 80 or 90 years, some even to nearly 100.

Emigration

Perhaps 50 or 60 persons emigrate annually to America from this parish, principally to Canada. The dread of innovations in religion is the chief cause of the emigrations of Protestants.

Remarkable Events

None. Skelton when rector of Donacavey wrote 4 volumes of sermons; whether worth reading or not, I don't know.

PRODUCTIVE ECONOMY

Employment

With the exception of the hammer mill for the formation of spades and shovels before mentioned, there is no other manufactorial establishment in the parish. The peasantry are employed in agricultural pursuits and the manufacture of linen cloth, most farmhouses having a loom, which is constantly at work in the winter months. From this district the bleach greens of counties Derry and Antrim are supplied with a large quantity of coarse brown linen, principally nine hundredths, ten hundredths and eleven hundredths, and seven-eights in width. The price from 8d to 1s 2d per yard, rarely higher. The market day for linen every other Friday.

Parish of Donacavey

Leases and Farms

By a reference to the table of townlands with the names of proprietors, it will be seen that this parish possesses the advantages of resident landlords, the family of Eccles having resided on their property near the town since it has come into their hands, and the excellent house which Samuel Vesey Esquire has just built at Derrybard is a sufficient guarantee that he does not intend to be much an absentee. The property in the Ecclesville estate is generally leased for lives and years and much of it, including the town of Fintona, on leases renewable for ever. Lord Belmore's property in this parish is almost all held on lease for 1 life or 21 years and the size of the farms generally is from 10 to 50 Irish acres at from 10s per acre up to 1 pound per Irish plantation acre. The Reverend Grey Porter of Kilskeery, proprietor of 7 townlands in the south west of the parish called the Bar, gives 1 life and 21 years in some cases where he thinks it would be advantageous, but in most cases the spirit of improvement now pervading that property is best carried on under his own eye by tenants at will, he expending the capital. The size of his farms varies from 3 to 20 acres of arable.

Use of Lime

The great impediment to the improvement of this district is the want of lime, the nearest deposit of which is at Claby in the county Fermanagh, the land carriage from which over a mountain road is a matter of serious inconvenience. Mr Porter supplies lime to all his tenants, the amount being repaid by instalments. [Insert note: marl was raised by Mr Porter on his estate in 1831].

Proprietors and Tenants

The principal proprietors are Charles Eccles Esquire, holding 48 townlands, 8 of which are abbey lands and are tithe free; the Reverend John Grey Porter of Kilskeery, proprietor of 7 townlands, the Earl of Belmore, proprietor of 5 townlands, Samuel Vesey Esquire, proprietor of 4 townlands, H.G. Edwards Esquire, proprietor of 2 townlands; 9 townlands are churchland, 6 of which are held under the see of Clogher by Samuel Evans Esquire of Dublin, and these are 2 glebes. The remaining townlands are the property of small proprietors. Taking the whole parish generally, the land is held in various ways, on leases for lives and years, on leases renewable for ever and on toties quoties leases. The average for the best land per Irish acre is about 30s, for middling land 25s, worst land 15s.

[Insert note: All the lands held on toties quoties leases and on leases renewable for ever are, as is usual with such cases, at a very reduced rent. The general size of the holdings is from 10 to 20 acres but in several cases they amount to 50 acres and upwards.

The system of middlemen is not and cannot be for a length of time entirely abolished, in consequence of the nature and length of the leases, but its injurious effects both to landlord and tenant are now so well known that subletting in no case is permitted on the renewal of leases. The system of duty men and service is still in some cases observed in this parish. When the landlord's turf is to be brought home, the tenants assemble with their cars and it requires a very active overseer to get a good day's work out of them. In fact they attend as in duty bound for the day or days and do as little work as they can.

The enclosures are generally speaking of a moderate and convenient size and well fenced, particularly in the northern end of the parish where quickset hedges are in general use. The tenants are subject to county cess, manorial cess and the tithe composition and but little difficulty has been hitherto experienced in the collection. The farm buildings are of the usual character in the north. They are generally built of brick or stone and some few cottages are of mud.

Soil and Geology

The soil partakes very much of the character of the rock and substratum on which it rests, namely a light red graywacke <grauwacke> approaching in character to the old red sandstone. It may be considered generally as a good light stony soil and frequently assumes a reddish hue from the colour of the decomposed rock which forms its basis. The stones scattered over the surface are generally speaking of the same material. Towards the west and on the rich holmes on the banks of the rivers some veins of clay appear, and in the northern townland of Donamona the soil is very gravelly in some parts from the vicinity of the gravelly eskragh which traverses that townland. [Insert note: The soil in the centre and west in several places rests on a cold clay till, very much opposed to the productive qualities of the soil from the difficulty of draining in such circumstances. Surface can then alone be resorted to to carry off the superabundant water which falls in such quantities in this moist climate].

At one point only is there the least appearance of lime: at the meeting of the 4 crossroads in the townland Edinafogry, an argillaceous shale with an admixture of carbonate of lime appears at a short depth below the surface. With this exception, I do not remember to have observed even a limestone pebble throughout the whole parish, the limestone and lime for agricultural and other economic purposes being all brought from Clabby near Tempo in the county of Fermanagh. 2 marl pits have been opened in the townland of Cavan and in many parts of the parish immediately beneath the turf bog appears a layer of white clay which deserves a closer examination than I at the time gave to it. If not marly in its composition, query, is it not very well adapted for making bricks or pottery

Crops

On the whole the soil is productive and is very capable of being greatly improved. Oats, flax and potatoes [superscript numbers indicate reverse order] are the general produce and the succession of crops in the above order. Sometimes a crop of potatoes is followed by 2, 3 and even 4 crops of oats in succession and the land is then suffered to run to lea without any assistance. Grass seed is rarely sown, and wheat in 1833 was scarcely seen in the parish: I saw but 2 very small fields in that year. [Insert note: a very small quantity of barley is grown. Such is the miserable system of farming followed through the whole parish, in which it may generally be considered that the land, after being run out by a succession of oat crops after potatoes, is left in a state of nature except in a few places when an improved system of agriculture is practised, especially on the demesne of Samuel Vesey Esquire of Derrybard House].

An average crop throughout the parish is from 250 to 300 bushels of potatoes per Irish acre, 40 bushels of oats per Irish acre, 48 stone of flax per Irish acre. Barley ripens in August, oats about a fortnight later. Potatoes from the end of August to October.

The principal markets for the produce are Omagh and Fintona, the latter being one of the best meal markets in the north. The general price of oats is from 6d to a shilling per stone according to the season, and it is taken to market by the country farmers on their own cars and carts.

Quarries and Stones

Before closing this report I may remark that quarries of sandstone fit only for roads and rough building materials are opened in every part of the parish. Recently a fine freestone has been discovered and quarried in the mountain in the south east of the parish close to the new road from Fintona to Fivemiletown. The bridges in its neighbourhood were built of it and it appears applicable to every building purpose.

In all the water courses flowing from the range of mountains on the south of the parish agates are found, some of them of a very fine quality and deserving of the attention of the lapidary. They are embedded in the conglomerate rock of which these mountains are composed, by the disintegration of which and the action of the winter floods they are washed down to the lower level and are found in the beds of gravel and pebbles on the sides of the rivers and rivulets.

HISTORY

Letter concerning Attack on Fintona Glebe House in 1797

Dear Sir, Though I willingly comply with your request to give you some account of the attack and defence of the Glebe House of Fintona in the year 1797, yet my many engagements compel me to be as brief as possible. The incumbent at that time was the Reverend James Johnston, who had been for some years chaplain to the British Embassy at the Court of Copenhagen under Mr Elliot, afterwards Lord Minto. In this situation he carried on an extensive correspondence with His Britannic Majesty's ministers, of which he left a large volume in manuscript containing copies of several important communications which he had made to His Majesty's government, and also several letters from the Marquis of Carmarthen, thanking him in His Majesty's name for the many important services he had rendered to his country. On his return he was collated (I presume on the recommendation of the government) by the Bishop of Clogher, Dr Hottram, to the living of Magheracross and subsequently to that of Fintona.

He appears to have been a man of real piety, learning and talents as well as of great courage and steady loyalty, but of remarkable eccentricity. He seemed desirous to shut himself completely out from the world, and accordingly erected a small house for his residence in Dundiven, the more distant and secluded of the glebes of the parish. This singular structure, of which I annex a rough sketch, was built between a steep hill on the one side and the river on the other, with a bog in front, without any means of communication with the high road. It was about 40 feet in length. A was the only entrance, B the only window of any size on the ground floor, having one of the same dimensions over it, flanked by portholes in the projecting towers, C the staircase and D a semicircular tower serving as a cellar on the ground floor and as a closet above. The remaining windows were very small and high from the ground so that they could not be easily entered, and there were no windows in the rear except single panes, and the towers and walls were pierced with 40 portholes. It was evidently built for defence, and being provided with several stand of arms was capable of making effectual resistance to any irregular attacking party.

The secret society of United Irishmen, originating from Belfast, had spread at that period extensively over Ulster. Mr Johnston was well aware of the dangers that surrounded him and was determined to oppose them. The disaffected sent him in the course of that year several messages desiring him to deliver up his arms and assuring him that if he complied they would not molest him; but he indignantly refused and then they determined to obtain by force what they could not extort by fear. One evening, when the rest of his family was in bed and he just on the point of retiring to rest, he heard the distant barking of dogs, which continually becoming nearer and more distinct gave unequivocal proof of the approach of a large party and soon the tread of feet was heard. He hastily summoned up a trusty man and a lad whom he had in the house. He placed the man on the staircase to defend the large window and the door and took his station in the larger room above in company with the lad, whom he employed in loading the muskets for him.

On his refusal to surrender, they poured successive volleys from behind a turf stack which stood near the house, which he returned with undaunted spirit. During the heat of the contest his daughter, at that time a mere child, said to her mother "Mamma, don't be afraid, papa is fighting for us and God will protect us, but indeed it is not God that they are thinking of." A word of encouragement spoken in season, for out of the mouth of babes and sucklings God ordained strength! The insurgents finding they could make no impression by a distant fire at last ventured from their covert and with a large sledge endeavoured to break open the door, but it was strongly secured by iron bars running across from post to post. On this change of attack Mr Johnston immediately came downstairs and forcing out a loose brick (which being plastered on the outside concealed a porthole immediately over the door) discharged a large blunderbuss heavily loaded into the midst of the crowd of assailants. "Sir", said the trusty man who told me, "It riddled them." The effect was instantaneous. The attack ceased, the wretches fled carrying off their wounded and dead. How many suffered on that occasion is unknown, but blood was found on the door and the line of retreat. One person, a respectable farmer in Aghentain, was buried privately by night in Clogher churchyard and to prevent exhumation a confession was made that he had been shot on that occasion. Another person was found dead in the mountain behind the demesne of the Bishop of Clogher. Within the house no casualty occurred, except that the dog was shot by the man's side on the staircase, telling him how near death had come, but the Lord delivered him.

The corps of yeomanry was at that time on guard in the town of Fintona, and it may be asked why they did not hasten immediately to the assistance of their respected rector. The fact was, it was part of the insurgents' system to make false alarms in distant parts of the parish in order to draw off the attention of the yeomanry to those points. Thus distracted and harassed, the corps, when they first heard the report of the firearms on that evening, conceived it to be one of the usual feints, until the successive volleys assured them that the affair was serious. They hastened then where the sound directed them to Mr Johnston's house, but some time before they reached it (for it was nearly 2 English miles distant), the gallant defenders had put their hundreds to flight. As they approached, however, the barking of dogs, the tramp of feet and sound of human voices alarmed the garrison, and thinking that the enemy had returned they were again prepared to give them a warm reception when the cry of "Friends" dissipated their each remaining fear and the doors were thrown open to exchange mutual congratulations.

The year after this noble defence, the Reverend Mr Johnston died suddenly of an apoplectic stroke, leaving his widow and 2 children very slenderly provided for. 400 pounds fell to the lot of the son, then an infant of a few months old. This was loosed by Allen and Company, Bankers in Edinburgh, in the hands of Messrs J.C. Beresford and Company for his use, but unfortunately the whole of it was lost by the failure of that firm. The unfortunate young man has passed through many trying scenes in the army and the police, and of late burdened with a large family has supported himself by the labour of his hands. Such are the strange vicissitudes of life! Who can contemplate the son of such a father fallen so low without his compassion being stirred within him, and feeling the full force of the apostolic direction, "Remember them which suffer adversity as being yourselves also in the body." The above particulars relative to the attack on Dundiven I learnt from the best authority, the testimony of the widow of the deceased Mr Johnston, and the 2 persons who assisted in the defence of the house. I am, my dear Sir, very faithfully, Yours W. Atthill, Ardess, Kesh, March 20 1836.

Note on Horse

James Tring: Dear brother, I intend running my <hoors> horse regular <raglur> [? anglier] on Saturday next <nex>. Brother if you choose <chuse> to see my horse <hors>. [Unfinished note scribbled on back of valuation report].

SOCIAL ECONOMY

Ecclesiastical Summary

[Table] Name Donacavey, diocese Clogher, province Armagh, rectory and vicarage, not a union, patron Bishop of Clogher, incumbent Reverend William Atthill, extent of glebe 2 townlands, 1 Donamonagh and 2 Dundiven: 1st 216 acres 3 roods 36 perches, 2nd 486 acres 3 roods 15 perches, total 703 acres 3 roods 11 perches. Tythes not impropriate, tithes belong to the rector. Under composition for 600 pounds yearly from 1st May 1828 for 21 years, [signed] R.J. Stotherd, Lieutenant Royal Engineers, 26th June 1835.

LAND DIVISIONS

Notes on Townlands

[Table giving name of townland, barony, manor, proprietors, remarks].

Annaghbo, Clogher, Castleleigh, Charles Eccles Esquire, abbey land and is tithe free. Annaghmurneen, Clogher, Castleleigh, Charles Eccles Esquire, abbey land and is tithe free. Ardatinny, Clogher, Castleleigh, Charles Eccles Esquire. Attaghmore, Omagh, Touchet, Mr Hugh Johnston. Aughadreenan, Omagh, Castleleigh, Charles Eccles Esquire. Aughafad, Clogher, Castleleigh, Charles Eccles Esquire. Augharonan, Clogher, Cope, Samuel Vesey Esquire.

Baronagh, Omagh, Touchet, Mr F. Crawford. Belnagarnon, Clogher, Touchet, Samuel Evans Esquire, churchland held under the see of Clogher and is tithe free. Blackfort, Clogher, Touchet, Samuel Evans Esquire, churchland held under the see of Clogher and is tithe free.

Carriglass, Clogher, Castleleigh, Reverend J.G. Porter. Carnalea, Clogher, Cope, [blank] Tagart Esquire, held in fee simple. Carnaroosk, Clogher, Castleleigh, Charles Eccles Esquire. Castletown, Clogher, Castleleigh, Charles Eccles Esquire, churchland held under the see of Clogher and is tithe free. Cator, Clogher, Cope, Hugh Gore Edwards Esquire. Cavan, Omagh, Touchet, James Wilson Esquire. Corbally, Clogher, Castleleigh, Charles Eccles Esquire. Corrisesk, Clogher, Castleleigh, Reverend J.G. Porter. Cranny, Omagh, Touchet, Earl of Belmore. Crocknaferbrague, Clogher, Castleleigh, the Reverend J.G. Porter. Cumber, Clogher, Castleleigh, C. Eccles Esquire, abbey land and tithe free.

Derrybard, Clogher, Cope, Samuel Vesey Esquire. Donacavey, Clogher, Cope, Samuel Evans Esquire, churchland and tithe free. Donamona, Omagh, Touchet, Major Crawford. Donamona Glebe, Clogher, Touchet, Reverend W. Atthill (1835), glebe of the parish. Drafton, Clogher, Castleleigh, C. Eccles Esquire. Drummond, Clogher, Castleleigh, C. Eccles Esquire. Drumlagher, Clogher, Castleleigh, C. Eccles Esquire. Drumwhisker, Clogher, Castleleigh, Samuel Evans Esquire, churchland held under the see of Clogher and is tithe free. Dundiven (Glebe), Clogher, Castleleigh, Reverend W. Atthill (1835), glebe of the parish, Dungorran, Clogher, Castleleigh, C. Eccles Esquire.

Ecclesville (Demesne), Clogher, Castleleigh, C. Eccles Esquire. Edinafogry, Omagh, Touchet, Earl of Belmore. Edinasop (East), Clogher, Castleleigh, C. Eccles Esquire. Edinsop (West) Clogher, Castleleigh, C. Eccles Esquire. Edinatoodry, Clogher, Castleleigh, C. Eccles Esquire. Fallagheran, Omagh, Touchet, Earl of Belmore. Feenan, Clogher, Castleleigh, C. Eccles Esquire, abbey land and tithe free.

Fintona, Clogher, Castleleigh, C. Eccles Esquire. Freighmore, Clogher, Cope, Mrs Perry.

Gargrim, Omagh, Castleleigh, C. Eccles Esquire. Garvola, Clogher, Cope, Samuel Vesey Esquire. Glennan, Omagh, Touchet, Charles Sproul Esquire. Gulladoo, Omagh, Castleleigh, C. Eccles Esquire.

Kilcootry, Clogher, Castleleigh, Mrs Hay, churchland held under the see of Clogher and is tithe free. Kilgort, Clogher, Cope, Mrs Perry. Killyberry, Clogher, Castleleigh, C. Eccles Esquire. Killyliss, Clogher, Castleleigh, C. Eccles Esquire. Killymoonan, Omagh, Touchet, Earl of Belmore.

Lacca, Clogher, Castleleigh, C. Eccles Esquire. Legamaghery, Clogher, Castleleigh, C. Eccles Esquire. Leggatiggle, Clogher, Castleleigh, C. Eccles Esquire. Lisavody, Clogher, Castleleigh, C. Eccles Esquire. Lurganboy, Omagh, Castleleigh, Reverend J.G. Porter. Lissconrea, Clogher,

Parish of Donacavey

Castleleigh, Reverend J.G. Porter. Lissdergan, Clogher, Castleleigh, C. Eccles Esquire. Lisky, Clogher, Castleleigh, C. Eccles Esquire, abbey land and tithe free. Lisnacrieve, Clogher, Castleleigh, C. Eccles Esquire. Lisnabulravy, Clogher, Castleleigh, C. Eccles Esquire. Lissnegardy, Clogher, Castleleigh, C. Eccles Esquire.

Mullanboy, Clogher, Castleleigh, Mr Samuel Evans, churchland held under the see of Clogher and tithe free. Mullaselega, Clogher, Castleleigh, C. Eccles Esquire. Mullawinny, Omagh, Touchet, several proprietors. Mullins, Clogher, Castleleigh, Mr Auchinleck.

Racrean, Clogher, Castleleigh, C. Eccles Esquire, abbey land and tithe free. Raneese, Clogher, Cope, Samuel Vesey Esquire. Rathfragan, Clogher, Cope, Mr Henry Harman, churchland held under the see of Clogher and tithe free. Raveagh, Clogher, Cope, H.G. Edwards Esquire. Rathwarran, Clogher, Castleleigh, C. Eccles Esquire, abbey land and tithe free. Roghan, Clogher, Castleleigh, Mr Auchinleck.

Screggagh, Clogher, Castleleigh, C. Eccles Esquire. Screen, Omagh, Touchet, C. Sproul Esquire. Sessiagh, Clogher, Touchet, Samuel Evans Esquire, churchland held under the see of Clogher and tithe free. Sionfin, Clogher, Castleleigh, C. Eccles Esquire. Sionnee, Clogher, Castleleigh, C. Eccles Esquire. Skelgagh, Omagh, Castleleigh, C. Eccles Esquire. Strabane, Clogher, Castleleigh, Reverend J.G. Porter. Stranisk, Clogher, Castleleigh, C. Eccles Esquire. Stratigore, Clogher, Castleleigh, C. Eccles Esquire.

Tatemoyle (Upper), Clogher, Castleleigh, the Reverend J.G. Porter. Tattymoyle (Middle), Clogher, Castleleigh, C. Eccles Esquire. Tattymoyle (Lower) Clogher, Castleleigh, C. Eccles Esquire. Tatymulmona, Omagh, Touchet, Earl of Belmore. Tonnaghbane, Clogher, Castleleigh, C. Eccles Esquire, abbey land and tithe free. Tonnaghbeg, Clogher, Castleleigh, C. Eccles Esquire. Tonnaghmore, Omagh, Castleleigh, C. Eccles Esquire. Tullyrusk, Clogher, Castleleigh, C. Eccles Esquire. Tullyvally, Clogher, Cope, Mrs Perry. Tyreenan, Clogher, Castleleigh, C. Eccles Esquire.

Ownership of Land

Aghafad, 300 acres, J.D. Eccles Esquire, resident. Aghnonan, 268 acres, Reverend Dr Vesey, non-resident. Ardatinny, 86 acres, J.D. Eccles Esquire. Belnagarnon, 142 acres, see of Clogher. Castletown, 96 acres, see of Clogher. Calor, 73 acres, Captain Edwards' residence. Corbelagh, 96 acres, Carnaroosk, 34 acres, J.D. Eccles Esquire. Carnaloe, 120 acres, Mr Taggart, non-resident. Corrysesk, 93 acres, Corryglass, 175 acres, Mr Quinn. Dunnamena, 130 acres, glebe of Fintona. Drumnoheskea, 153 acres, see of Clogher. Derrybard, 130 acres, Reverend Dr Vesey. Dunderrin, 80 acres, glebe of Fintona. Drafton, 169 acres, Dungorran, 130 acres, Drumlaghan, 98 acres, Drummons, 151 acres, Cumber, 89 acres, Ednatroody, 18 acres, Ednasor, 35 acres, Feenan, 112 acres, J.D. Eccles Esquire. Freeghmore, 148 acres, George Perry Esquire, resident. Garvola, 221 acres, Reverend Dr Vesey. Gargrim, 136 acres, J.B. Eccles Esquire. Kilcootry, 85 acres, see of Clogher. Kilgort, 170 acres, G. Perry Esquire. Killyliss, 152 acres, Killyberry, 95 acres, Lacca, 138 acres, Leggamaghry, 78 acres, Lisnacreive, 215 acres, Leggetiggle, 108 acres, J.D. Eccles Esquire. Lisnabulravey, 31 acres, Liskey, 46 acres, Lisnagardy, 47 acres, Lislagan, 30 acres, J.D. Eccles. Mullanboy, 151 acres, see of Clogher. Riveagh, 95 acres, Captain Edwards. Sionee 140 acres, Sianfin 159 acres, Sengagh, 82 acres, Sluckgore 53 acres, Stranisk 217 acres, Slettymoyle 267 acres, Mullisclogagh 56 acres, Roghan 123 acres, Rathwarren 74 acres, J.D. Eccles Esquire. Rathfraggan 181 acres, see of Clogher. Ranoes 237 acres, Reverend Dr Vesey. Tannaghbeg 118 acres, Tannaghbane 65 acres, Tullyrusk 106 acres, J.D. Eccles Esquire. Tattyratty 136 acres, G. Perry Esquire. Tyreenan 123 acres, J.D. Eccles. There is about 900 acres of mountain on Mr Eccles' estate. [This paragraph inserted from Clogher memoir].

Classification of Soil

[Table giving name of townland, quantity of bog, woods and plantations, rough and heathy pasture, mountain, heather and wasteland, marsh, water, arable and pasture, total area].

Annaghbo, bog 17 acres 1 rood 24 perches, arable and pasture 29 acres 3 roods 8 perches, total 47 acres 32 perches. Annaghmurneen, bog 26 acres 2 roods 16 perches, arable and pasture 15 acres 3 roods 1 perch, total 42 acres 1 rood 17 perches. Ardatinny, bog 97 acres 32 perches, rough and heathy pasture 3 acres 3 roods 8 perches, arable and pasture 142 acres 3 roods 26 perches, total 243 acres 3 roods 26 perches. Attaghmore, bog 103 acres 2 roods 32 perches, rough and heathy pasture 2 roods 32 perches, arable and pasture 258 acres 3 roods 30 perches, total 363 acres 1 rood 14 perches. Aughadreenan, bog 21 acres 1 rood 24 perches, rough and heathy pasture 2 acres 32 perches, arable and pasture 78 acres 39 perches, total 101 acres 3 roods 15 perches. Aughafad, bog 304 acres 3 roods 8 perches, rough and heathy pasture 25 acres 16 perches, arable and pasture 706 acres 2 roods 3 perches, total 1,036 acres 1 rood 27 perches. Augharonan, bog 97 acres 2 roods 16 perches, woods and plantations 7 acres 2 roods 16 perches, rough and heathy pasture 13 acres 1 rood 8 perches, marsh 1 acre 16 perches, arable and pasture 586 acres 3 roods 11 perches, total 706 acres 1 rood 27 perches.

Baronagh, bog 52 acres, woods and plantations 1 acre 2 roods 16 perches, arable and pasture 325 acres 1 rood 7 perches, total 378 acres 3 roods 23 perches. Belnagarnan, bog 8 acres 3 roods 24 perches, woods and plantations 1 acre 2 roods 16 perches, arable and pasture 138 acres 32 perches, total 148 acres 2 roods 32 perches. Blackfort, bog 20 acres, arable and pasture 163 acres 2 roods 20 perches, total 183 acres 2 roods 20 perches.

Carriglass, bog 18 acres 2 roods 16 perches, woods and plantations 2 roods 16 perches, rough and heathy pasture 7 acres 1 rood 8 perches, mountain, heather and wasteland 314 acres, water 3 roods 24 perches, arable and pasture 247 acres 3 roods 14 perches, total 589 acres 38 perches. Carnalea, bog 15 acres 2 roods 16 perches, arable and pasture 214 acres 1 rood 13 perches, total 229 acres 3 roods 29 perches. Carnaroosk, bog 1 acre, arable and pasture 45 acres 1 rood 28 perches, total 46 acres 1 rood 28 perches. Castletown, bog 13 acres 32 perches, arable and pasture 202 acres 1 rood 37 perches, total 215 acres 2 roods 29 perches. Cator, bog 25 acres 2 roods 32 perches, arable and pasture 166 acres 1 rood 23 perches, total 192 acres 15 perches. Cavan, bog 81 acres, woods and plantations 4 acres, water 3 acres 2 roods 32 perches, arable and pasture 330 acres 2 roods 31 perches, total 419 acres 1 rood 23 perches. Corbally, bog 44 acres 32 perches, rough and heathy pasture 9 acres, marsh 1 acre 1 rood 24 perches, arable and pasture 212 acres 2 roods 14 perches, total 267 acres 30 perches. Corrisesk, bog 8 acres 3 roods 8 perches, arable and pasture 144 acres 16 perches, total 152 acres 3 roods 24 perches. Cranny, bog 174 acres, rough and heathy pasture 1 acre, marsh 2 roods 16 perches, arable and pasture 335 acres 18 perches, total 510 acres 2 roods 34 perches. Crocknaferbrague, bog 2 acres 32 perches, rough and heathy pasture 1 acre, mountain, heather and wasteland 102 acres 2 roods, arable and pasture 125 acres 2 roods 39 perches, total 231 acres 1 rood 31 perches. Cumber, bog 48 acres 3 roods 8 perches, arable and pasture 148 acres 1 rood 12 perches, total 189 acres 20 perches.

Derrybard, bog 1 acre 32 perches, woods and plantations 68 acres, rough and heathy pasture 1 rood 24 perches, arable and pasture 250 acres 1 rood 14 perches, total 319 acres 3 roods 30 perches. Donacavey, arable and pasture 38 acres 8 perches, total 38 acres 8 perches. Donamona, bog 60 acres, rough and heathy pasture 3 roods 8 perches, marsh 1 acre 2 roods, arable and pasture 461 acres 30 perches, total 523 acres 1 rood 38 perches. Donamona Glebe, bog 2 acres 1 rood 8 perches, arable and pasture 214 acres 2 roods 28 perches, total 216 acres 3 roods 36 perches. Drafton, bog 7 acres 3 roods 8 perches, marsh 3 acres, arable and pasture 275 acres 3 roods 8 perches, total 286 acres 2 roods 16 perches. Drummond, bog 14 acres 3 roods 8 perches, rough and heathy pasture 2 roods 16 perches, arable and pasture 218 acres 2 roods 36 perches, total 234 acres 20 perches. Drumlagher, bog 13 acres, rough and heathy pasture 4 acres 3 roods 8 perches, arable and pasture 143 acres 3 roods 25 perches, total 161 acres 2 roods 33 perches. Drumwhisker, bog 13 acres 1 rood 8 perches, arable and pasture 161 acres 3 roods 21 perches, total 175 acres 29 perches. Dundiven (Glebe), woods and plantations 1 acre 2 roods, mountain, heather and wasteland 320 acres 3 roods 8 perches, arable and pasture 159 acres 2 roods 7 perches, total 486 acres 3 roods 15 perches. Dungorran, bog 5 acres 32 perches, rough and heathy pasture 8 acres, mountain, heather and wasteland 105 acres 2 roods 16 perches, arable and pasture 186 acres 3 roods 15 perches, total 305 acres 2 roods 23 perches.

Ecclesville (demesne) bog 6 acres 1 rood 8 perches, woods and plantations 34 acres 32 perches, rough and heathy pasture 7 acres 1 rood 8 perches, arable and pasture 181 acres 36 perches, total 229 acres 4 perches. Edinafogry, bog 46 acres 16 perches, water 16 perches, arable and pasture 167 acres 1 rood 28 perches, total 213 acres 2 roods 20 perches. Edinasop (East), bog 32 perches, woods and plantations 1 rood 24 perches, arable and pasture 23 acres 22 perches, total 23 acres 2 roods 38 perches. Edinasop (West), water 32 perches, arable and pasture 25 acres 1 perch, total 25 acres 33 perches. Edinatoodry, mountain, heather and wasteland 106 acres 3 roods 24 perches, arable and pasture 182 acres 4 perches, total 288 acres 3 roods 28 perches.

Fallagheran, bog 67 acres 1 rood 8 perches, arable and pasture 101 acres 2 roods 9 perches, total 168 acres 3 roods 17 perches. Feenan, bog 19 acres 16 perches, arable and pasture 135 acres 2 roods 8 perches, total 154 acres 2 roods 24 perches. Fintona, arable and pasture 17 acres 33 perches, total 17 acres 33 perches. Freighmore, bog 4 acres

2 roods 16 perches, woods and plantations 3 acres 3 roods 24 perches, arable and pasture 331 acres 25 perches, total 339 acres 2 roods 25 perches.

Gargrim, bog 2 acres 32 perches, rough and heathy pasture 6 acres 3 roods 8 perches, arable and pasture 208 acres 1 rood 22 perches, total 217 acres 1 rood 22 perches. Garvola, bog 80 acres 1 rood 8 perches, woods and plantations 5 acres 2 roods 16 perches, rough and heathy pasture 6 acres, marsh 2 roods 16 perches, arable and pasture 415 acres 1 rood 24 perches, total 507 acres 3 roods, 24 perches. Glennan, bog 28 acres, arable and pasture 189 acres 2 roods 32 perches, total 217 acres 2 roods 32 perches. Gulladoo, bog 36 acres 2 roods 32 perches, arable and pasture 160 acres 1 rood 30 perches, total 197 acres 22 perches.

Kilcootry, arable and pasture 274 acres 27 perches, total 274 acres 27 perches. Kilgort, bog 36 acres 32 perches, arable and pasture 258 acres 3 roods 24 perches, total 295 acres 16 perches. Killyberry, bog 12 acres 16 perches, rough and heathy pasture 5 acres 16 perches, mountain, heather and wasteland 52 acres 1 rood 8 perches, arable and pasture 136 acres 20 perches, total 205 acres 2 roods 20 perches. Killyliss, bog 16 acres 2 roods 16 perches, arable and pasture 214 acres 3 roods 9 perches, total 231 acres 1 rood 25 perches. Killymoonan, bog 54 acres 3 roods 8 perches, marsh 1 acre, arable and pasture 152 acres 21 perches, total 207 acres 3 roods 29 perches.

Lacca, bog 83 acres 1 rood 8 perches, rough and heathy pasture 3 acres 2 roods, arable and pasture 209 acres 17 perches, total 295 acres 3 roods 25 perches. Legamaghery, bog 62 acres 32 perches, mountain, heather and wasteland 83 acres 1 rood 8 perches, arable and pasture 145 acres 11 perches, total 290 acres 2 roods 11 perches. Leggatiggle, bog 70 acres 16 perches, arable and pasture 232 acres 3 roods 3 perches, total 302 acres 3 roods 19 perches. Lisavaddy, bog 4 acres 2 roods 32 perches, arable and pasture 33 acres 1 rood 15 perches, total 38 acres 7 perches. Lurganboy, bog 10 acres 32 perches, arable and pasture 131 acres 3 roods 3 perches, total 141 acres 3 roods 35 perches [insert marginal query: Lurganbuoy?]. Lisconrea, bog 13 acres 1 rood 24 perches, arable and pasture 133 acres 2 roods 12 perches, total 146 acres 3 roods 36 perches. Lisdergan, arable and pasture 23 acres 9 perches, total 23 acres 9 perches. Lisky, bog 5 acres 3 roods 8 perches, arable and pasture 83 acres 5 perches, total 88 acres 3 roods 13 perches. Lisnacrieve, bog 57 acres, rough and heathy pasture 18 acres 3 roods 8 perches, arable and pasture 429 acres 1 rood 26 perches, total 507 acres 1 rood 26 perches. Lisnabulravy, bog 4 acres 2 roods 32 perches, arable and pasture 54 acres 3 roods 34 perches, total 59 acres 2 roods 26 perches. Lisnagardy, bog 4 acres 3 roods 24 perches, arable and pasture 102 acres 1 rood 35 perches, total 107 acres 1 rood 19 perches.

Mullanboy, bog 81 acres 3 roods 8 perches, arable and pasture 396 acres 2 roods 17 perches, total 478 acres 1 rood 25 perches. Mullaselega, bog 26 acres 1 rood 24 perches, rough and heathy pasture 3 roods 24 perches, arable and pasture 116 acres 3 roods 5 perches, total 144 acres 13 perches. Mullawinny, bog 60 acres, arable and pasture 351 acres 2 roods 1 perches, total 411 acres 2 roods 1 perch. Mullins, rough and heathy pasture 1 acre 3 roods 24 perches, arable and pasture 80 acres 1 rood 12 perches, total 82 acres 36 perches.

Racrean, bog 11 acres 1 rood 24 perches, arable and pasture 62 acres 9 perches, total 73 acres 1 rood 33 perches. Raneese, bog 10 acres 16 perches, woods and plantations 8 acres 2 roods 32 perches, rough and heathy pasture 4 acres 16 perches, arable and pasture 396 acres 1 rood 36 perches, total 419 acres 1 rood 20 perches. Rathfraggan, bog 51 acres 1 rood 24 perches, arable and pasture 341 acres 3 roods 33 perches, total 393 acres 1 rood 17 perches. Raveagh, bog 53 acres 32 perches, marsh 12 acres 3 roods 8 perches, water 3 roods 8 perches, arable and pasture 173 acres 3 roods 2 perches, total 240 acres 2 roods 10 perches. Rathwarren, bog 36 acres 3 roods 24 perches, arable and pasture 191 acres 3 roods 21 perches, total 228 acres 3 roods 5 perches. Roghan, bog 14 acres 2 roods, rough and heathy pasture 2 roods 32 perches, arable and pasture 90 acres 2 roods 27 perches, total 105 acres 3 roods 19 perches.

Screggagh, mountain, heather and wasteland 355 acres 2 roods 16 perches, arable and pasture 153 acres 3 roods 35 perches, total 509 acres 2 roods 11 perches. Screen, bog 13 acres, arable and pasture 188 acres 3 roods 24 perches, total 201 acres 3 roods 24 perches. Sessiagh, bog 17 acres 32 perches, arable and pasture 89 acres 3 roods 36 perches, total 107 acres 28 perches. Sionfin, bog 34 acres 1 rood 24 perches, rough and heathy pasture 3 acres 3 roods 24 perches, arable and pasture 211 acres 27 perches, total 249 acres 1 rood 35 perches. Sionnee, bog 15 acres 3 roods 8 perches, rough and heathy pasture 5 acres 32 perches, arable and pasture 169 acres 3 roods 24 perches, total 190 acres 3 roods 24 perches. Skelgagh, bog 56 acres 3 roods 24 perches, rough and heathy pasture 1 acre 2 roods, marsh 1 rood 24 perches, arable and pasture 176 acres 31 perches, total 234 acres 3 roods 39 perches. Strabane, bog 12 acres 2 roods, arable and pasture 123 acres 3 roods 23 perches, total 136 acres 1 rood 23 perches. Stranisk, bog 12 acres 1 rood 8 perches, rough and heathy pasture 2 acres, mountain, heather and wasteland 553 acres 2 roods 16 perches, arable and pasture 211 acres 13 perches, total 778 acres 3 roods 37 perches. Stratigore, arable and pasture 111 acres 3 roods 29 perches, total 111 acres 3 roods 29 perches.

Tatemoyle (Upper), bog 3 acres 2 roods 16 perches, woods and plantations 1 acre 32 perches, rough and heathy pasture 3 acres 3 roods 8 perches, mountain, heather and wasteland 258 acres 3 roods 24 perches, water 2 roods 32 perches, arable and pasture 200 acres 13 perches, total 468 acres 1 rood 5 perches. Tatemoyle (Middle), bog 4 acres 3 roods 24 perches, mountain, heather and wasteland 420 acres 1 rood 8 perches, arable and pasture 136 acres 1 rood, total 561 acres 1 rod 32 perches. Tatemoyle (Lower), bog 5 acres 3 roods 24 perches, mountain, heather and wasteland 341 acres, arable and pasture 155 acres 1 rood 17 perches, total 502 acres 1 rood 1 perch. Tatymulmona, bog 45 acres 1 rood 24 perches, arable and pasture 196 acres 21 perches, total 241 acres 2 roods 5 perches. Tonaghbane, bog 4 acres 2 roods, arable and pasture 34 acres 1 rood 39 perches, total 38 acres 3 roods 39 perches. Tonnaghbeg, bog 63 acres, arable and pasture 164 acres 33 perches, total 227 acres 33 perches. Tonnaghmore, bog 51 acres 32 perches, arable and pasture 266 acres 35 perches, total 317 acres 1 rood 17 perches. Tullyrusk, bog 29 acres 16 perches, rough and heathy pasture 4 acres 1 rood 24 perches, arable and pasture 165 acres 1 rood 34 perches, total 198 acres 3 roods 34 perches. Tullyvally, bog 45 acres 2 roods, arable and pasture 237 acres 2 roods 31 perches, total 283 acres 31 perches. Tyreenan, bog 10 acres 1 rood 24 perches, rough and heathy pasture 1 acre 3 roods 8 perches, arable and pasture 238 acres 3 roods 16 perches, total 251 acres 8 perches. [Totals] Quantity of bog 2,790 acres 1 rood 24 perches, woods and plantations 141 acres 16 perches, rough and heathy pasture 155 acres 2 roods 32 perches, mountain, heather and wasteland 3,019 acres 3 roods 8 perches, marsh 22 acres 1 rood 24 perches, water 6 acres 1 rood 24 perches, arable and pasture 16,916 acres 2 roods 33 perches, total 23,052 acres 2 roods 1 perch.

Tithe Applotment and Cess in 1774

[Table] applotment of 12 pounds cessed on the parish of Donacavey at a vestry held on Monday the 4th day of July 1774, being 5d farthing half farthing per pound valuation. James West, John Buchanan [bracketed together], assessors.

1, Aghafad, valuation 13 pounds, cess 5s 9d 3 farthings. 2, Agharonan Upper, valuation 6 pounds, cess 2s 7d ha'penny. 3, Agharonan Lower, valuation 12 pounds, cess 5s 4d ha'penny. 4, Arditinny, valuation 5 pounds 10d, cess 2s 5d ha'penny. 5, Attaghmore, valuation 10 pounds 10s, cess 4s ha'penny. 6, Aghadreenan, valuation 2 pounds, cess 11d ha'penny. 7, Bollnagarnan, valuation 6 pounds, cess 2s 7d ha'penny. 8, Baranagh, valuation 12 pounds, cess 5s 4d ha'penny. 9, Castletown, valuation 11 pounds, cess 4s 11d ha'penny. 10, Cattor, valuation 5 pounds 10s, cess 2s 5d ha'penny. 11, Carriglass, valuation 6 pounds 10s, cess 2s 11d. 12, Corbolly, valuation 6 pounds, cess 2s 8d. 13, Carnarusk, valuation 2 pounds 10s, cess 1s 2d. 14, Carnalea, valuation 6 pounds 10s, cess 2s 11d ha'penny. 15, [?] Cranny, valuation 12 pounds 10s, cess 5s 7d ha'penny. 16, Cavan, valuation 11 pounds, cess 4s 11d ha'penny. 17, Corrishesk, [bracketed with Crocknaferbrague, Lurganboy and Strabane], valuation 14 pounds 10s, cess 6s 6d ha'penny.

18, Drumwhisker, valuation 10 pounds, cess 4s 6d. 19, Derribard, valuation 9 pounds 10s, cess 4s 1d. 20, Draughton, valuation 6 pounds 10s, cess 2s 11d ha'penny. 21, Dundivin, valuation 6 pounds 10s, cess 2s 11d ha'penny. 22, Dungoran, valuation 6 pounds, cess 2s 8d. 23, Drumlaghan, valuation 5 pounds, cess 2s 3d. 24, Drummon, valuation 6 pounds 15s, cess 3s ha'penny. 25, Donamonay Upper, valuation 6 pounds 10s, cess 2s 11d. 26, Dunamonay Lower, valuation 12 pounds, cess 5s 4d ha'penny. 27, Ecclesville, valuation 2 pounds 10s, cess 1s 2d. 28, Edenforgery, valuation 6 pounds, cess 2s 8d. [Subtotal of valuation 220 pounds 5s]. 29. Feenan and Cumber, valuation 11 pounds, cess 4s 11d ha'penny. 30, Frughmor, valuation 11 pounds, cess 4s 11d ha'penny. 31, Fullaghearn, valuation 4 pounds 10s, cess 2s. 32, Garvolagh, valuation 9 pounds, cess 4s ha'penny. 33, Garvolagh Lower, valuation 4 pounds, cess 1s 9d ha'penny. 34, Gargrim, valuation 5 pounds 15s, cess 2s 7d. 35, Glenan and Screen, valuation 13 pounds, cess 5s 10d. 36, Golladough, valuation 5 pounds, cess 2s 3d.

37, Killcootry, valuation 12 pounds, cess 5s 4d ha'penny. 38, Killgort, valuation 9 pounds 10s, cess 4s 3d. 39, Killaberry, valuation 5 pounds, cess 2s 2d. 40, Killaliss, valuation 7 pounds 10s, cess 3s 5d. 41, Killamoonan, valuation 6 pounds 10s, cess 2s 11d ha'penny. 42, Lissharmebrew, valuation 6 pounds 13s 4d, cess 3s. 43, Lisnacrieve, valuation 12 pounds 10s, cess 5s 7d. 44, Ligamagary, valuation 2 pounds 15s, cess 1s 3d. 45, Lakagh and Edinatoodry, valuation 12 pounds 10s, cess 5s 7d

Parish of Donacavey

ha'penny. 46, Lisnarbulreavy, valuation 1 pound 10s, cess 8d ha'penny. 47, Ligatigle, valuation 6 pounds 15s, cess 3s ha'penny. 48, Liskey, valuation 3 pounds 10s, cess 1s 7d. 49, Mullanboy, valuation 12 pounds, cess 5s 4d ha'penny. 50, Middlesess, valuation 3 pounds 6s 8d, cess 1s 6d. 51, Mullaghsillagh, valuation 4 pounds, cess 1s 9d ha'penny. 52, Mullan and Roghan, valuation 6 pounds 15s, cess 2s 11d ha'penny. 53, Mullawinney, valuation 12 pounds, cess 5s 4d ha'penny. 54, Refragan, valuation 12 pounds, cess 5s 4d ha'penny. 55, [name illegible], valuation 12 pounds 10s, cess 5s 5d. 56, Lisnagardy and Ednasop, valuation 9 pounds, cess 3s 11d ha'penny. [Subtotal of valuation 221 pounds 10s].

57, Revagh, valuation 7 pounds, cess 3s 2d. 58, Rewaran, valuation 8 pounds, cess 3 pounds 7d. 59, Shanefinn, valuation 6 pounds 10s, cess 2s 11d. 60, Scregagh, valuation 7 pounds, cess 3s 2d. 61, Strannisk, valuation 11 pounds, cess 4s 11d ha'penny. 62, Shannee, valuation 6 pounds, cess 2s 7d ha'penny. 63, Strattygore, valuation 4 pounds, cess 1s 9d ha'penny. 64, Skelgagh, valuation 5 pounds 10s, cess 2s 5d ha'penny. 65, Tullivallevy, valuation 9 pounds 10s, cess 4s 1d ha'penny. 66, Tattymoyle, valuation 15 pounds, cess 6s 9d. 67, Tyrarnan, valuation 6 pounds, cess 2s [7d ha'penny ?]. 68, Tonaghbeg, valuation 5 pounds 10s, cess 2s 5d. 69, Tattymalmona, valuation 8 pounds 10s, cess 3s 9d. 70, Tonagh, valuation 6 pounds 10s, cess 2s 10d ha'penny. 71, Tonaghbeg, valuation 4 pounds 15s, cess [?] 2s. 72, Tullyrusk, valuation 4 pounds 10s, cess 2s 1d. [Place-names now replaced by personal names]. 73, Thomas Buchanan, valuation 10s, cess 3d. 74, William Buchanan, valuation 1 pounds 10s, cess 9d ha'penny. 75, John Buchanan, valuation 10s, cess 3d. 76, Widow Creery, valuation 10s, cess 3d. 77, Richard Segerson, valuation 10s, cess 3d. 78, James Robinson, valuation 10s, cess 3d. 79, James Anderson, valuation 1 pound 10s, cess 8d ha'penny. 80, Michael Jones, valuation 10s, cess 3d. 81, Widow Worthington, valuation 1 pounds 10s, cess 8d ha'penny. 82, Claud Finigan, valuation 10s, cess 3d. 83, [name illegible], valuation 10s, cess 3d. 84, Charles Worthington, valuation 1 pounds 10s, cess 8d ha'penny. [Subtotal of valuation 125.5 pounds]. [Signed] John Simson, [?] John Boyd, Thomas [?] Folsidde, Alexander Auchenleck [? curate], [? Andrew Hamill], James [Flemming ?], churchwardens.

Applotment laid out at Vestry 1833

Applotment of 85 pounds 11s laid on at Easter Vestry 1833, parish cess. [Table gives name of townland, sometimes followed by a letter, amount of cess, name of landlord].

Aghafad, E, 1 pound 19s, Eccles. Agharonan Upper, 18s. Agharonan Lower, 1 pound 16s. Ardatinny, 16s 9d. Balnagarnon, B, 18s. Castletown, B, 1 pound 13s, query. Cator, query, 16s 8d, Edwards. Corbelagh, 18s. Carnaroosk, 9s. Carnalea, 19s 9d, query. Corrisesk, P, 1 pound 7d. Crocknafirbrague, P, 4s 10d. Corryglass, P, 19s 9d, query. Cumber, A, 16s 7d. Dennamona Upper, 18s, glebe. Drumwhisker, B, 1 pound 10s. Derrybard Upper, 14s 4d. Derrybard Lower, 14s 4d. Drafton, 19s 9d. Dundiven, 19s 9d, glebe. Dungorran, 18s. Drumlaghan, 15s, query. Drummona, 1 pound 4d. Ednatoodry, 18s 10d. Ednasop, 12s. Feenan, A, 16s 8d. Frughmore, 1 pound 13s, Perry. Garvola Upper, 1 pound 7s. Garvola Lower, 12s. Gargrim, 17s 4d. Kilcootry, B, 1 pound 16s. Kilgort, 1 pound 8s 8d, Perry. Killaless, 1 pound 2s 8d. Killyberry, 15s. Lacca, 18s 10d. Leggamaghery, 18s 4d [query]. Liskermalane, B, 19s 2d. Legnacrieve, 1 pound 18s. Leggatiggle, 1 pound 4d. Lisky, 10s 8d. Lisnabulravey, 4s 8d. Lisnagardy, 16s 8d. Lisdergan, 7s 8d. Lurganboy, P, 11s, query. Mullanboy, B, 1 pound 16s. Middlecess, B, 10s 2d query. Mulliseligagh, 12s, query. Mullins, 10s 3d, Auchinleck. Roghan, 10s 3d, Auchinleck. Rathwarren, 1 pound 4s, query abbey land? Rathfragan, B, 1 pound 16s. Ranees Upper 18s 10d. Ranees Lower, 18s 10d, query. Reveagh, E, 1 pound 1s, Edwards. Estrabane, P, 7s 6d. Sionnee, 18s. Stratigore, 12s. Sionfin, 19s 9d. Scregagh, 1 pound 1s. Stranisk, 1 pound 13s. Tatymoyle Upper, P, 15s; Tatymoyle Lower, E, 15s; Tatymoyle Middle, P, 15s, [all queried]. Tonnaghbeg, 16s 8d. Tullyrusk, 13s 8d. Tonnaghbane, 14s 4d. Tullyvalley, 1 pound 8s 8d, Perry. Tyreenan, 18s. Fintona, 1 pound 10s. Attaghmore, 1 pound 11s 9d, [name illegible]. Aghadreenan, 6s. Baronagh, 1 pound 16s, F. Crawford. Cavan, 1 pound 13s, J. Wilson. Cranny, 1 pound 18s, Lord Belmore. Dunnamona Lower, 1 pound 16s, Major Crawford. Edenfogry, 18s, Lord Belmore. Fallagheran, 13s 8d, Lord Belmore. Glennan, 19s 9d query. Gulladoo, 15s. Killymoonan, 19s 9d, Lord Belmore. Mullawinny, 1 pound 16s, various. Screen, 19s 9d query. Skelgagh, 16s 8d. Tatymulmona, 1 pound 6s, Lord Belmore. Tonnaghmore, 19s 9d. W. Tomes, applotter.

Names of Townlands

[Footnote] Names of townlands in parish of

Donacavey, mentioned in the original grant to John Lee by Charles II, which have no similtude to the present names of any of the townlands in the parish.

Tonagheitra, Shriaghduffgower (query Gulladoo or Gulladuff). Gasonory alias Garwory. Tonnaghenew or Tonaghenewe. Syonhugh or Syonhue. Dromheruke alias Drumhurke. Shriaghmarke alias Shriaghmiske, query Stranisk. Derryaghnan. Aghebrassell, Aghabrasill. Tatefadda alias Taghfadda. Derryaghnan. Dromherick alias Drumhurke. Garronory alias Gawory. Taterrewe or Tatecrewe. Derryaghnan. Drumherick alias Dromhurke. Shraghduffgower. Tonaghheitra. By letters patent, sexto die Augusti anno regni nostri Septimo, Carolus II. [Signed] R. Stotherd, Lieutenant Royal Engineers, 26th June 1835.

Notes on Townlands

DIVISIONS

Notes on Townlands

With regard to situation of townlands taken from the maps. Townland of Donamona, 1 schoolhouse and 1 ancient fort. Bounded on the north side by the parish of Drumragh.

Screen, situated about 4 miles north west of the town of Fintona, bounded on the north west end by the parish of Drumragh.

Baronagh, situated about 3 and a half miles north west of Fintona, bounded on the north by the parish of Drumragh. There is 1 ancient fort planted with fir trees.

Tatymulmona, situated about 2 and a half miles north of Fintona, bounded on the north and east sides by the parish of Drumragh.

Edinafogry, situated about 2 and a half miles north of Fintona.

Glennan, situated about 3 and three-quarter miles north west of Fintona, bounded on the north west by the parish of Drumragh. There is 1 ancient fort situated on the highest point of the land.

Mullawinny, situated about 3 and a quarter miles north west of Fintona, bounded [remainder blank]. There is 1 schoolhouse and an old fort.

Cavan, situated about 1 and a half miles north west of Fintona, the south west boundary passing through a mill dam adjoining a main road, leading into the parish of Dromore and close by a meeting house in the townland of Cavan. There is a mill immediately under [blank] Dickson's Esquire, towards the north west end of the townland and in townland.

Attaghmore, situated about 2 and a half miles north west of Fintona and 1 small schoolhouse in it.

Cranny, situated about 1 and a half miles north west of the town of Fintona. There is an ancient fort in it.

Fallagheran, situated about 2 miles north west of Fintona.

Killymoonan, situated about 1 and three-quarter miles north of Fintona, bounded on the north east side by the parish of Drumragh and on the east by the barony of Clogher.

Mullanboy, situated about half a mile north of Fintona, the main road from Fintona to Omagh passing through it from south to north. It is bounded on the west side by the barony of Omagh and on the north by the parish of Drumragh.

Annaghmurneen, situated about three-quarters of a mile north west of Fintona.

Annaghbo, situated about half a mile north of Fintona.

Black Fort, situated about 2 and three-quarter miles north east of Fintona. There are 2 ancient forts, 1 schoolhouse and 1 mill in this townland. It is bounded on the west, north and east sides by the parish of Drumragh.

Sessiagh, situated about 1 and a half miles north of Fintona and bounded on the north west by the parish of Drumragh.

Drumwhisker, situated about 1 mile north east of Fintona.

Donacavey, situated about 1 mile north east of Fintona. There is the ruins of an old church towards the south west called Donacavey old church.

Belnagarnon, situated about half a mile north east of Fintona, towards the south east of this townland. Near to a river being the boundary of this and Kilcootry townlands is a small mill for manufacturing spades.

Rathfragan, situated about 1 and three-quarter miles north east of Fintona. There are 2 ancient forts in it. It is bounded on the north east side by the parish of Drumragh.

Tullyvally is situated about 1 and three-quarter miles north east of Fintona, having 1 ancient fort in it. It is bounded on the north by the parish of Drumragh and on the east by the parish of Clogherny <Clogherney>.

Kilgort, situated about 1 and three-quarter miles north east of Fintona, having 1 ancient fort in it.

Notes on Townlands

[Continuation of list].

Kilcootry, situated about 1 mile north east of Fintona. There is 1 ancient fort in it.

Castletown, situated in the north of Fintona,

Parish of Donacavey

having a portion of Fintona town, the church and the ruins of an old castle.

Feenan, situated about three-quarters of a mile north west of Fintona.

Cumber, situated about 1 mile north west of Fintona, having 1 school in it towards the west and very convenient to the boundary.

Drummond, situated about 1 and a quarter miles north west of Fintona. It is bounded on the north west by the parish of Dromore, on the north by the barony of Omagh.

Carnalea, situated half a mile north east of Fintona and has 1 ancient fort in it.

Donamona Glebe, bordering on the east side of Fintona.

Carnaroosk, situated 1 and a quarter miles east of Fintona.

Derrybard, situated 1 and three-quarter miles east of Fintona and contains the seat of the Reverend Dr Vesey.

Liskey, situated on the west side of Fintona, containing a small portion of the south west part of the town.

Racrean, situated quarter of a mile north west of Fintona. There is 1 ancient fort on it.

Fintona contains the town of Fintona.

Liggatiggle, situated on the north west of Fintona about 2 miles and has 1 schoolhouse in it. It is bounded on the west by the parish of Dromore and barony of Omagh.

Killyliss, situated on the west side of Fintona about 1 and a quarter miles. There are 2 ancient forts in it. It is bounded on the south west by the barony of Omagh.

Skelgagh, situated 2 and a quarter miles south west of Fintona. The north is bounded by the parish of Dromore and east by the barony of Clogher.

Aughadreenan, situated about 3 miles west of Fintona. It is bounded on the north west and south west by the parish of Dromore.

Tonnaghmore, situated about 3 miles south west of Fintona. There are 2 forts and a mill in the townland. It is bounded on the west by the parish of Dromore and on the south by the barony of Clogher.

Gulladoo, situated about 2 and a half miles south west of Fintona. It is bounded on the south east side by the barony of Clogher.

Tyreenan, situated about 2 and a quarter miles south west of Fintona. It is bounded on the north by the barony of Omagh.

Tonnaghbeg, situated about 1 and a quarter miles south west of Fintona. There is 1 ancient fort in it and is bounded on the north west by the barony of Omagh.

Sionnee, situated about 1 and a quarter miles south west of Fintona.

Roghan, situated about 1 mile west of Fintona.

Rathwarran, situated about three-quarters of a mile west of Fintona. There is 1 ancient fort towards the south east end and planted.

Notes on Townlands

[Continuation of list]

Stratigore, situated about half a mile south west of Fintona.

Ecclesville Demesne, the seat of C. Eccles Esquire. There are 3 ancient forts and a Roman Catholic chapel. It is situated on the south of Fintona.

Tullyrusk, situated 1 and a half miles south west of Fintona.

Lisnabulravy, situated three-quarters of a mile south west of Fintona and having 1 ancient fort in it.

Lisdergan, situated about three-quarters of a mile south of Fintona.

Sionfin, situated about 1 mile south of Fintona. There is 1 ancient fort in it.

Lisavady, situated about three-quarters of a mile south of Fintona.

Lissnegardy, situated about half a mile south of Fintona. There are 2 ancient forts in it.

Edinasop (West) is bounded on the north west by the town of Fintona. There is a meeting house and a mill in it.

Edinasop (East), situated about a quarter of a mile south east of Fintona.

Carnarook, situated about 1 and a quarter miles east of Fintona.

Gargrim, situated about 1 and a half miles south east of Fintona.

Drafton, situated about three-quarters of a mile south east of Fintona. There is a schoolhouse and an ancient fort in it.

Lisnacrieve, situated about one and a half miles south east of Fintona. There is 1 fort and 1 schoolhouse in it.

Freighmore, situated about 2 miles north east of Fintona. There are 2 ancient forts in it. It is bounded on the north east side by the parish of Clogherny.

Raneese, situated 2 and a quarter miles east of Fintona. There is 1 ancient fort in it. It is bounded on the north east by the parish of Clogherny.

Garvola, situated 2 and three-quarter miles east of Fintona. Towards the north of this townland is a mill. It is bounded on the north and north east by the parish of Clogherny.

Augharonan, situated about 3 miles south east

of Fintona. It is bounded on the north east by the parish of Clogherny.

Raveagh, situated about 4 miles south east of Fintona with a mill in it. It is bounded from north east to south by the parish of Clogher.

Cator, situated about 3 and three-quarter miles south east of Fintona. It is bounded on the south by the parish of Clogher.

Aughafad, situated about 2 and a quarter miles south east of Fintona. There are 2 ancient forts in it. It is bounded from east to south by the parish of Clogher.

Lacca is situated about 2 and a quarter miles south east of Fintona. There is a corn mill towards the north of it. It is bounded on the south east by the parish of Clogher.

Notes on Townlands

[Continuation of list]

Dundiven Glebe, situated south of Fintona about 2 miles, the seat of the Reverend W. Tomes, curate. There are 2 ancient forts in it. It is bounded on the south and south east by the parish of Clogher.

Edinatoodry, situated south of Fintona, 1 and three-quarter miles. It is bounded on the south by the parish of Clogher.

Legamaghery, situated 3 and three-quarter miles south east of Fintona. It is bounded from north west to south west by the parish of Clogher.

Dungorran, situated about 2 miles south of Fintona. There is 1 ancient fort in it.

Scregagh, situated about 2 and a quarter miles south west of Fintona. It is bounded on the south by the parish of Clogher.

Drumlaghar, situated about 2 and a quarter miles south west of Fintona.

Killyberry, situated about 2 miles south west of Fintona.

Stranisk, situated about 2 and a half miles south west of Fintona. It is bounded on the south by the parish of Clogher.

Mullaselaga, situated about 2 miles south west of Fintona.

Lower Tatemoyle, situated about 2 and three-quarter miles south west of Fintona. There is an ancient fort towards the north west end and a school. It is bounded on the south by the parish of Clogher.

Corbally, situated about 2 and three-quarter miles south west of Fintona.

Middle Tatemoyle, situated about 3 and a quarter miles south west of Fintona. It is bounded on the south east by the parish of Clogher and on the south by the parish of Enniskillen.

Upper Tatemoyle, situated about 3 and three-quarter miles south west of Fintona. Towards the north of this townland there is a mill and pond. It is bounded on the south by the parish of Enniskillen.

Strabane, situated about 3 and a half miles south west of Fintona. It is bounded on the north west side by the parish of Dromore.

Lurganbuoy, situated about 4 and a quarter miles south west of Fintona. It is bounded on the west by the parish of Dromore.

Corrisesk, situated about 3 and a half miles south west of Fintona.

Lissconrea, situated 3 and three-quarter miles south west of Fintona. There are 2 ancient forts in it. It is bounded on the north west by the parish of Dromore.

Crocknaferbrague, situated about 4 and a half miles south west of Fintona towards the south west of this townland. Close to the boundary of the parish is a chalybeate well, with a house by its side for the convenience of such people who choose to benefit by the spring.

Carriglass, situated about 4 miles south west of Fintona. There is 1 schoolhouse and a pound.

Mullins, situated about 1 mile north west of Fintona.

Tonnaghbane, situated about a quarter of a mile south west of Fintona.

Townland Names and Orthography for Fintona (Donacavey) Parish

Table of Townlands

[Table contains the following headings: list of names to be corrected if necessary, orthography as recommended to be used in the new plans, other modes of spelling the same name, authority for these other modes of spelling, when known, situation, descriptive remarks or other general observations which may be considered of interest].

[Insert note: The authority for the mode of spelling in the column "other spellings of the same name" is derived from an old charter of Mr Eccles' property. I would, however, not recommend the adoption of that mode of spelling universally as it has become quite obsolete in many instances, but rather let the names be spelled as they are found in the adjoining column. I have only altered them when they appeared to me to be spelled incorrectly [signed] W. James].

Annaghmurnin, orthography recommended Annaghmurnun, parish of Fintona, barony of

Parish of Donacavey

Clogher, manor of Castleleigh, proprietor John Dickson Eccles, leased for years.

Annaghneboe, orthography recommended Annaghbo, parish of Fintona, barony of Clogher, same manor and proprietor, leased for lives and years.

Ardatinny, other spellings Ardetony, parish of Fintona, barony of Clogher, same manor and proprietor, leased for lives and years.

Attymore, orthography recommended Attaghmore, parish of Fintona, barony of Omagh, proprietor Hu[gh] Johnston, manor Touchet.

Aughadreenan, parish of Fintona, barony of Clogher, manor of Castleleigh, proprietor J.D. Eccles.

Aughafad, other spellings Tatefadda, parish of Fintona, barony of Clogher, manor of Castleleigh, proprietor J.D. Eccles, leased for lives and years.

Augharonan, parish of Fintona, barony of Clogher, proprietor Doctor Vesey, (manor Cope, I believe [last 2 words crossed out]).

Balnegarnan, orthography recommended Belnagarnon, parish of Fintona, barony of Clogher, proprietor Samuel Evans, held under the see of Clogher.

Barronagh, orthography recommended Baronagh, parish of Fintona, barony of Omagh, proprietor Andrew Crawford, manor Touchet.

Blackforth, orthography recommended Blackfort, parish of Fintona, barony of Clogher, proprietor Samuel Evans, half under the see of Clogher.

Carrickglass, orthography recommended Carriglass, parish of Fintona, barony of Clogher, manor of Castleleigh, proprietor Reverend John Grey Porter.

Carnalea, parish of Fintona, barony of Clogher, proprietor half William Teggart and half to children of late Samuel Tegart.

Carnaroosk, parish of Fintona, barony of Clogher, manor of Castleleigh, proprietor J.D. Eccles, leased for years.

Castletown, parish of Fintona, barony of Clogher, held by J.D. Eccles under the see of Clogher, partly leased for years and partly for years renewable.

Cattore, orthography recommended Cator, parish of Fintona, barony of Clogher, proprietor Hugh Gore Edwards, manor Cope.

Cavan, parish of Fintona, barony of Omagh, proprietor James Wilson, manor of Touchet.

Coveysesk, orthography recommended Corrisesk, other spellings Corrycesky, parish of Fintona, barony of Clogher, manor of Castleleigh, proprietor Reverend John Grey Porter.

Corbally, other spellings Corbally, parish of Fintona, barony of Clogher, manor of Castleleigh, proprietor J.D. Eccles, half leased for lives renewable, half for 1 life only.

Cranny, parish of Fintona, barony of Clogher, proprietor Earl of Belmore, manor Touchet.

Cumber, parish of Fintona, barony of Clogher, manor of Castleleigh, proprietor J.D. Eccles, leased for lives and years.

Table of Townlands

[Continuation of list].

Derrybard, parish of Fintona, barony of Clogher, proprietor Reverend Doctor Vesey, manor Cope.

Donacavey, parish of Fintona, barony of Clogher, proprietor Samuel Evans, held under the see of Clogher.

Donamona, barony of Omagh, parish of Fintona, proprietor Jones Crawford, manor Touchet.

Donamona (Glebe), parish of Fintona, barony of Clogher, Reverend William Atthill.

Drafton, other spellings Derryaghnan, parish of Fintona, barony of Clogher, manor of Castleleigh, proprietor J.D. Eccles, leased for lives and years.

Drumlagher, orthography recommended Drumlaghan, other spellings Dromlaghan, parish of Fintona, barony of Clogher, manor of Castleleigh, leased for lives renewable.

Drommond, other spellings Mullinadroman or Ballinadroman, parish of Fintona, barony of Clogher, manor of Castleleigh, proprietor J.D. Eccles, leased for years and lives.

Drumwhisker, barony of Clogher, proprietor Samuel Evans, held under see of Clogher.

Dundiven Glebe, barony of Clogher, parish of Fintona, proprietor Reverend William Atthill.

Dungorran, other spellings Dongorran, barony of Clogher, parish of Fintona, manor of Castleleigh, proprietor J.D. Eccles, leased for years.

Ecclesville (demesne), barony of Clogher, parish of Fintona, J.D. Eccles.

Edinatoodry, other spellings Edentooderry, barony of Clogher, parish of Fintona, manor of Castleleigh, leased for years renewable.

Ednafogry, orthography recommended Edinafogry, parish of Fintona, barony of Omagh, proprietor Earl of Belmore, manor Touchet.

Ednasop, orthography recommended Edinasop, other spellings Edenesopp, parish of Fintona, barony of Clogher, manor of Castleleigh, proprietor J.D. Eccles, held by proprietor.

Fallaghearan, orthography as recommended, Fallagheran, parish of Fintona, barony of Omagh, proprietor Earl of Belmore, manor Touchet, I believe.

Feenan, parish of Fintona, barony of Clogher, manor of Castleleigh, proprietor J.D. Eccles, leased for years and lives.

Fintona, parish of Fintona, barony of Clogher, manor of Castleleigh, proprietor J.D. Eccles, leased for ever.

Freighmore, other spellings Froughmore, parish of Fintona, barony of Clogher, proprietor Mrs Mary Perry, manor Cope.

Gargrim, other spellings Gargrom, parish of Fintona, barony of Omagh, proprietor J.D. Eccles, manor of Castleleigh, leased for years and lives.

Garwallagh, orthography recommended Garvola, parish of Fintona, barony of Omagh, proprietor Reverend Dr Vesey.

Glannon, orthography recommended Glennan, parish of Fintona, barony of Omagh.

Gulladhue, orthography recommended Gulladoo, parish of Fintona, barony of Omagh, manor of Castleleigh, proprietor J.D. Eccles, leased for years and lives.

Table of Townlands

[Continuation of list].

Kilcootry, parish of Fintona, barony of Clogher, proprietor Mrs Hay, held under see of Clogher.

Kilgort, parish of Fintona, barony of Omagh, proprietor Mrs Mary Perry, manor Cope.

Killyberry, other spellings Killiberry, parish of Fintona, barony of Omagh, manor of Castleleigh, proprietor J.D. Eccles, leased for years and lives, part for lives renewable.

Killyliss, other spellings Killalussie, parish of Fintona, barony of Omagh, manor of Castleleigh, proprietor J.D. Eccles, leased for lives and years.

Killymoonan, parish of Fintona, barony of Omagh, proprietor Earl of Belmore, manor Touchet.

Knocknefarbreagea, orthography recommended Crocknaferbrague, parish of Fintona, barony of Clogher, proprietor Reverend J.G. Porter, manor Castleleigh.

Lackagh, orthography recommended Lacca, other spellings Lackaboy, parish of Fintona, barony of Clogher, manor of Castleleigh, proprietor J.D. Eccles, leased for years and lives.

Legamaghry, orthography recommended Leggamaghery, parish of Fintona, barony of Clogher, manor of Castleleigh, proprietor J.D. Eccles, leased for lives renewable.

Ligatiggle, orthography recommended Leggatiggle, other spellings Loggetigill, parish of Fintona, barony of Clogher, manor of Castleleigh, proprietor J.D. Eccles, leased for years and lives and some of it for lives renewable.

Lissbuoy, parish of Fintona, barony of Clogher.

Lissconrea, parish of Fintona, barony of Clogher.

Lissdergan, parish of Fintona, barony of Clogher, manor of Castleleigh, proprietor J.D. Eccles, partly held by proprietor and partly leased for years.

Lissnegardy, other spellings Lissegarduffe, parish of Fintona, barony of Clogher, manor of Castleleigh, proprietor J.D. Eccles, partly leased for lives and years.

Lissebaddy, orthography recommended Lisavady, parish of Fintona, barony of Clogher, manor of Castleleigh, proprietor J.D. Eccles, partly leased for lives and years.

Lisskey, orthography recommended Lisky, parish of Fintona, barony of Clogher, manor of Castleleigh, proprietor J.D. Eccles, leased for ever.

Lissnacreive, orthography recommended Lisnacrieve, other spellings Tatecrewe or Lissnecrew, parish of Fintona, barony of Clogher, manor of Castleleigh, proprietor J.D. Eccles, leased for years and lives.

Lissnebalreavey, orthography recommended Lisnabulravy, parish of Fintona, barony of Clogher, leased for years.

Mullanboy, parish of Fintona, barony of Clogher, proprietor Samuel Evans, held under see of Clogher.

Mullans, orthography recommended Mullins, parish of Fintona, barony of Clogher, proprietor J.D. Eccles, manor of Castleleigh, leased for ever.

Mullasellegga, orthography recommended Mullaselega, other spellings Mullasilage, parish of Fintona, barony of Clogher, manor of Castleleigh, proprietor J.D. Eccles, leases for lives renewable.

Mullawinny, parish of Fintona, barony of Clogher, proprietors Hugh Johnston and Hugh Warnock, manor Touchet.

Table of Townlands

[Continuation of list].

Raneese, parish of Fintona, barony of Clogher, proprietor Reverend Doctor Vesey, manor Cope.

Rathfraggan, orthography recommended Rathfragan, parish of Fintona, barony of Clogher, proprietor H.J. Harman, held under see of Clogher.

Rathwarran, other spellings Ravarran, parish of Fintona, barony of Clogher, manor of Castleleigh, proprietor J.D. Eccles, leased for lives and years.

Raveagh, parish of Fintona, barony of Clogher, proprietor Hugh Gore Edwards, manor Cope.

Recreane, orthography recommended Racrean, parish of Fintona, barony of Clogher, manor of Castleleigh, proprietor J.D. Eccles, leased for years and lives.

Parish of Donacavey

Roughan, orthography recommended Roghan, parish of Fintona, barony of Clogher, manor of Castleleigh, proprietor J.D. Eccles, leased for ever.

Scionfin, orthography recommended Sionfin, parish of Fintona, barony of Clogher, manor of Castleleigh, proprietor J.D. Eccles, leased for years and lives and partly for lives renewable.

Screggagh, orthography recommended Scregagh, other spellings Skreggagowre, parish of Fintona, barony of Clogher, manor of Castleleigh, proprietor J.D. Eccles, leased for years.

Screen, orthography recommended Screen, parish of Fintona, barony of Clogher, proprietor Charles Sproul, manor Touchet, I believe.

Sessagh, orthography recommended Sessiagh, parish of Fintona, barony of Clogher, proprietor Samuel Evans, held under the see of Clogher.

Shannee, orthography recommended Sionnee, other spellings Syonhugh, parish of Fintona, barony of Clogher, proprietor J.D. Eccles, manor of Castleleigh, held for years and lives.

Skelgagh, orthography recommended Skelgagh, other spellings Ballynaskelgie, parish of Fintona, barony of Omagh, proprietor J.D. Eccles, manor of Castleleigh, leased for years renewable.

Strabane, parish of Fintona, barony of Clogher, proprietor Reverend J.G. Porter, manor Castleleigh.

Straniskey, orthography recommended Stranisk, parish of Fintona, barony of Clogher, manor of Castleleigh, proprietor J.D. Eccles, leased for years and lives.

Strattygore, orthography recommended Stratigore, parish of Fintona, barony of Clogher, manor of Castleleigh, proprietor J.D. Eccles, leased for years and lives.

Tonaghbawn, orthography recommended Tonnaghbane, parish of Fintona, barony of Clogher, manor of Castleleigh, proprietor J.D. Eccles, partly held by proprietor J.D. Eccles and partly leased for years and lives.

Tonaghbeg, parish of Fintona, barony of Omagh, manor of Castleleigh, proprietor J.D. Eccles, leased for years and lives.

Tonaghmore, parish of Fintona, barony of Omagh, manor of Castleleigh, proprietor J.D. Eccles, leased for years and lives.

Tattymoile (Upper), orthography recommended Tatimoyle, other spellings Tatemoyle, parish of Fintona, barony of Clogher, proprietor J.D. Eccles, manor Castleleigh.

Tattymoile (Middle), parish of Fintona, barony of Clogher, proprietor J.D. Eccles, manor Castleleigh.

Tattymoile (Lower), parish of Fintona, barony of Omagh, proprietor Reverend J.G. Porter, manor Castleleigh.

Tattymulmona, orthography recommended Tatymulmona, parish of Fintona, barony of Omagh, proprietor Earl of Belmore, manor Touchet.

Tillevally, orthography recommended Tullyvally, parish of Fintona, barony of Clogher, proprietor Mrs Mary Perry, manor Cope.

Tullyrush, other spellings Tollerish, parish of Fintona, barony of Clogher, manor of Castleleigh, proprietor J.D. Eccles, leased for years and lives.

Tyreenan, other spellings Tyregrenan, parish of Fintona, barony of Clogher, manor of Castleleigh, proprietor J.D. Eccles, leased for years and lives.

Parish of Donaghedy, County Tyrone

Unfinished Memoir, May 1836

NATURAL FEATURES

Hills

The principal hills in the parish of Donaghedy <Donagheady> are Meendamph, Craignagopple, Cavanhill, Main mountain, Loughash, Slievkirk and Dullerton.

1st, Meendamph is one of the principal mountains in the Sawel or Monterlony chain. Its height is 1,890 feet above the level of the sea and the southern boundary of the parish passes over its top. The slopes of this mountain are vast, steep and smooth and it affords indifferent grazing for cattle in summer.

2nd, Craignagopple and Cavanhill are also situated in the southern part and on the boundary of the parish. They are properly speaking the same hill, form part of the above mentioned range and run in a northern and southern direction. The height of the point Craignagopple is 1,200 feet and of Cavanhill 1,313 feet above the level of the sea.

3rd, Main mountain forms one of the western boundaries of Donaghedy. Its height above the sea is 918 feet. The slopes of this mountain are very smooth.

4th, Loughash mountain is 892 feet in height. It forms part of a minor range (along with the Main mountain) which runs from Dart in the direction of Dunnamanagh village or to the north west.

5th, Slievekirk rises very abruptly towards the summit. It forms the north eastern boundary of the parish and is [blank] feet in height. The range to which it belongs is in the county of Londonderry.

6th, Dullerton is rather an isolated feature and forms the north western boundary of the parish until it enters the River Foyle. Its height above the sea is 726 feet and it is cultivated nearly to the top and is in fact the only one of those mentioned above which is of any value at present, the others being for the most part covered with heather.

Lakes

There are two viz. Lough Moor and Loughash. The first of these is situated in the south western part of the parish, is 31 chains long and 19 broad. It contains or covers 42 acres 3 roods 20 perches and its depth is not known. Only part of it, 30 acres 2 roods 12 perches, is in Donaghedy and the rest is in Leckpatrick. It is 600 feet above the level of the sea.

The latter lake (Loughash) is situated in the centre of the eastern half of the parish. It contains 41 acres 1 rood 39 perches, is 41 chains long and 15 broad. Its depth not known. Its height above the sea is 500 feet and there are no islands either in it or Lough Moor. The latter, however, is said to contain very good trout but the fish will only rise during a southerly wind.

PRODUCTIVE ECONOMY AND MODERN TOPOGRAPHY

Mills

[Table contains the following headings: situation and description, date of erection, proprietor, type and dimensions of water wheel, machinery, observations].

Corn mill in the townland of Bunowen, a cabin in good repair, proprietor Sir James Bruce; breast wheel, diameter of water wheel 13 feet, breadth 2 feet, diameter of cog wheel 4 feet, single geared, machinery wood; supplied well by the Bunowen stream, works about 7 months in the year.

Flax mill in the townland of Bunowen, a mud cabin, erected about 1800, proprietor Sir James Bruce; breast wheel, diameter of water wheel 12 feet, breadth 2 feet, diameter of cog wheel 4 feet, single geared, machinery wood; water supplied in sufficient quantity during the year by the Bunowen stream, works about 4 months on an average.

SOCIAL ECONOMY

Table of Schools

[Table contains the following headings: name, situation and description, when established, books read, visited by, number of pupils subdivided by age, sex and religion, name and religious persuasion of master and mistress].

Loughash national school, 3 miles south east of Dunnamanagh, built in 1820, under the National Board in 1834; books published by the Commissioners of Education for the Irish national schools, visited once by the Episcopal clergyman and twice by the Roman Catholic clergyman since its commencement; number of pupils: males, 33 under 10 years of age, 4 from 10 and 15, 37 total males; females, 35 under 10 years of age, 10 from 10 and 15, 45 total females; total number of pupils 82, 6 Protestants, 18 Presbyterians, 58 Roman Catholics; masters: James Kilgore, Protestant, James Moon, Roman Catholic.

Parish of Donaghedy

Roosky school, under the patronage of the London Hibernian Society, 1 mile south of Dunnamanagh, established October 1819; books are obtained gratis from the London Hibernian Society, visited by the Reverend James Hazlett, curate; number of pupils: males, 18 under 10 years of age, 21 from 10 to 15, 3 above 15, 42 total males; females, 24 under 10 years, 19 from 10 to 15, 11 above 15, 54 total females; total number of pupils 96, 17 Protestants, 56 Presbyterians, 23 Roman Catholics; master William Young, Presbyterian.

Answers to Queries from the North West Agricultural Society, by James Haslett, Curate, 6 October 1821

NATURAL STATE

Locality

Answers to the queries proposed by the North West Agricultural Society by the rector of the parish of Donaghedy <Donagheady>. [Query number in brackets].

Donaghedy is situated in the county of Tyrone, lower part of the barony of Strabane, in the diocese of Londonderry, patron the Marquis of Abercorn, present incumbent Andrew Thomas Hamilton.

PRODUCTIVE ECONOMY

Proprietors

(4th) The only fee simple landed proprietors under the Crown in this parish are the Marquis of Abercorn, Colonel Enery, Mr Ball and Mr Hutton, none of whom reside under the Marquis and Colonel Enery. There are several gentlemen who have considerable property, none of whom are resident except the Reverend Richard Nesbit of Cloghogal and Robert McCrea of Glencush, Esquire. For towns and lands see appendix.

Farms

(5th) Farms in general about 20 acres, very few are enclosed. Potatoes are the general preparation crop throughout this parish. The usual rotation as follows, according to the soil: potatoes, barley, flax, oats, potatoes, oats, flax, oats, potatoes, oats, oats. Flax is never sown after potatoes except near the mountains. Draining and enclosing the land would very much contribute to the improvement of the soil throughout this parish.

(6th) There is very little pasture land here unless near the mountains.

NATURAL FEATURES

Mountains

(7th) The mountains of this parish are Belags, Ballyneary, Doorat, Lignagopag and some others of inferior note, most parts of which are pasturable, and cultivation is rapidly advancing up their sides.

Bogs

(8th) The principal bogs are Callan, Balaghalair, Maghareagh and Cooby, and in all the mountainous parts turbary is abundant. Oak and fir are found in most of the bogs from 6 to 9 feet in depth.

Woods

(9th) There is nothing in this parish which can, with propriety, be called a wood. There are 4 banks extending on each side of the River Denit for a considerable distance, which, with the little planting about my place, contribute to the beauty of the place. There are many orchards of small extent throughout the parish, very few plantations.

(10th) Trees of every description if well secured from cattle thrive here.

PRODUCTIVE ECONOMY

Rents

(11th) The best arable land is let at 1 pound 14s per acre, the middling at 1 pound 2s 9d, the worst at 12s. Ditto in the mountains. The best is let at 1 pound, middling 12s, worst at 6s.

(12th) Tenants are not charged for turbary here.

Farm Techniques

(13th) The only improvement as to tillage is planting potatoes with the plough. In enclosures none, fences none. Scotch ploughs and carts are much used.

(14th) Hawthorn and furze fences are in most use and in my opinion suit best.

Employment

(15th) In spring and harvest employment is abundant; want of capital prevents farmers giving employment at other seasons, for which there is an ample field in this parish as there is much boggy and barren ground which might easily be reclaimed.

(16th) Labourers if boarded get from 2 pounds to 2 pound 10s for 6 months, day labourers without board from 10d to 1s 1d a day according to the season of the year.

Crops

(17th) There are no green crops cultivated except on a small scale by me.

(18th) Rye and the common white grass are sown by some of the most respectable farmers in this neighbourhood along with clover.

Draining and Manures

(19th) In the mountainous parts, mostly surface, in the other, under draining.

(20th) Composts of dung, bog, clay and lime are used for manure. The mode of burning clay or soil is not practised here unless it be so mixed with bog as to be easily consumed without the trouble of putting it into kilns, and is not so prevalent as composts of lime and clay.

(21st) Irrigation of meadows and other lands is practised in this parish.

Types of Farming

(22) No dairies have been established.

(23) None are used [oxen].

(24) No spade tillage is practised.

Markets and Measurements

(25) Barley and oats, for which there is no fixed price as yet. Londonderry <Londerry> is the principal market for the inhabitants of this parish, from the greater part of which it is about 6 miles distant.

(26) The Marquis of Abercorn, who is the principal proprietor, computes by the Irish and I believe all others compute by the Scotch acre.

Livestock

(27) The black cattle here are of an inferior kind, no care whatever being taken to improve them.

(28) A few cows are fattened, but for the most part young cattle are the stock which they sell in fairs except such as are kept for their own use.

(29) No sheep are reared here except the old Irish breed.

(30) In the most arable part of the parish horses bred from blood stallions and draught mares are used, no good draught stallion being in the country. In the mountainous parts a mixture between the small Ragheries and the small Irish breed.

(31) A mixture between the English and Irish [swine].

SOCIAL ECONOMY

Census

(32) Referred to the person appointed on the population acts as I could not answer this query otherwise than by consulting him and could not by any means find an opportunity. [Number of inhabitants, acres and livestock].

(33) No improvement has been made in the different breed of horses, black cattle, sheep and swine within the last 20 years.

NATURAL FEATURES

Rivers and Lakes

(34) There is only one, the River Denit in this parish which, issuing from its north eastern boundary and taking a north western course augmented by other small streams, empties itself into the Foyle about 5 miles from Strabane.

2 lakes, Ash and Moore, the last of which abounds with trout.

2 ferries over the Foyle, Donelong and Grange.

Mines and Stone Quarries

(35) No metallic mines yet discovered.

(36) Stones for building are conveniently found throughout the entire parish. There is also a slate quarry near the mail coach road, distant 6 miles from Londonderry and 5 from Strabane.

(37) Limestone of a blue colour in many parts of this parish, which is burnt in kilns with peat fire at about 10d per barrel expense.

(38) No coal has yet been discovered.

(39) No mineral springs.

(40) No marl has been discovered.

SOCIAL ECONOMY

Habits of the People

(41) Indifferent as to comforts, well inclined to industry and fond of earning money could they get it to earn.

(42) The people poor and consequently unable to procure those cabin <cabbin> comforts as to clothing, food, and necessaries.

(43) Fuel: peat and plenty, seldom bought and when [bought] about 1s 8d per load.

Food

(44) [Farmers] potatoes, milk and butter. Seldom any animal food.

(45) Manufacturing class ditto, ditto.

(46) [Labourers and poor] potatoes and buttermilk and often salt only.

Parish of Donaghedy

Schools and Education

(47) A general wish for education prevails through all classes.

(48) Schools are numerous. There are 4 Hibernian Society schools and 6 others besides the parish school. Expense of education between 2s to 5s per quarter.

(49) The society's schools have not been [able?] to answer here, as the masters are unable to teach so great a number of pupils, which in some amount to 150, and the more kind they are to the inspectors, the greater number of pupils pass his examination.

Health

(50) The inhabitants are hardy and healthy, the climate damp, and from its mountainous situation, subject to rain. The prevalent diseases are pleurisy, rheumatism and weakness in the limbs.

Friendly Societies

(51) No friendly societies are established here for that purpose.

MODERN TOPOGRAPHY

Villages

(52) Only one village, namely Dunnamanagh <Demomana>.

SOCIAL ECONOMY

Improvements

(53) Want of capital and high rent prevent the people from any turn for improvement.

(54) There are no experimental farmers in this parish worthy to be called so.

PRODUCTIVE ECONOMY

Linen Manufacture

(55) Increased [manufacture of linen].

(56) One bleach green.

(57) Land is prepared for a flax crop by twice ploughing, one in the month of December, the other about the middle of April. Flax succeeds barley or a crop of oats is first taken off, lea and then flax. What they are not able to consume at home is sold for exportation or seed is saved.

(58) By mills and fire is used in preparing it [flax].

Cost of Prepared Flax

(59) From 2 and a half hanks to 5 hanks in the pound for what is termed fine yarn; for a spangle spinning 1s or 3d per day.

(60) Yarn commonly sells at from 2s or 2s 6d per spangle and partly used at home and partly sold for exportation.

(61) They [spinners] grow it [flax].

(62) It has not been introduced here [double spinning wheel].

(63) It is purchased unprepared by the spangle and prepare it at about 4d per spangle expense [yarn].

(64) No yarn greens.

(65) The linen here is of strong rather than a delicate texture and for the most part three-quarters to seven-eighths width and in quality runs from what is called an 1,100 to a 1,300 varying in price from 1s 5d to 11d per yard brown and three-quarters breadths from 8d to 1s, ditto sold in Londonderry.

(66) No woollen manufacture here.

(71) No cotton manufactory.

Kelp and Fisheries

(73) No kelp manufacture.

(76) Salmon fishery, one.

(79) 4 boats and from 10 to 15 men to each boat on the River Foyle.

(80) The greater part are sent off iced to Liverpool and the residue are sent to Strabane and Londonderry markets.

DIVISIONS

Appendix of Townlands and Proprietors

Altrest, Sir J. Hamilton, Allshane, Lord Belmore, Ardcame, Sir H. Bruce, Aughebrack, Mr Knox, Aughafad, Mr Knox, Ardmore, Sir J. Hamilton, Aughtermoy, Mr Knox.

Bennelly, Mr Knox, Bonone, Sir H. Bruce, Baron, Sir J. Hamilton, Belnaboe, Robert McCrea, Ballyheather, Lord Abercorn, Belnamalaght, Mr Knox, Bellybeney, Lord Abercorn, Brosney, Robert McCrea, Balaghalan, Sir J. Hamilton, Bellynenac, Mr Lyle, Belbennett, Sir J. Hamilton, Belags, Sir J. Hamilton, Burndinnett, Lord Abercorn.

Churchhill, Sir H. Bruce, Carrickayeon, Sir J. Hamilton, Cloghagal, Lord Abercorn, Coolmaghery, Sir J. Hamilton, Carnagribban, Mr Lyle, Cleggan, Sir J. Hamilton, Clegan Altnacree, Mr Lyle, Carickatain, Lord Abercorn, Clogherney, Sir J. Hamilton, Cloghbeg, Lord Abercorn, Cullin, Lord Abercorn, Creagheer, Lord Abercorn, Castlemellan, Lord Abercorn, Castlewarren, Lord Abercorn.

Doorat, Sir J. Hamilton, Donelong, Lord Abercorn, Drean, Sir J. Hamilton, Drumgally, Lord Abercorn, Drummenny, Mr Ball and Austin, Dunemana, Sir J. Hamilton, Drummon, Sir J. Hamilton, Doolertown, Sir J. Hamilton, Duneboe, Lord Abercorn.

Eden, Lord Abercorn.

Glengannow, Sir J. Hamilton, Gortwey, Lord Abercorn, Graystone, Lord Abercorn, Gortmonley, Sir J. Hamilton, Gortileck, Lord Abercorn, Grange, Austin or Hudson, Gorticlare, Lord Abercorn, Gortmesson, Lord Abercorn, Glandstown, Robert McCrea, Gobnascale, Sir J. Hamilton, Glencush, Sir J. Hamilton.

Killycurry, Sir J. Hamilton, Killiney, Sir J. Hamilton, Killdonough, Lord Abercorn, Killycloney, Sir J. Hamilton.

Lisbotweeney, Sir J. Hamilton, Leatrim, Sir H. Bruce, Liscleen, Mr Lyle, Lisnanon, Sir J. Hamilton, Leat, Sir J. Hamilton, Lisdivin, Lord Abercorn, Loughash, Sir J. Hamilton.

Menaghill, Lord Abercorn, Mountcastle, Lord Abercorn, Moneykenon, Mr Lyle, Magheramason, Lord Abercorn, Mayagh, R. McCrea, Maghereagh, Lord Abercorn.

Ruskey, Sir J. Hamilton.

Sandvile, Lord Abercorn, Stoneyfalds, Sir J. Hamilton, Solis, Lord Abercorn.

Tamnaghbready, Lord Abercorn, Tip Connelly, Mr Lyle, Tamnakeary, Lord Abercorn, Tylleard, Lord Abercorn, Tamnaclare, Lord Abercorn, Tyrkernaghan, Mr Lyle, Tamnabrean, Lord Abercorn.

Windy Hill, Sir J. Hamilton.

SOCIAL AND PRODUCTIVE ECONOMY

Number of Inhabitants and Cattle

Not having received the account of the population from the person appointed according to act until today, I take the liberty of transmitting it to you by this post. The number of inhabitants in this parish is 10,290. The number of houses, inhabited and uninhabited, is 1,961. The number of acres according to the best information I have received is, in the inland part of the parish 20,000 and most part of it arable and meadow, and in the mountainous part 10,000 or thereabouts, besides mountain that cannot be conveniently ascertained at present, which we may suppose may amount to 6,000 acres. As to cattle in the inland part of this parish, they amount to from 2 to 3,000, besides young ones which are now on the mountains but did not come under inspection at present. Horses in the inland part amount to 1,800. As to the upper manor or mountainous part, the horses are very few. As to grazing cows, I was not accurate in taking the amount, as perhaps the proprietors live at a distance and some of them at other parishes. If any more accurate information should occur I will be very happy in transmitting it to you as soon as possible. Your most obedient humble servant, (signed) James Haslett, curate of the parish of Donaghedy, 6 October 1821. Directed to the right Honourable George F. Hill, President of the North West Agricultural Society, Londonderry.

Parish of Dromore, County Tyrone

Answers to the Statistical Questions of the North West Farming Society

PRODUCTIVE ECONOMY

Farms

County of Tyrone, barony of Omagh and diocese of Clogher, parish of Dromore, Viscount Lifford, incumbent. [Each query number in brackets].

(4) The general size of farms is about 16 acres, enclosed with ditches, some quicked and others not. Cultivation is performed by ploughing first and trenching afterwards with a spade. Good farmers usually lime their lands before ploughing. In reclaiming new land they use from 60 to 80 barrels per acre, and some from 40 to 60 barrels per acre. Some mix lime, mud and dung made up in composition heaps for potatoes.

Crops

Oats and potatoes are our principal crops. The different kind of oats used here are Blantyre <Blanter>, Prussian brown, black, lightfoot, early white, Moselle and of late some Friesland <Freezeland>. The kind of potatoes in use here are English red tolies, seedlings, cups, monkies, Scotch downs and farmers. Some require less manure than others, particularly cups, foleys and monkies, for they are frequently planted on mud alone, from which we have an abundant crop.

Manures

We find from experience a great means of improving land, and easily procured, by laying mud or moss in pretty large quantities upon stiff clay land, or by drawing stiff clay upon that which is deep with moss. This is found very useful either for potatoes or for making meadow. Another way of raising crops and improving land is by burning ashes of the soil, composed of both bog and clay. Lime and mud are used either by themselves or mixed together with farmyard or other manure. Any or all of these are useful as manure, yet in some places where marl can be got it is used, however, very rarely.

Pasture

(5) In this parish there are no farms solely appropriated to pasture, but mixed with tillage. Even in those tracts mostly adapted to grazing, which is in the mountainous parts of this parish, some parts of them are occupied in raising potatoes and oats.

NATURAL FEATURES

Mountains and Hills

(6) The large mountains are Glengeen, Skeogue, Grennan, Dullahan, Carnalea, Aughadulla and Letteree. Our principal hills are Mulnacross, Shanmullagh, Aughnamoe, Drumskiny, Lettergess, Kildrum and Corlaghdergan.

Bogs

All parts of this parish are capable of improvement, except those places which are too deeply covered with moss; and those, by burning the moss into ashes and liming, <it> may be reclaimed from a state of nature. However, this is attended with considerable expense from the inconvenience of limestone.

(7) The principal bogs are Drumlish, Dullaghan, Mullaghbawn, Killdrum, Esker, Shanmullagh, Dressogue, Dernaseer, Grennan, Mullenboy, Straduff, Corlaghdergan, Shanerah.

There is some timber found in our bogs, commonly called bog fir and oak, at various depths from 6 to 10 feet. There has been an immense quantity found in Shanmullagh bog, principally fir. Notwithstanding being raised from the depth above mentioned, [it] is in some parts touched with fire and the fir thus found without [not] being in any way materially impaired but rather improved.

Woods

(8) There is nothing here which deserves the name of woods, no large timber except some hedgerows. There are some nurseries and plantations in Aughnamoe, Aughlish, Gardrum, Drumconnis, Dressogue, Grennan, Mullenboy and Goland, as also in Gortnagullen, Lisanadin and Esker. No orchards except those in Aughnamoe and Aughlish.

(9) The ash, sycamore, larch and black sallow seem to be the most thriving and profitable trees here. Oak and Scotch [fir ?] are esteemed, but the rapid progress of the former is more admired in this part.

PRODUCTIVE ECONOMY

Rents

(10) The highest acreable land in this parish is about 1 guinea and a half per acre, the middle kind

about 25s and the inferior about 18s to 20s per acre. The mountains calculating reclaimed and unreclaimed are estimated at 20d an acre and under, but those fields adjoining the town of Dromore, on account of their convenience to the town and good hedges and enclosures and also their improved state, are valued from 1 guinea to 1 pound 10s per acre.

Fuel

(11) Farmers are for the most part supplied with turf bog without any particular charge. Those who are not farmers pay from 2s 6d to 5s for what is called a day's cutting.

Improvements

(12) The people seem inclined to improve, which is quite evident from the number of crops raised after liming. In the townland of Ahadara not less than 25 crops of good oats have been raised after it. The spade is found to improve the land and crop by trenching after ploughing, for it keeps the land in heart and deepens the soil, especially when done early before the frost comes, which purifies the stiff clay and makes it mellow, bringing it to a proper temper and fertility. Thus the holders of large farms get their land ploughed early in order to receive the benefit of the frost. The ridges are trenched deep and raised high in the middle so that they may be kept dry.

The landholders who have the means generally ditch and quick to make enclosures, considering them a great advantage to shelter their lands, cattle and crops from the great winds which are very destructive, particularly to the latter, of which we have many instances but especially about 2 years ago when the wind and storm beat so violently on our crops as to break the straw and hinder them from filling, making them ripen too fast before they came to perfection. I consider this new plan of making ditches along the highway to be attended with many advantages with regard to the safety of persons and property: that is, by throwing the back of the ditch to the road.

(13) We have no new implements of husbandry in this parish.

Labour and Roads

(14) The labourers here have not constant employment except farming. The method that appears most useful and to afford general employment to the labouring class would be to have several new roads laid out, avoiding the high hill, which could be easily done so that a safe conveyance of goods might be carried on and a secure passage for carts and carriages, to the great benefit of the country at large. I consider that the best method of making roads is by breaking hard stones upon them to a certain size and putting a sufficient quantity of them on, instead of the bad sort of gravel mixed with clay as we have at present.

Wages

(15) Servant men have from 40s to 50s for half a year, servant maids from 20s to 25s and labourers from 6d ha'penny to 8d per day. There is not any labour performed here by the piece.

Green Crops

(16) There are no green crops cultivated here except some small clover plots and some cabbages planted in the side of the potatoe ridges, and in the gardens where we have turnips, beans, peas, onions, carrots, parsnips, cucumbers and celery. Grass seed is sown in some parts of this parish.

Drainage

(17) Surface and under-draining are both in use. Surface draining is performed by trenching with the spade and under-draining by sinking a trench below the spade or plough's usual action, which is denominated French draining.

Manures

(18) The principal manure here for the land is lime, which is usually put on the grass by itself but often intermixed with clay, soil, farmyard manure and mud in order to make meadow. Clay and soil is frequently burned for manure, sometimes by throwing it up with the spade until it is dry and fit for burning and will produce a great quantity of ashes.

Irrigation

(19) Farmers generally are in the habit of watering their meadows, which they consider a great advantage as the winter rains bring down from the hills a quantity of soil, clay and sand, forming a very good manure for the surface of meadow.

Dairy Produce

(20) Some farmers here have 20 cows and some less, and generally can make a vessel of butter from each new milk cow which they send to market, together with a large quantity of milk.

Parish of Dromore

(21) There are no oxen used here in the husbandry.

Tillage

(22) There is no spade tillage used here except in trenching the furrows, which is usually done after ploughing and is found exceedingly useful as it deepens the soil and keeps it dry all winter. This advantage is principally gained by those who plough and trench early before the frost. In some cases, owing to the distress of the landholder where he cannot afford to hire a horse, tillage is done by the spade.

Crops

(25) In the answer to (5) you will find described the different kinds of oats commonly used here. In the aforesaid number we did not write of barley, rye or wheat, yet they are sown in small quantities but least of all the wheat. Rye does better in moss ground than any other. The want of flour mills in our parish is a great preventative to our farmers sowing wheat.

Prices

The price of grain is as follows: oats from 20s to 25s per sack, barley from 9d to 10d per stone. Owing to the scarcity of wheat and rye, none is offered for sale. Oatmeal from 12s to 13s 6d per cwt, potatoes from 2d to 2d ha'penny, mutton from 4d to 4d ha'penny per lb, beef from 3d ha'penny to 4d per lb, butter from 8d ha'penny to 9d farthing per lb.

Land Measurement and Stock

(26) Land is computed here by the Irish or plantation acre.

(27) Cows and heifers are of the middle size and are well adapted to the soil, as this place is not abundant in grass or meadow.

(28) Young heifers, bullocks, dry cows, young horses, sheep, tame and wild fowl and pigs, the latter in great abundance.

Sheep

(29) The common small mountain sheep which are very nice when fat. We have also some merinos which are of a very low broad shape having fine wool, and very productive, bringing forth some 2 and some 3 lambs at a birth.

Livestock

(30) The horses are of a middle size, with some mules and asses.

(31) The swine are of a large size, of which this country feeds vast numbers. No family in the parish but have one or more in possession, some 20 or 30.

(32) Stock is as follows viz. cows 2,500, horses 800, pigs 2,500, sheep 1,500, heifers 1,500, bulls 50, calves 1,000.

The chief improvement I wish to suggest would be that farmers might be encouraged to raise green crops such as clover and good hay seed mixed, and that they should pay more attention to the making of meadow, for if we had plenty of good feeding, the stock of every description would improve accordingly.

(33) Not much improvement in the breed of horses, black cattle, sheep or pigs, yet nothing worse for the last 20 years.

NATURAL FEATURES AND NATURAL HISTORY

Rivers

(34) There are no large rivers in this parish but two, Goland and Aughlish, both of which unite in the townland of Shanerah. Goland rises in Dullaghan and passes through Greenan to Dernaseer, where it is joined by a small river from Corbally which is indebted for its source to Doohragh lake and another small stream coming down to Corbally mill. Aghlish river is formed from one running from Glengeen and [a] river coming from the parish of Fintona.

Lakes and Fish

Aughnamoe, Aughlish, Doohrah, Drumskiny and Galbolly. Their productions are pike, trout, perch, roach and eel, with some salmon.

Minerals

(35) I have heard of no mines being discovered.

(36) There are no freestone quarries found here. There are many quarries of very good building stone adjoining the townland of Dromore and many other parts of this parish.

Limestone

(37) There is no limestone found in this parish. The inhabitants travel from 5 to 7 miles for it, which is of a blue colour and makes good lime either for building or land and is burnt by turf. The expense is not great as we have turf in great abundance.

(38) I have heard of none being found [coal].

Springs

(39) There are some chalybeate <calybeate> springs

(but seldom used) in Shanmulla, Killdrum and Mahagaret, which is the largest in this parish.

Marl

(40) Marl has been discovered in different parts of this parish, particularly in Oughterard, Coyah and Aughnamoe. I believe it is of the calcareous and argillaceous kind, [and] is put or spread on to the grass as lime.

SOCIAL ECONOMY

Situation of the People

(41) Poor to a great degree. Their domestic comforts are very limited, yet they are not discontented but are well disposed and habituated to a laborious manner of living. I think if they were not oppressed with heavy rents they would soon be comfortably situated. Their chief way of earning money is by labouring the land and following their usual trades, particularly the linen manufacture. The present general depression of trade and commerce appears to arise from the heavy burden laid on the farmer, to which the price of grain and cattle are no way proportionate.

Habits of the People

(42) The general condition of the farm and cottage houses as to their state of repair, cleanliness and internal comforts is very different in many respects. However, the desire and inclination of the labouring class to improve their houses almost exceed our expectation. The better sort of farmer are also very industrious and desirous of improving their houses and land by those means which they have, but the great distance they have to draw the limestone and heavy rents and taxes are great preventatives. In this parish alone about 1,400 pounds per annum is paid in county cess, including the 16 townlands in the parish of Fintona that usually pay with this parish, on account of being, I suppose, in the same barony.

Roads are very bad. There are excellent materials in this parish to make roads if encouragement were given. The people are very industrious and pay great attention to the moral conduct of their children, for many of them at the early age of 6 years old are taught to spin. The emoluments arising from such exertion are by no means adequate to afford them a competent subsistence, owing chiefly to the reduction of the markets. The males are generally hired out either to herd when young or to do those things their age and abilities capacitate them for. Some very poor of late, who by the blessing [of] God on their continued industry and application to their business, have arisen to comfort and wealth.

Fuel

(43) Fuel is very plenty and convenient and farmers pay nothing for turf as they have plenty of bog attached to their farms.

Food

(44) The general food of farmers is indeed not of costly materials, as they cannot afford it. However, a good many of them live very comfortably, having plenty of beef and bacon and abundance of tame and wild fowl, and some of them have good mutton of their own feeding besides a great variety of vegetables. Many of the labouring class have no better than potatoes and milk.

(45) The general food of the manufacturing class is little superior to that of the poorest farmer, but some of them endeavour to live better. At the same time they save nothing.

(46) I believe the fare of the labouring class is very poor indeed.

Education

(47) There seems to be a general desire among all classes to educate their children. However, in some cases the Roman Catholics are prevented from attending the Sunday and Hibernian schools as they are taught to believe such schools to be designed to bring all to the Protestant faith.

(48) I believe children pay from 1s 3d to 2s 6d per quarter for spelling, reading from 2s 6d to 3s per quarter, writing and arithmetic 3s 4d to 3s 9d, book-keeping from 5s 5d to 7s 6d per quarter.

(49) Wherever education prevails the difference in the state of the people is obvious, but it is so limited in this country that I cannot see any.

Health

(50) The state of health is generally good. Fevers and other occasional diseases prevail in some degree. We often see people live here to a very advanced age of life.

(51) I know of none [banks].

Improvements

(52) Our principal town is Dromore, situate in the centre of the parish and nearly in a direct line between Enniskillen and Omagh, which is our post town.

Parish of Dromore

(53) The people are certainly inclined to improve their land, especially by liming and watering their meadows. If gentlemen of landed property were to stir up the spirit of active improvement, chiefly by proposing premiums to the most deserving tenants, it would be a great means of improving our parish.

PRODUCTIVE ECONOMY

Farmers

(54) The names of the practical farmers in this parish are as follows: (X) John Corry of Munelbuy, (X) Thomas Osborne of Corbully, (X) Henry Blaney of Aughterard, (X) Thomas Anderson of Mullaghbane, Archbald Osborne of Dernaseer, Robert Hamilton Esquire of Lakemount, William Hamilton of Maghagart, Nevill McFarland of Newpark, (X) John Stephenson of Munelbuy, James Osborne of Dressogue, Daniel Colter of Killdrum, (X) Thomas Alexander of Dromore, John Osborne of Mossfield, (X) Francis Gibson of Tohirdoe, Robert Warnock of Tullyclenah, Hugh Johnstone of Lisnadin, (X) Lieutenant Moorehead, Aughlish, (X) Nathaniel Smith, Drumconis, William Young of Shanmullagh, William Wilson of Shanvera, Robert Crawford of Esker and John Charlton of Knockaravin. Those marked thus (X) are most likely to be intelligent and useful correspondents to the North West Farming Society.

Omagh is our post town.

Linen

(55) Linen manufacture is greatly increased. There is much more linen made now in this place than has been in the memory of the oldest inhabitants.

(56) None [bleach greens].

Rotation of Crops

(57) The land is prepared here in general by planting potatoes first and the ensuing year flax seed is sown. Sometimes a crop of barley is taken off before the flax. Very little of our flax can be spared for exportation. Some seed is saved in dry seasons.

Flax

(58) There are no mills in this parish. The flax is manufactured by manual labour and dried on flax kilns by the fire, and prepared by beetling and scutching. There are also cloves used by men which renders the flax softer and finer.

(59) [Warp yarn] very coarse. I believe from 2 and a half to 3 hanks grist is considered fine, some from 3 to 5 hanks per lb. Spinners can earn no more than from 2d ha'penny to 3d per day, owing chiefly to the reduction of the markets.

(60) [Fine yarn] as above. Some used for home manufacture and some for exportation. Flax yarn sells here from 1s 8d to 2s 6d per spangle.

(61) The very poorest grow their own flax but not in sufficient quantities for the demand, for some are obliged to go to market where they can be abundantly supplied. All cultivate their own flax.

Weaving

(62) It has not been introduced [double spinning wheel].

(63) The weaver, I believe, purchases the yarn green and prepares it himself by boiling, bleaching, spooling and warping. We have a few warp mills. The expense of preparing yarn for the weaver is from 3s 6d to 4s per web of 52 yards.

(64) [Yarn greens] There are none in this neighbourhood. If yarn was carefully attended to in such greens, the establishment of them would be very useful to facilitate as well as improve the manufacture.

(65) The description of linen manufactured here is from 48 to 52 bier. The price is from 10d to 1s 3d per yard. Fintona and Omagh and Newtownstewart are our linen markets.

Woollen Goods

(66) There is no woollen manufacture in this parish except a little for their own use, such as <a> grey webs, home-made blankets, drugget, flannel and stockings.

(67) No woollen staples.

(68) Our wool is spun on the small wheel.

(69) Females do not make woollen stockings for the market, but knit them for pay and earn about 4d per day.

(70) Farmers shear their sheep only once a year. However, we have some instances of them being shorn <shorne> twice a year. The season for shearing is generally in May for large sheep. Lambs are usually shorn in the month of August.

Cotton

(71-2) Very little cotton manufactured here. We have cotton and linen intermixed <intermixt>, also a little knit for female stockings.

Kelp and Fishing

(73-5) No kelp of any description is made here.

(76-81) As we live not upon the sea coast and

only 2 rivers convenient, with 1 large lake and 4 small ones, no fisheries of consequence. We have some trout, pike, eel, perch, roach and, rarely, a few salmon.

DIVISIONS

Townlands

[Table contains the following headings: townland, number of houses and inhabitants, arable acres, acres of mountain and bog, name of proprietor].

1, Aghlish, houses 15, inhabitants 111, arable acres 126, bog 6, proprietor Mrs Bunbury, non-resident.

2, Aughadarra, houses 40, inhabitants 227, arable acres 312, bog 60, proprietor Earl of Belmore, non-resident.

3, Aughadulla, houses 29, inhabitants 139, arable acres 300, mountain 300, bog 40, proprietors Mr John Spillers, Reverend Mr Creighton, the former [resident] in Omagh and the other near it.

4, Augher, houses 10, inhabitants 60, arable acres 99, bog 45, proprietor the Earl of Belmore, non-resident.

5, Aughnamoe, houses 45, inhabitants 284, arable acres 390, bog 60, proprietor Robert Hamilton, resident.

6, Bodony, houses 27, inhabitants 152, arable acres 180, bog 30, proprietor Charles Sprout Esquire, resident.

7, Camdry, houses 5, inhabitants 28, arable acres 40, bog 20, proprietor Lord Belmore, non-resident.

8, Carnalea, houses 25, inhabitants 88, arable acres 80, mountain 50, bog 50.

9, Corbolly McCaron, houses 32, inhabitants 161, arable acres 198, mountain 50, bog 60.

10, Corbolly Hamilton, houses 41, inhabitants 207, arable acres 199, mountain 40, bog 60.

11, Corlaghdergan, houses 30, inhabitants 178, arable acres 229, bog 50.

12, Cornamucklagh, houses 20, inhabitants 133, arable acres 189, bog 44, proprietor Earl of Belmore, non-resident.

13, Cornamuck, houses 16, inhabitants 89, arable acres 146, bog 35, proprietors Mrs Osborne, John Osborne and A. Osborne, resident.

14, Corryheskum, houses 13, inhabitants 83, arable acres 140, mountain 10, bog 100, proprietor Mr McClintock, non-resident.

15, Corgah, houses 16, inhabitants 90, arable acres 152, bog 40, proprietor the rector and Mrs Bunbury.

16, Cranny English, houses 9, inhabitants 75, arable acres 116, bog 11, proprietor Mrs Bunbury, non-resident.

17, Cranny Scott, houses 3, inhabitants 21, arable acres 50, bog 4, proprietor Mrs Bunbury, non-resident.

18, Cranny Slevin, houses 6, inhabitants 34, arable acres 52, bog 5, proprietor Mrs Bunbury, non-resident.

19, Derrylawn, houses 16, inhabitants 78, arable acres 101, mountain 25, bog 15, proprietor Major Irwin, non-resident.

20, Dergany Neville, houses 8, inhabitants 42, arable acres 90, bog 10, proprietors Mr George Neville and Mr William Neville, non-resident.

[1st subtotal]: houses 406, inhabitants 2,280, arable acres 3,189, mountain 475, bog 745.

21, Dergany McGuire, houses 11, inhabitants 79, arable acres 85, bog 10, proprietor Reverend Mr Wade, non-resident.

22, Doughrock, houses 30, inhabitants 149, arable acres 190, mountain 50, bog 50, proprietor Major Irwin, non-resident.

23, Dressogue, houses 15, inhabitants 95, arable acres 234, mountain 10, bog 180, proprietor Earl of Belmore, non-resident.

24, Dromore, houses 94, inhabitants 417, arable acres 70, bog 10, proprietor Mrs Bunbury, non-resident.

25, Drummarit, houses 17, inhabitants 103, arable acres 74, bog 40, proprietor Earl of Belmore, non-resident.

26, Drumconnis, houses 6, inhabitants 33, arable acres 49, bog 20, proprietor Reverend Mr Creery, non-resident.

27, Drumderg, houses 22, inhabitants 139, arable acres 170 and a half, bog 40, proprietor the rector, non-resident.

28, Dullahan, houses 32, inhabitants 188, arable acres 134, mountain 266, bog 90, proprietors George and Charles Sproul Esquires, resident.

29, Drumlish, houses 9, inhabitants 53, arable acres 60, mountain 10, bog 120.

30, Drumsheal, houses 17, inhabitants 92, arable acres 113, bog 10, proprietor Earl of Belmore, non-resident.

31, Drumskiny, houses 57, inhabitants 331, arable acres 365, bog 60, proprietors Major Richardson and Mr Percival, non-resident.

32, Ednagone, houses 7, inhabitants 31, arable acres 101, bog 13, proprietor General Archdall, non-resident.

33, Esker, houses 24, inhabitants 135, arable acres 247, bog 80, proprietor Earl Belmore, non-resident.

34, Fartagh, houses 10, inhabitants 40, arable

Parish of Dromore

acres 55, bog 20, proprietor Major Irwin, non-resident.

35, Galbolly, houses 28, inhabitants 125, arable acres 180, bog 50, proprietor General Archdall, non-resident.

36, Gardrum, houses 16, inhabitants 77, arable acres 128, bog 10, proprietor Mrs Bunbury, non-resident.

37, Glengeen, houses 38, inhabitants 183, arable acres 186, mountain 200, bog 70, proprietor Earl of Belmore, non-resident.

38, Goland Upper, houses 8, inhabitants 39, arable acres 60, bog 15, proprietor Colonel Cuff, non-resident.

[2nd subtotal]: houses 847, inhabitants 4,589, arable acres 5,690 and a half, mountain 1,011, bog 1,633.

39, Goland Lower, houses 5, inhabitants 33, arable acres 54, bog 10, proprietor Colonel Cuff, non-resident.

40, Grennan, houses 18, inhabitants 124, arable acres 200, mountain 300, bog 70, proprietor Earl of Belmore, non-resident.

41, Killdrum, houses 14, inhabitants 105, arable acres 150, bog 90, proprietor Reverend Mr Creery, non-resident.

42, Knockaravan, houses 10, inhabitants 57, arable acres 72, bog 15.

43, Lisenadin, houses 19, inhabitants 121, arable acres 156, bog 30, proprietor Earl of Belmore, non-resident.

44, Letteree, houses 20, inhabitants 107, acres, arable 112, mountain 180, bog 40, proprietor Charles Sprout Esquire, non-resident.

45, Lettergesh, houses 9, inhabitants 62, arable acres 84, mountain 30, bog 60, proprietor Earl of Belmore, non-resident.

46, Mahagart, houses 36, inhabitants 175, arable acres 264 and a half, bog 40, proprietors General Archdall, Major Richardson and Mr Percival, non-resident.

47, Minigar, houses 30, inhabitants 184, arable acres 192, mountain 30, bog 50, proprietor Reverend A. Hamilton, non-resident.

48, Mulnagoe, houses 14, inhabitants 69, arable acres 120, bog 6, proprietor Mrs Bunbury, non-resident.

49, Minigone, houses 12, inhabitants 77, arable acres 119, bog 30, proprietor Reverend Mr Wade, non-resident.

50, Mullenbuy, houses 9, inhabitants 65, arable acres 105, bog 40, proprietor Colonel Cuff, non-resident.

51, Mullaghbane, houses 34, inhabitants 218, arable acres 324, mountain 10, bog 120, proprietors Mrs Roberts, Mrs McWarnock and Mrs Scott, residents.

52, Newpark, houses 19, inhabitants 104, arable acres 170, bog 20, proprietor Reverend Mr Wade, non-resident.

53, Oughill, houses 17, inhabitants 74, arable acres 48, bog 10, proprietor Earl of Belmore, non-resident.

54, Oughcurragh, houses 8, inhabitants 43, arable acres 28, bog 8, proprietor Earl of Belmore, non-resident.

55, Oughterard, houses 22, inhabitants 160, arable acres 180, bog 30, proprietor Colonel Cuff, non-resident.

[3rd subtotal]: houses 1,143, inhabitants 6,367, arable acres 8,068, mountain 1,561, bog 2,302.

56, Pulfore, houses 25, inhabitants 143, arable acres 161, bog 40, proprietor Pierce Hamilton Esquire, non-resident.

57, Rakerenbeg, houses 4, inhabitants 40, arable acres 65, bog 9, proprietor Earl of Belmore, non-resident.

58, Rahawney, houses 34, inhabitants 222, arable acres 402, bog 60, proprietor Earl of Belmore, non-resident.

59, Shanerah R., houses 33, inhabitants 175, arable acres 230, bog 110.

60, Shanerah W., houses 31, inhabitants 167, arable acres 211, bog 110, proprietor Reverend Mr Criggan, non-resident.

61, Skeages, houses 15, inhabitants 104, arable acres 188, mountain 170, bog 40, proprietor General Archdall, non-resident.

62, Shanmullagh, houses 8, inhabitants 43, arable acres 70, bog 8, proprietor the rector, non-resident.

63, Straduff, houses 14, inhabitants 80, arable acres 94, mountain 10, bog 100, proprietor Samuel Galbraith Esquire, non-resident.

64, Tatticor, houses 25, inhabitants 156, arable acres 132, bog 35, proprietor Earl of Belmore, non-resident.

65, Tumery Gal, houses 35, inhabitants 210, arable acres 227, bog 50.

66, Tumery Teag, houses 37, inhabitants 164, arable acres 210, bog 30, proprietor Counsellor Spear, non-resident.

67, Tullywee and McGeagh, houses 30, inhabitants 169, arable acres 122, bog 20, proprietor Counsellor Story, non-resident.

68, Tullyclenah, houses 10, inhabitants 80, arable acres 118, bog 14, proprietor Earl of Belmore, non-resident.

[Overall totals]: houses 1,044, inhabitants 8,120, arable acres 10,298, mountain 1,741, bog 2,928,.

Memoir by W. Hemans, received 30 November 1835

NATURAL FEATURES

Hills

The most northern extremity of the parish of Dromore, where the boundary runs up into a triangular point, is the highest spot of ground in the parish i.e. 959 feet above the level of the sea and averaging about 500 feet above the average height of ground on the parish surface. The ridge this elevation belongs to is part of a range of high ground, the principal point of which called Dooish is situated in the adjoining parish of West Longfield. The rest of the parish is a wide surface of ridgy hills of monotonous appearance and slightly varied heights, the average of which might probably be considered as between 400 and 500 feet above the sea.

Lakes

Lough Mulnagoagh or Sheep Hill lough occupies portions of 3 townlands: Aghalisk, Mullnagoagh, Magheragart (Donnell), 329 feet above the level of the sea, depth uncertain. Area 10 acres 3 roods, no islands. Lough [blank].

Rivers

A small river, formed by the conjunction of numerous streams in the parish, runs from south west taking a sweep towards east and, joining with a similar stream coming from south east, forms in the parish of Drumragh a course of more importance taking the name of the Drumragh river. Its distance from the sea is about 36 miles. This river is shallow and rapid and its overflows are of small extent and less consequence. Its height above the sea, taken at the spot where it first assumes the appearance of some importance, which is at the bridge in the townland of Shannaragh, is 900 feet. Its banks are very low.

Bogs

This parish contains a great quantity of bog, dispersed in very small patches all over its surface, but is nowhere to be found in any continued spread. These patches furnish all the fuel burnt in the parish, and the depth of peat is still far from exhausted. This depth varies much: some 12 feet, some 20 feet, others as deep as 30 feet.

Woods

There are no natural woods in the parish.

MODERN TOPOGRAPHY AND SOCIAL ECONOMY

Town of Dromore

Dromore, situated in the centre of the parish, is 86 miles from Dublin, in latitude 54 degrees 30 minutes north, 7 degrees 25 minutes west longitude. The main road between Fintona and Irvinestown passes through it. The town in length is 240 yards and in breadth 200 yards. Its situation offers nothing remarkable, either for local advantages or picturesque effect.

Public Buildings: Church

There are no public buildings within the town nor any gentlemen's residences. A little to the west there are near the town some traces of a ruined abbey and the base of an old stone cross. The parish church is close upon the south west end of the town. It is a plain stone building without a steeple. Its shape and dimensions are [ground plan, main dimensions 72 by 44 feet, "T" shape]. It will accommodate from 500 to 800 persons. The average attendance on Sundays is from 500 to 600 people. It was built in about 1680, expense unknown, which was defrayed by some of the followers of King William who destroyed the Roman Catholic chapel which formerly stood in the vicinity.

Streets

The streets, of which there are 2 nearly at right angles to each other, the principal running north to south, are very dirty and kept in bad repair. The houses, of which there are 29 of 1-storey, 68 of 2-storeys and 5 of 3-storeys, are mostly built of stone. A few are roughcast over the front but none of them have a neat or clean appearance. 27 are slated, the remainder thatched. No new houses have been lately built nor are there any building at present. At a short distance from the town on an eminence the present incumbent of the parish is finishing a new and handsome glebe house of a large size.

Habits of the People

In a small and unpatronised village such as Dromore, the habits of the people are easily described in a few words. Their sole employment being to make out life as well as they can, they have not leisure or inclination to turn their thoughts to improvement or cultivation. They are reckless of all appearance of neatness either in the houses or persons, and indigence is, with them, an all-sufficent

Parish of Dromore

excuse for dirt. About one-third are employed in petty retail dealing, the remainder are artisans and day labourers. They have no savings bank or news room nor any other provision of the poor of the parish than the assistance afforded by the dispensary, which was established in August 1832 and is supported by subscriptions and a grant from the grand jury. It is open on Tuesdays and Fridays from 12 at noon to 3 p.m. Its effects have been very visible in the improved state of health among the poor. The average number of patients relieved each year up to the present date has been between 400 and 500.

There is a school in the town, see table of schools for the parish. Neither horses nor post conveyances of any description are to be had for hire. There is no hotel nor any better inn in the town than a miserable ale and whiskey house. The town is not improving, nor has it been recently improved. The police force stationed here consists of a sergeant <serjeant> and 4 men of the Omagh district.

Occupations

[Table] grocers and spirit dealers 2, grocers 9, surgeons 1, general dealers 1, bakers 2, butchers 1, lodging houses 1, spirit dealers 17, milliners 1, shoemakers 3, tailors 1, reedmakers 1, huxters 2, carpenters 1, smiths 1. Note, it may be noticed under the head "Habits of the People" that there is a quantity of whiskey drunk <drank> in this small place quite disproportionate to the number of the inhabitants, as the above table containing 19 spirit shops out of 44 tradesmen's houses will testify.

Modern Topography

Public Buildings: Roman Catholic Chapel

A Roman Catholic chapel, situated on one of the roads from Dromore to Irvinestown, a third of a mile from the former town; it is now rebuilding on the scale of 104 feet by 44 feet. The cost is estimated at about 525 pounds. It will, when finished, accommodate 600 persons. Galleries are to be added inside when a sufficient sum can be collected, which will render the chapel capable of containing many more. The cost of the present erection has been obtained from the present congregation by subscriptions. The style of the building is a simple rectangle.

Covenanters' Meeting House

A Covenanters' meeting house, on the old road from Dromore to Trillick about half-way between the 2 towns; a plain rectangular building, cost and date of erection cannot be ascertained, capable of containing 400 to 500 persons.

Meeting House

A meeting house in the townland of Gardrum was built in the year 1755 at the expense of the congregation. Frequent alterations and repairs have since been made to the amount of about 400 pounds, original cost forgotten; accommodates 400 persons, plain rectangular building, slated roof.

The parish church has been noticed under the head of Dromore.

Gentlemens' Seats

Lakemount, townland Aghnamore, [is] a plain whitewashed building, the residence of Colin Hamilton Esquire. The crossroad in front of the house has been planted on both sides with alder and fir trees which give the appearance of an avenue, and added to the plantations around the house, which though small are thriving, give this spot a pleasant look.

The Glebe House, the residence of the present rector the Reverend [blank] St George, is close to the town of Dromore. It is not yet completed, having been only begun 3 years ago, but will be a spacious fine house when finished.

Mills

No bleach greens nor manufactories.

Townland of Tannarragh, corn mill, wheel 12 feet diameter, undershot.

Tummery, corn mill, wheel 11 feet diameter, undershot.

Aghadulla, corn mill, wheel 12 feet 6 inches, undershot.

Canderry, corn mill, wheel 12 feet 2 inches diameter, breast wheel.

Cavan, corn mill, wheel 12 feet 6 inches diameter, breast wheel.

Communications

About 3 and a half miles from Fintona to Dromore are contained in the parish. It is hilly and by no means in good repair.

About 4 and a third miles from the main road Enniskillen to Drumquin are contained in this parish. This road is hilly, narrow and stony.

2 and a half miles of the road from Dromore to Trillick; this is a new and judiciously made good road.

About 4 miles of the road from Dromore to Irvinestown: very indifferent road as well as the 3 miles of road from Dromore to Omagh.

It is notorious in the parish that half the number of the roads actually contained in it would be more serviceable if kept in good repair than all the wretched lines which now intersect it in all directions.

There is a bridge of 4 arches on a by-road from Fintona to Drumquin, which passes through this parish over the river before mentioned. It is [blank] feet long and [blank] feet broad.

There are other small bridges mostly in bad repair over the minor streams in the parish.

ANCIENT TOPOGRAPHY

Giant's Grave

There is a giant's grave in the parish at the point where the south boundary of the parish joins the west boundary of the county, of which the accompanying sketch may give an idea. See sketch no. 2, parish of Dromore. [Insert note on cover sheet: sketch of giant's grave alluded to in the Memoir not received].

MODERN TOPOGRAPHY

General Appearance

Of this little can be said. There is as before mentioned one point of high ground at the northern extremity, but the rest of the parish presents a monotonous though not unfertile series of low bumpy ridges and round hills, on whose sides a good deal of corn is planted and whose bases are generally encircled by little intersecting streams which run in all directions.

SOCIAL ECONOMY

Early Improvements

There has been little improvement in the parish of any kind for many years.

Obstructions to Improvements

The absence of proprietors and of the rector of the parish, who had not lived in it for 40 years back, until 3 years ago [when] the present incumbent arrived and built the Glebe House he now resides in, on the site of the cabin which formerly answered to that name.

Local Government

Petty <petit> sessions for this parish are held at Trillick and Omagh, there being no resident magistrates nor any within a nearer reach than Trillick. A sergeant of police and 4 men of the Omagh district are stationed in the town of Dromore.

Dispensaries

Dispensaries: see Artificial State, town of Dromore.

Schools

[Table contains the following headings: name, situation and description, when established, income and expenditure, physical, intellectual and moral education, number of pupils subdivided by age sex and religion, name and religion of master or mistress. No physical education].

Tummery school, a small cottage beside a cross lane, built in 1824; income: from Education Society 8 pounds per annum, from pupils 1d per week; master's salary 8 pounds, other expenses none; intellectual education: Kildare Society books; moral education: Authorised Version read; number of pupils: males 52, females 27, total 79, 5 Protestants, 74 Presbyterians.

Dromore parish school, a small cottage near the church, not known when established; income: Hibernian Society 14 pounds per annum, rector of parish 4 pounds, Lady Bunbury 3 pounds 3s, from pupils 1d per week; intellectual education: Kildare Society books; moral education: frequent visits from rector, Authorised Version taught; number of pupils: males, 18 under 10 years of age, 21 from 10 to 15, total 49; females, 65 under 10 years of age, 7 from 10 to 15, total 72; total number of pupils 121, 63 Protestants, 35 Roman Catholics, 17 Presbyterians, 6 others; master James Lendrum, Church of England.

There are many hedge schools in the parish, but there being general holidays during the potatoe digging, October to November, particulars could not be had [initialled] WH.

Poor

No charitable institutions in the parish for the poor, aged or infirm.

Religion

It is a singular fact that almost all the parishioners belonging to the Church of England are at heart mere Methodists, and though they appear at church in the morning, never fail to season the information they have derived there with a little Methodistical rant in the evenings. The worst consequence of this is that far from receiving any

Parish of Dromore

useful instruction from these meetings, the ignorant and fanatic preachers only bewilder and frighten the poor people without improving them. All persons of this description may be classed under the general head "Protestants" and form about half the population. The rest are Roman Catholics.

Habits of the People

The generality of cottages in this parish are of a very wretched description. Numbers are built of mud with a miserable thatch, some half mud, half brick, others are built of rough stones, never more than 1-storey high and no slated houses are to be seen except a solitary farmer's here and there which arrive at the dignity of 2-storeys. Turf is the only fuel used in the parish, of which the numerous patches of bog afford an ample supply.

One instance of peculiarity of costume prevails in this as well as in the surrounding parishes of this part of Tyrone, that is, the great prevalence of red cloaks and shawls among the women. At a fair or any other concourse of people this remark cannot fail of occurring to the stranger. Its effect is very pleasing in the crowd. It gives a great air of liveliness and brilliance to the fairs.

There is a small spring gushing out of the base of the rock on which the parish church is built, which is considered holy by the Roman Catholics, who visit in numbers at some periods and drink of the water, which they suppose to be a cure for all diseases. There is nothing remarkable in all its appearance, being a simple stream running out of a small fissure in the rock.

Emigration

Emigration prevails to a considerable extent to New South Wales and America. A family left their farm in the parish during the last week, October 1835, for New South Wales, with a sum of 2,400 pounds capital. No more than 1 or 2 labourers leave the parish in the year for the English harvest.

Parish of Drumragh, County Tyrone

Statistical Report by Lieutenant William Lancey, 7th March 1834

NATURAL STATE

Locality and Extent

The parish of Drumragh <Drumreagh> is situated in the county Tyrone, barony of Omagh and diocese of Derry. It is surrounded by the parishes of Ardstraw, Cappagh, Clogherny, Donacavy, Dromore and East Longfield, and contains 20,160 acres.

NATURAL FEATURES

Hills

This parish is for the most part a low country of round hills called "drums" with raths or forts on their summits, from whence its name of Drumrath is derived. Towards East Longfield it attains at Corridinna the height of 972 feet, but this is the only mountain in the parish. The greater part is under cultivation, and the soil is far preferable to that of the adjacent parishes.

General Appearance

The general appearance of Drumragh indicates superior wealth, industry and good management. Having the advantages of good land and a ready market, there is every encouragement for an outlay of money. Much has been done of late years, but fencing, ditching and draining are still a good deal neglected; but the parish taken collectively is in a more civilised state than those adjoining it.

Rivers and Lakes

Two small streams called the Owenreagh and Quiggery unite above the old church and take the name of the Drumragh river which at Omagh mingles with the Camowen <Cammon> which divides this parish from Cappagh.

The Fairy water bounds a portion of the north of Drumragh. It is celebrated for fine pearls, some of which are scarcely inferior to those of the East. They are found in fresh water mussels <muscles> which abound in the streams round Omagh. Pearls in the summer season can always be obtained in Omagh and are not confined to the Fairy water. The Drumragh, Camowen and Strule <Strewel> produce them and some of the best are found in Mountjoy forest. They can be purchased for a trifle: the finest, about the size of a pea, for 4 or 5 shillings.

Lakes

[Insert addition: There are 4 lakes situated in Lough Muck, Firreagh, Kivlin and Rylands. The two former are the principal, that of Lough Muck being the largest, and contains [blank] acres. It is prettily situated and famous for pike, eels and perch. That at Firreagh is also celebrated for pike. A boat on Lough Muck is a great attraction to the people of Omagh. It belongs to Mr Campbell].

MODERN TOPOGRAPHY

Buildings in Omagh

The principal buildings in Drumragh are [in] the county town of Omagh, in which are included the court house of assize, gaol, infirmary, the church, 2 meeting houses, Methodist chapel <chaple>, Roman Catholic chapel and barracks.

Court House

The court house stands on the hill at the head of the main street. It is a handsome plain building of cut freestone, with a Doric portico of 4 columns with a pediment. It contains a large vestibule opening into Crown and civil courts, retiring rooms for the judge and juries, a large room for the grand jury and a handsome dining and drawing room for their accommodation, with a kitchen and lock-up place for prisoners on the underground floor. The Crown court has 2 galleries for the accommodation of the public and one for the grand jury, whose official room opens into it. The civil court is small, without a gallery, and has little space appropriated to the people. This building was erected on the site of the old gaol in 1814. The portico was added in 1820 and the whole cost by county presentments, 17,000 pounds. The freestone for its erection was obtained from West Longfield and the columns from Mulnatoosnog in Drumragh.

Gaol

The county gaol stands at the west end of the town on the Derry road. It consists of the old and new gaols. The former was built in 1796 of common stone and is now used as the women's and debtors' prison. The new part was erected in 1823 of cut freestone in a semicircular form, divided into [blank] wards, each having a separate yard for the

Parish of Drumragh

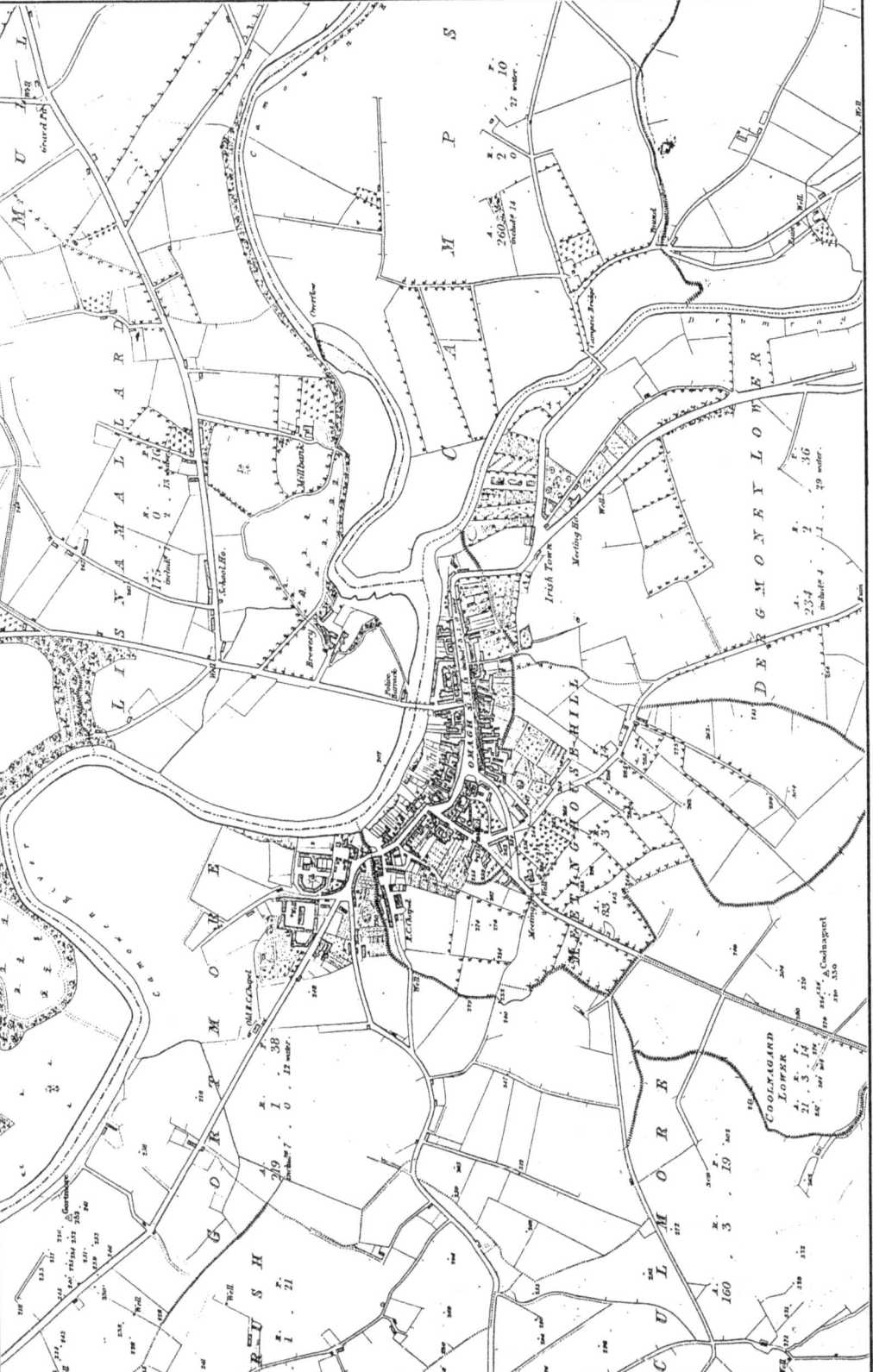

Map of Omagh from the first 6" O.S. Maps, 1830s

different classes of prisoner. Both old and new gaols are 3-storeys high. In front of the old building an open space has lately been enclosed for the prisoners to work in, and the whole building is surrounded with a high stone wall to prevent their escape.

This establishment can accommodate 300 prisoners and is guarded by 14 keepers. The numbers for trial in 1829 were 113, in 1830 172, in 1831 144, in 1832 93, in 1833 137, total tried 659. Of these none suffered the extreme penalty of the law. 34 were transported for life, 5 for 14 years and 94 for 7 years, amounting to 133 transports.

The governor's house stands in the centre of the arc formed by the new gaol and looks into each yard. His salary has lately been reduced to 150 pounds a year. The keepers receive gaol <goal> allowance and 1s 6d a day wages.

The tread mill is of small dimensions and its power is only applied to raise water for the building from a deep well adjacent to it.

SOCIAL ECONOMY

Police

There is a lock-up house in the new market, a police barrack over the bridge and one close to the church for the internal peace of the town. 2 officers of the constabulary are stationed in Omagh.

Infirmary

The county infirmary, situated in the town, is a building of small extent for such a purpose. It is supported by a grant from government of 100 pounds Irish, by county presentments and by private subscriptions. The number of patients for 1833 was 234. The prevailing diseases are scrofula, lues veneria, ulcers and accidents. The surgeon's salary is 120 pounds Irish and the annual expenditure between 700 and 800 pounds per annum. It would be well if this building were sold and one better suited to the purpose erected in the county.

Dispensary

The dispensary is supported by presentments and private subscriptions. The number relieved last year were 1,217, at an expense of 90 pounds. The surgeon's salary is 50 pounds and the usual diseases fevers, dyspepsia and pectoral complaints.

MODERN TOPOGRAPHY

Places of Worship: Church

The parish church, situated in the town, is very inconveniently placed for the greater part of the parish. It is a neat building with a high spire. It was built about 100 years ago and the spire added in 1810. In 1818 a new roof was put on the church and in 1827 it was enlarged at an expense of 145 pounds and a second commodious gallery added. It can contain 1,000 people and in the summer any festival is generally well filled. Since 1792 the sum of 1,300 pounds has been assessed on the parish for the repairs of the church.

Presbyterian Meeting Houses

There are 2 Presbyterian places of worship: one, called the old meeting house, with 3 half galleries, stands on the Dublin road. It was built in 1717 and cost 800 pounds. It had a thatched roof replaced by a slated one about 10 years ago, and was fully repaired in 1830.

The new meeting house without galleries cost 600 pounds and stands on the road to Dromore. The first Presbyterian congregation, worshipping in the old house, are accommodated to the amount of 800 persons, the second congregation in the new house to the amount of 372. In the summer they are generally full. The new house was built by subscription in 1754 and was repaired amd ceiled in 1830 at an expense of 62 pounds. The stipend of the minister is 30 pounds with 50 regium donum added. The stipend of the minister of the first congregation is 60 pounds, with 100 pounds regium donum.

Methodist Chapel

This place of worship is a neat building. [It] has a gallery and is nearly opposite the church. It was built in 1812 and pays 5 pounds a year ground rent. It is pewed and well fitted out and can contain 250 people. It is usually well filled by persons of various denominations, the number of Methodist families not exceeding 60. There is a good house attached for the resident preacher. Omagh and Newtownstewart are in the same circuit.

Roman Catholic Chapel

The Roman Catholic chapel in Brook Street is a modern building erected in 1829, the former place of worship being on the Derry road beyond the barracks. It cost 700 pounds and can contain 1,500 persons, having a gallery on 3 of its sides.

Barracks

The barracks at Gortmore is divided from the gaol by a narrow lane. It was an ordnance barrack for 1

Parish of Drumragh

troop of horse artillery, for which there was every convenience for officers, men, horses and guns. It is now occupied by a detachment of infantry, consisting of 2 officers and 44 rank and file, a detachment of 1 officer and 26 men being stationed at Lifford. Infantry to the amount of 8 officers, 110 rank and file and 60 horses could if necessary be quartered in this barrack at present. There are also quarters for a barrack-master and sergeant, officers' mess-room, hospital, engine house and a good well.

Town of Omagh

The county town of Tyrone consist[s] of 1 main street with 4 avenues leading to the adjacent bridges. It is situated on the left bank of the Camowen river, 86 miles from Dublin and 26 from Derry. The centre of the town, in which the church and court house are situated, stands on a hill, which is a great inconvenience to travellers. There are several good private houses and numerous good mercantile establishments, with 2 hotels who let post horses. Jaunting cars can also be hired from 2 other houses at cheaper rates than at the hotels.

The daily public conveyances are the Derry and Dublin mail up and down, a chaise marine to and from Derry and a mail car to and from Gortin. A day coach from the White Hart runs to Dublin every Monday, Wednesday and Friday, and returns the alternate days. An opposition coach from Derry to Dublin runs the same days as the Omagh coach. [Insert marginal note: a chaisemarine leaves Omagh for Enniskillen on Monday, Wednesday and Friday and returns the following days].

SOCIAL AND PRODUCTIVE ECONOMY

Markets

A weekly market is held on Saturday, every alternate week being a large market and every first Saturday in the month a fair. The cloth market is held every fortnight opposite the White Hart Inn, the corn and potato markets in Brook Street and the new market near Bridge Lane. Meal and butter are also sold in this square. The sheep markets are in front of the infirmary and at the corner of Church Street. Pigs are sold in the open space near the court house and the last mentioned sheep market. The cattle market is between the church and the new Presbyterian meeting house, and the horse fair at the Dublin end of the town. There are meat shambles of an inferior kind, but on market days it is exposed for sale in the public streets. The markets are all good and families can have all their wants supplied. Beef sells at 3d ha'penny a pound, mutton at 4d, butter at 7d ha'penny, bread, a 4lb loaf for 12d.

Proprietors

The principal proprietors of the town are General Archdale of Fermanagh, who has the ground rent but only 2 tenements. The houses chiefly belong to Mrs Spiller, John and George Buchanan, James Greer and the orphans Hamilton, the heirs of Alexander Campbell and John and Samuel Galbraith. The inhabitants are estimated at 2,400, one-half of whom are Protestants. Many have attained to independence. They dress and live well. Some of them are moral and some few religious.

Schools

There are good schools for all ranks of the inhabitants. The curate educates 40 boys in classics at the rate of 30 guineas a year for boarders, and 8, 6 and 4 guineas for day scholars. This school is of immense advantage to the town as the respectable merchants can educate their children well, under their own eyes, at a cheap rate.

Respectable female children are instructed by Mrs Duncan, who has 16 day scholars at the rate of 8 guineas per annum, music and drawing included, with a separate charge for the French language.

Miss McArthur's preparatory school for male and female children contains 36 scholars at 4 guineas a year; Mr Alcrow's school 36 male children, English and arithmetic for 4 guineas per annum.

The church free school supported by the rector educates 80 male and 40 female scholars, principally Roman Catholics. The master receives 13 pounds a year, assessed at parish vestry annually, and does not reside in the house, which stands at the church door.

A London Hibernian school under the management of Mrs Spiller is built at her garden gate. There are 40 scholars. The society grants 4 pounds and she pays the rest of the expenses, amounting to about 16 pounds per annum. The mistress resides and on the Lord's day assists in instructing 60 scholars.

MODERN TOPOGRAPHY

Country Places of Worship

The principal buildings not in town are the Seceders' houses in Gillygooley and Ballynahatty and Drumragh Roman Catholic chapel in Firreagh.

The Gillygooley house is fully pewed, that at

Ballynahatty is partly pewed. Neither has galleries, and they would hold about 150 persons each. The minister receives 50 pounds bounty and 20 pounds stipend and performs service in each house every other Sunday.

Drumragh chapel is the old parish place of worship for the Roman Catholics. It is partly thatched and partly slated. It has 1 gallery and will hold about 900 persons.

Rectory and Newgrove

The rectory at Tattyreagh Glebe and Newgrove, the residence of Samuel Galbraith Esquire. The rectory was built by Dr Richard Stack about 25 years ago and cost 2,000 pounds, 100 of which was paid by the Board of First Fruits. It is a commodious house with every requisite for a person of wealth.

Newgrove has been lately enlarged and the demesne comprising 100 acres much improved.

Village of Ballynahatty

The only village is that of Ballynahatty, a small place of no importance. Audley Mervyn, its ancient proprietor, had it in contemplation to build the town there, after the destruction of Omagh by fire in 1745.

Dwellings

There are many very respectable houses belonging to the better class of farmers, and the buildings generally in this parish are of a superior description to those of the immediate vicinity. The cabins are thatched and usually whitewashed.

ANCIENT TOPOGRAPHY

Monastery

The site of an old monastery is shown at the pound near the dry bridge in Omagh, said to have been built in the 14th century by the O'Neill family and in modern times occupied by Audley Mervyn, who was the proprietor of Omagh and a large territory around it. The ruins of this monastery, converted into a castle, were in existence 50 years ago, but were taken down to obtain stones for rebuilding the town, which had been accidently burned on the 4th May 1743. This castle was an extensive pile of building, but now no vestige remains of it.

Castle and Fort

Audley Mervyn also had a large castle at Ballynahatty, the site of which is still known, the remaining stones having been removed to erect a modern house within these few years. A garrison of King James' troops held Omagh from January to July 1689. A fort at that time stood on the elevated ground near the present site of the court house. This garrison fled from the town before the forces of King William.

Old Church

Drumragh old church is pleasantly situated on the river of that name, and has the walls and gables yet standing. No account can be obtained respecting its history, except that it was burned in Cromwell's time, rebuilt and is now a ruin.

Old Bell

An old bell about 9 inches long was dug up by the ancestors of a family called McAnkill in the neighbourhood of the graveyard. It has been handed down to the present generation and is always rung for the corpses of their family when on the road to and at the place of interment <internment>. They state that two of their ancestors in company with a third person, on leaving the burial place, heard the ringing of this bell under their feet, but the ears of the third were holden. On turning up the ground they found the bell, which will not sound for any but one of the McAnkills. It is kept by the oldest of the race and always rings the morning of the approaching death of any of the family. The lord of the soil took the bell, but as he could not get it to ring he returned it to the McAnkills. This family claims descent from that of St Columbkill and are of the Roman Catholic faith.

Chapel

Near the fort called the Mass House Hill Fort, at the back of Mr Rodger's house in Cavanacaw, a Roman Catholic chapel was erected 100 years ago by a famous priest named Father Terence McCawell. This chapel was afterwards taken down and removed to Mulloughmore and subsequently erected in Firreagh, its present situation.

Holy Wells

There is a well in Mullaghmenagh called Tubberdoney, said of old to be good for sore eyes. It is now unfrequented. There is also a well at Cornabracken, where the people dip their sick children at Midsummer's Eve, and one at Tattykeel above the mill where they wash themselves for ulcers. These are only frequented by the Roman Catholics.

Parish of Drumragh

Forts and Giant's Grave

There are many forts in Drumragh, one in Drumconnelly with 3 parapets and 2 ditches. Others have single ditches: a large one of this kind is behind Mr Rodger's house in Cavanacaw, and a very commanding one at Beagh, one at Loughmuck, one at Makeeragh, one in Gillygooley, one in Tullyhenry, one in Tattyreagh Glebe and many others whose situations will be seen on the plans. There are no legends respecting them, except the usual one attributing their erection to the Danes. Attempts have been made to discover gold in these forts, but whether they have been attended with success it is difficult to say; but I have been informed by respectable authority that Mr Watson of Mullaghmenagh dug out of the fort on his land silver coins of an ounce weight which he disposed of.

A giant's grave stands on the mearing of Cornabracken and Deerpark and one in Loughmuck.

SOCIAL ECONOMY

Landlords

There are no resident landlords except Mr Samuel Galbraith of Newgrove, George Buchanan of Tattykeel and Mr Rodgers of Cavanacaw. Others possessing property in Drumragh reside near the parish, and much of the land has the benefit of the personal inspection of those who derive their wealth from its inhabitants: Lord Belmore of Castlecoole, Sir James Stronge of Tynan Hall, Sir Hugh Stewart of Ballygawley, Sir James Bruce of Downhill, Reverend Hamilton Stewart of Buncrana, Reverend Lowery of Somerset, Lieutenant-General Hamilton of London, Mervyn Stewart Esquire of Ballygawley, John Galbraith Esquire of Greenmount, Sir John Burgoyne of Strabane, Mrs Spiller of Omagh, Alexander Hudson Esquire of Dublin, Thomas Armstrong of Fellow's Hall, Armagh, with the residents mentioned above are the principal possessors of the soil.

Inhabitants

Many of the inhabitants not living in the town are wealthy and independent. They are industrious, civil and anxious to improve. There is generally work for the poor, and absolute poverty might here be almost unknown. About one-half are Roman Catholics, who generally comprise the poorer classes. Few migrate for harvest either to England or Scotland.

Schools

Besides the schools mentioned in connection with the town of Omagh, there is one at Corlea having 66 male and 44 female children, the master residing near the house; one at Tattykeel, 25 males and 22 females, master resides. Drumragh school has 36 males and 21 females, master and mistress reside; Sir James Bruce gives them 5 pounds annually and an acre of land. Cavanaca, 80 males and 54 females, master resides amongst the scholars. Gillygooley, 52 males, 48 females, master resides. Dressog school (lately maliciously burnt down); Ballynahatty private school, 30 males and females (Latin taught) and Tattykeel private school for Latin and English, 20 boys. The Society scholars pay 6s a year and the Latin pupils 2 pounds. The Protestants and Catholics go to the same teachers and no school under the new National Board has yet been opened in Drumragh.

Dispensary

The dispensary in the town of Omagh already described supplies the medical wants of the poor of this parish.

PRODUCTIVE ECONOMY

Farms, Rent and Tenure

The size of farms varies from 5 to 60 acres, the average being 25 acres. Any land less than 5 acres is generally held by the labourer under the large farmer, and the rent paid either by work or money as agreed on. The average rent of good arable land varies from 3 half guineas to 30s down. It is held for 3 lives or 31 years, or 2 lives and 21 years, bishop's land as usual for 21 years and some is renewable for ever. General Hamilton's estate is an old lease now depending on an aged life, and lets for 13s an acre. This property returns to the proprietor only 350 pounds, which sum will be doubled at least on the death of the above life. There is no grazing farm in Drumragh and very little mountain for the farmers' young cattle. Some of the farms are kept in excellent order. Amongst the best are those of Joseph Moore on Sir James Bruce's estate and Mr Osborn's on Lord Belmore's property.

Crops

The usual rotation of crops is first potatoes, then oats, barley, flax, forced grass and wheat. Mr Moore crops his land with oats, then potatoes, wheat or barley, flax and grass seed, hay and 2 years grazing. Iron ploughs are very general.

Manures

The chief manures are lime mixed with farmyard manure. The lime is purchased at Kilmore quarry at the rate of 2s 6d a ton, and that obtained from West Longfield for 5d a cartload for as much as they can draw with 1 horse out of the quarry. It is not unusual for the farmers to draw out much more than they can remove to their farms and leave it on the side of the road for a future opportunity. 1 ton of stone burns into 10 barrels of lime.

There is an old quarry in Mullaghmenagh on General Hamilton's estate, but it is nearly exhausted.

Livestock

Cattle, the old Irish breed, some Ayrshire and some of the Devonshire breed, but the best come from Fermanagh. They sell in the Omagh market from 4 pounds to 7 pounds a head and there is usually a large supply. The farmers raise their own calves, some 10, 8 or 6 head annually.

Good farm horses with occasionally good roadsters are to be found in Drumragh. The former sell from 10 to 20 pounds, the latter depend on their quality, but there are none of superior breeding. The markets of Enniskillen and Moy are the usual places where good horses are sought for in this neighbourhood.

The best breed of sheep comes from Fermanagh. These when ready for market sometimes sell for 3 pounds a head, the usual price being about 40s. Country sheep vary from 20s to 35s, but as the soil is principally cropped there are few kept in this parish.

Pigs abound at a price varying from a few shillings to 5 pounds; a few of the Dutch breed in the parish.

Fish and Game

Salmon, trout, perch, pike and eels, partridges and snipe are not rare, but hares and woodcock are scarce. A few pheasants are met with at Newgrove and the vicinity of Ballynahatty.

Orchards

There are a few orchards of small extent adjacent to the farmers' or gentlemen's houses. Those of Newgrove and Riverland are the principal. Common fruit is sold in Omagh market at the rate of half a quart for gooseberries and 30 apples for a penny. The chief supply is brought from Loughgall and purchased in the Aughnacloy market, and transported by cars and carts to Omagh.

Mills

The corn mills are situated in Blacksessagh, Ballynahatty, Edergoole, Loughmuck, Drumshanely, Tattysallagh, Aghydulla, Tattykeel, Dressog, Gillygooley, Coolaghy and Rathnelly. The usual dimensions of the wheels are 10 feet in diameter. Some are undershot, others overshot.

The flax mills are in Blacksessagh, Loughmuck, Gillygooley and Coolaghy. Their wheels are less than 10 feet and are adapted to their situations with respect to the fall of the water. The mill at the Omagh brewery is much used by the neighbouring residents of Drumragh.

Manufactures, Prices and Wages

The chief manufacture is linen cloth. About 17,000 webs, 52 yards each, are sold annually in the Omagh market and average 9d ha'penny a yard, which amounts to 34,991 pounds 13s 4d. The trade is declining. The weavers usually earn from 10s to 15s, but some make 24s by 10 days work. This chiefly depends on the quality of the article. The farmers grow their own flax and make their own linen, but journeymen who work for others are the best paid in the linen trade. Grey country cloth is only manufactured to a small extent as it can be purchased cheaper than most farmers can make it. It sells from 2s 6d to 4s 6d a yard. Blankets and flannels are made for country use and bring from 9d to 11d a yard. Stockings are knit in almost every farmhouse and sell from 1s to 2s a pair.

The usual manufactures of shoes and hats are carried on in Omagh as in other towns. All the common articles of wearing apparel are made for country purposes and every description of English dress can be purchased in the shops. There are 2 tanneries in town which manufacture a good deal of leather. Bricks are made in Ballygowan and sell from 13s to 15s a thousand. The soil is well calculated for this branch of trade and sometimes 100,000 have been made in one season. The price of labour is the same as in Cappagh. Men receive 50s to 63s a half year, women 24s to 30s; daily wages from 8d to 12d a day.

MODERN TOPOGRAPHY

Communications

The mail road from Dublin to Derry passes through Omagh. It has been alluded to in the statistics of Cappagh. The principal crossroads in Drumragh run to Fintona, Dromore, Ballynahatty and Drumquin; they are all in tolerable repair.

A new line of road from Omagh to Enniskillen

Parish of Drumragh

passing through Dromore and Irvinestown has lately been opened, which will avoid many of the hills. A chaise marine has been established on it, which leaves Omagh for Enniskillen on Monday, Wednesday and Friday and returns the following days. A conveyance of the kind has been long wanted on this line, and no doubt if conducted with care and attention will bring profit to the proprietors and very much accommodate the public.

The country roads are tolerably well kept and there are sufficient of them.

NATURAL FEATURES

Woods and Plantations

There are few plantations and no woods in the parish. There used to be oak woods in General Hamilton's property in Mullaghmenagh, Gillygooley and Corlea, and that of George Buchanan's at Tattykeel, but they have been all destroyed, some 60, some 30 and some 20 years. Young plantations in Tattykeel, Ballynahatty and Newgrove have lately been put down, but nothing to any extent. Many of the good farmhouses have a few trees about them, which considerably enlivens their appearance.

Fuel

Turf and bog wood are the general fuel of town and country. Scotch coal can be purchased at Strabane, and that from Dungannon is brought to Omagh and sells at 20s a ton. Turf is 5d a box, the same dimensions as that described in Cappagh.

Rocks

The lowlands of Drumragh lie on the south on a strata of clay sandstone, on the north on strata of silicious sandstone, towards the east the lowest strata of mountain limestone are quarried, and the mountain of Corridinna on the west is composed of talcose slate. A basaltic dyke traverses West and East Longfield and is seen in the south west end of Drumragh. The soil is good, of a clayey nature and appears to be highly productive.

SOCIAL ECONOMY

Need for Church and Mills

A second church is very much wanted: the Protestant population is extensive and many of them remain at home on the Lord's day, pleading their distance from the parish church or the want of sufficient good clothing to appear where the congregation is so well dressed, a very mistaken but very prevailing notion. There is a good site for a church at Riverstown or Mullaghmore on the estate of Samuel Galbraith Esquire, who offered to give 100 pounds and an acre of land if the late Bishop of Derry would allow him to present to the curacy during his life. This was refused and the church not built.

Corn and flax mills are much wanted in the neighbourhood of Drumragh. There is a good site for one at the old bridge. The culture of wheat is increasing very much and there being no mills nearer than Dungannon or Strabane, a good wheat mill might not prove a bad speculation near Omagh. [Signed] William Lancey, Lieutenant Royal Engineers, 7th March 1834.

Replies to Queries of the North West Farming Society

NATURAL STATE AND NATURAL FEATURES

Name and Features

Answer to queries for the information of the North West Society of Ireland.

Section 1. Name, parish of Drumragh, townlands 52, soil 8,000 acres arable, mountains 2,000 acres, rivers 1, lakes 3, sea coasts none, plantations Newgrove, the seat of Samuel Galbraith Esquire.

Quarries

Section 2. Mines none, minerals none, quarries yes; different kinds of stone, limestone, freestone and building stone.

MODERN TOPOGRAPHY

Buildings

Section 3. Modern buildings: court house, hospital and gaol. Towns: Omagh, population 1864. Gentlemen's seats: Samuel Galbraith Esquire, Newgrove, Reverend Robert Burrowes, Riverland. Scenery: hill and vale, skirted with mountain. Inns: 2 principal inns, David Gree's and John Harkin's.

Roads: The country is well intersected with useful and convenient roads.

ANCIENT TOPOGRAPHY

Ancient Buildings

Section 4. Ancient buildings: 2. Churches: one in the townland of Drumragh, of which there is no history extant. Castles: one, supposed to be built in the year 1400.

SOCIAL ECONOMY

Comforts and Health

Section 5. Food: potatoes, meal, milk, butter, beef and mutton and bacon. Fuel: turf. Diseases: none peculiar to this place. Instances of longevity: John O'Neill, late of Omagh, died at the advanced age of 104 years.

Character and Customs of Inhabitants

Section 6. Genius <genious> and disposition of inhabitants: as to genius, though good, nothing very particular. As to disposition, generous, good-natured and most amenable. Language: English. Manners, customs, christenings, marriages, wakes, funerals, traditions: the same as in the other parts of Ulster.

Education

Section 7. Education and employment of children: reading and assisting in farming and weaving. Schools: 14; collection of books: none; manuscripts: none of such consequence as is thought worthwhile to insert.

Religion

Section 8. State of religious establishment: [blank]. Tithes: 530 pounds per annum. Churches 1, meeting houses 4, chapels Roman Catholic 2, chapels Methodist 1.

PRODUCTIVE ECONOMY

Agriculture

Section 9. Modes of agriculture: [blank]. Rotation of crops: potatoes, barley, flax and oats, whilst the land will bear a crop. Horses: a vast number of horses for agriculture, but few of a good breed. Black cattle: the cows in general are not of a good kind. Sheep: sheep in general not of a good kind. Pigs in general not of a good kind. Fairs and markets: 11 fairs in the year in Omagh and weekly markets in Ballinahatty. A weekly market in Omagh on Saturday, which is well supplied with linen and every article of provision. Wages and price of labour: from 10d to 1s per day for a labourer [and] horse and [cart] from 4s 2d to 5s per day.

Commerce

Section 10. Trades: carpenters, tailors, weavers, shoemakers, saddlers. Manufactories none, no commerce except by woollen ware, house, groceries' shops and large quantities of brown linen purchased on market days. Navigation none.

SOCIAL ECONOMY

Eminent Men

Section 11. Natural curiosity none, remarkable occurrence none. Eminent men: the Dean of Cork; writers: the Dean of Cork.

Improvements

Section 12. Suggestions for improvement and means of ameliorating the condition of the poor: no improvement in the agriculture in the parish for upwards of 20 years, except in a very few instances, for want of a spirited and resident gentry.

Parish of Kilskeery, County Tyrone

Memoir by J.R. Ward

NATURAL FEATURES

Hills

The only high ground in the parish of Kilskeery is a ridge along the south eastern boundary, which is little more than the finishing belt of a mass of mountains whose tops and principal features are in the adjoining county of Fermanagh. The rest of the parish is an irregular surface of low but occasionally steep gravel and sand hills. The average height of the south eastern ridge above mentioned is between 800 and 1,000 feet above the sea level [insert query: 1,000 feet].

Lakes

There are 2 small lakes in the parish (viz.) Relagh lough and Maghera lough. The first occupies portions of the townlands of Makenny and Relagh-Guinness. It is 200 feet above the sea, 8 acres 2 roods 16 perches in extent and is said to be from 2 to 20 feet deep. The second occupies portions of 3 townlands (viz.) Magheralough, Corlea and Drumash. It is 340 feet above the sea, 16 acres 1 rood in extent and from 10 to 40 feet deep. These lakes are well stocked with pike, trout and perch, and the Maghera lough is used as a mill dam.

Rivers

Kilskeery river flows through the centre of the parish in a south west direction; its breadth varies from 15 to 40 feet. It rises in the adjacent parish of Dromore and is useful for drainage and water power. There are no considerable falls or rapids on it. The average fall is 25 feet in a mile. It is not subject to any destructive floods. It impedes communication. The bed is varied, being in some parts rocky and in others of a gravelly nature. The banks are well cultivated but the scenery is uninteresting. This river forms part of the parish and county boundaries for 1 mile.

There are also a great number of smaller streams, some of which are used for turning mill wheels and all are useful for draining. There are no mineral or hot wells in the parish. Good spring water is not abundant.

Bogs

Small patches of bog occur in almost every townland. They are from 200 to 400 feet above the sea. Timber is found indiscriminately scattered through them. Oak, fir and birch are most common. The first is generally in good preservation and the peasants use it in building their cabins. The depth of these bogs is from 4 to 10 feet.

Woods

No natural woods in the parish.

PRODUCTIVE ECONOMY

Crops

The principal crops are oats, barley, flax and potatoes. The two first are sown in May and cut in September. Flax is sown in April and May and pulled in August. Potatoes are set in April and May and dug in October and November. Very little wheat is cultivated in the parish. The time for sowing is December and reaping in August and September.

MODERN TOPOGRAPHY

Town of Trillick

Trillick, situated in the east of the parish 82 Irish miles from Dublin, is in the diocese of Clogher, and the main road between Fintona and Enniskillen passes through it. The town is composed of one street a quarter of a mile in length. Its situation offers nothing remarkable for picturesque beauty.

Present State as to Buildings

The public buildings in the town are a Wesleyan Methodist meeting house, a Church Methodist meeting house and a court house. The first meeting house is a plain rectangular building 45 feet long and 25 feet broad. It was built in 1831. The expense, 150 pounds, was defrayed by public subscription. It will accommodate 200 persons, the general attendance is 100.

The second meeting house is at present building. It is 30 feet long and 20 broad, the cost, which is to be made by subscriptions from the public, will be 150 pounds and it is to accommodate 150 persons.

The court house is a plain plastered <plaistered> building 30 feet long and 20 feet broad. There is a market place underneath it. There are 2 good inns in the town, and a house at the south west end is occupied by the police.

There are 50 houses of 1-storey, 26 of 2 and 4 of

3-storeys. They are all built of stone and some few roughcast and whitewashed. 25 are slated and the remainder thatched. They have mostly a dirty appearance.

Social and Productive Economy

Local Government

Petty <petit> sessions are held in the town once in each fortnight. Quarter sessions are held in Omagh, 14 Irish miles distant. The greater part of the inhabitants are employed as labourers, the remainder in retail dealing.

Markets

Markets are held on every Tuesday and fairs on the 14th of each month. The traffic, which is much the same for both, is good for the size of the town. It principally consists of cattle, pigs, sheep and horses. Grain, butter and soft goods are not sold to a great extent. Tolls are paid to the landlord, General Mervyn Archdall.

Conveyances

There are 2 public conveyances through the town. They are named the Rover and the Tallyho. The first is a species of caravan and the second a double outside jaunting car. They are each drawn by 2 horses. These cars leave Omagh every morning at 5.30, arrive at Trillick at 9, proceed on to Enniskillen, and on their return arrive at Trillick at [sic] 5 a.m.

Dispensary

The parish dispensary is in the town.

Trades and Callings

A list of trades [table]: apothecary 1, grocers 6, general dealers 1, innkeeper 2, tanner 1, chandler 1, leather cutters 2, spirit shops 5, cooper 1, butcher 1, carpenter 1, smiths 2, nailers 2, tailor 1, shoemaker 1, reed maker 1.

Modern Topography

Public Buildings

Besides those mentioned in the town, there is an Episcopalian church and a Roman Catholic chapel. The church, situated in Kilskeery Glebe, is a neat plastered building with a square tower and freestone spire. The body of the church is 90 feet long and 30 feet broad. It is neatly fitted up inside with pews and a gallery and will accommodate 500 persons; the average attendance on each sabbath is from 400 to 700 persons. It was erected in 1772. The expense was defrayed by the incumbent of that period, the Reverend Archdeacon Hastings, but the amount is not known.

The chapel, situated in Stranacummer townland, is a plain plastered building 90 feet long and 36 feet broad. [Insert note: The priest promised further information but neglected to give it].

Gentlemen's Seats

The Glebe House, situated in Kilskeery Glebe, is the residence of the Reverend Thomas Porter, rector of the parish. It was built in 1774.

Relagh, the seat of Counsellor James Story, is a small neat double cottage situated in the townland of Relagh.

In Castle Mervyn demesne there is a shooting box of General Mervyn Archdall's.

Bleach Greens, Manufactories and Mills

There are no bleach greens or manufactories. There is a tannery in Trillick. A table of mills [contains the following headings: name of townland where situated, nature of the mill, dimensions and nature of wheel].

Scallen, corn mill, 13 feet diameter, 1 foot 9 inches breadth, undershot wheel.

Tullyincrin, corn mill, diameter 12 feet, breadth 1 foot 9 inches, undershot wheel.

Shanmullagh East, corn mill, diameter 12 feet, breadth 1 foot 8 inches, undershot wheel.

Corlea, corn mill, diameter 12 feet, breadth 1 foot 8 inches, breast wheel.

Drumsonus, corn mill, diameter 13 feet, breadth 1 foot 6 inches, breast wheel.

Corkragh, corn mill, diameter 12 feet, breadth 2 feet, breast wheel.

Cordromedy, corn mill, diameter 10 feet 6 inches, breadth 1 foot 6 inches, undershot wheel.

Carannamaragh, corn mill, diameter 13 feet, breadth 1 foot 4 inches, breast wheel.

Communications

The main road between Fintona and Enniskillen (passing through Trillick) traverses the parish south west for 6 and a half miles. The average breadth is 30 feet. It is very well laid out and kept in good repair. Another road branches from this, crossing the river by means of Kilskeery bridge, traversing north west and is the line of communication between Trillick and Irvinestown. There are 2 and a half miles from its junction (with the above road)

Parish of Kilskeery

to the parish boundary and it is greatly in want of repair. The average breadth is 26 feet.

The road between Trillick and Fivemiletown, traversing south east from the first, is very hilly and in great want of repair. There are 3 miles in the parish and the average breadth is 26 feet.

A road traversing the parish south from Trillick to Tempo (county Fermanagh) is very hilly and in bad repair. There are 3 miles in the parish and the breadth is 26 feet.

There are besides a good supply of by-roads in tolerably good repair.

Bridges

Kilskeery bridge crosses the Kilskeery river about 300 yards west of the church. It has 2 arches, is 40 feet long and 25 feet broad and is in good repair.

General Appearance and Scenery

This parish has very little to expatiate upon in point of general appearance. Scenery there is none; looking down from the high ridge of ground along the south east boundary, the parish presents an irregular bumpy surface, divided nearly across the centre from north to south by a rather conspicuous stream with occasional craggy banks. There is a general aspect of fertility, but very little wood except about the Glebe House and Relagh Cottage.

SOCIAL ECONOMY

Early Improvements and Obstructions to Improvement

The greatest obstruction to improvement is the want of leases. The farmers in general complain of having to pay higher rents according to the improvements they make.

Local Government

There are 4 magistrates residing in the parish (none of them stipendiary). Their names and residences are James Story Esquire, Relagh, the Reverend Thomas Porter, Kilskeery Glebe, the Reverend Arthur Irwin, [blank] and Robert Atthill Esquire, dispensary surgeon, Trillick. [Insert footnote: Mr Atthill has, since the above was written, resigned his commission of the peace, February 1836 [initialled] [?] JRW]. They are firm and respected by the people. The constabulary force is a sergeant and 3 men stationed in Trillick, in which town petty <pettit> sessions are held once each fortnight; 2 or 3 magistrates are generally in attendance [queried]. Outrages are decreasing. Illicit distilling is not carried on. Insurances are not common.

Dispensaries

The dispensary in Trillick has been of great service to the poor of the parish and diseases are diminishing. The surgeon would not give me any information regarding the number of diseases. [Signed] J.R. Ward.

Table of Schools

[Table contains the following headings: name of townland where situated, religion and sex of pupils, remarks as to how supported, when established].

Makenny, 24 Protestants, 6 Catholics, 16 males, 14 females, 30 total; the pupils pay from 1s to 3s per quarter, 1828.

Kilskeery Glebe, 20 Protestants, 18 males, 2 females, 20 total; supported by the Society for Discountenancing Vice, 1815.

Relagh, 58 Protestants, 17 Catholics, 59 males, 16 females, 75 total; Samuel Story Esquire, Relagh, gives 10 pounds per annum and the pupils pay from 1s to 3s per quarter, 1820.

Crossan, 5 Protestants, 5 females, 5 total; the pupils pay from 1s to 2s per quarter, 1819.

Scallen, 40 Protestants, 40 Catholics, 40 males, 40 females, 80 total; supported by the Hibernian Society, 5 pounds salary for mistress, date not known.

Keenogue, 36 Protestants, 45 Catholics, 54 males, 27 females, 81 total; supported by the pupils at the usual rate, date not known.

Ballyard, 28 Protestants, 8 Catholics, 32 males, 4 females, 36 total; the pupils pay from 1s to 4s per quarter, 1832.

Killyblunick Glebe, 8 Protestants, 42 Catholics, 38 males, 12 females, 50 total; the Reverend Thomas Porter, rector of the parish, gives the schoolhouse free of rent and the pupils pay from 1s to 3s per quarter, date not known.

Poor

No provision made for the poor.

Religion

The Roman Catholic persuasion bears a proportion of 3 and a half to 1 to the Protestants and Protestant Dissenters. The clergy of the Church of England are supported by tithes and glebe lands which are very considerable: the tithe is about 800 pounds per annum. Among the Dissenters, the

Methodists (of which there are 2 sects, Wesleyan and Church) are the most prevailing. They have no regular preachers but are attended by strollers whose salary is from 14 pounds to 16 pounds per annum, besides which they receive coals and candles, and are seldom put to any expense in travelling as they generally board themselves and horses with the richest of their several congregations. Those who are married receive 10 pounds extra per annum and 5 pounds for each child. The loudest preachers are most preferred. The Catholic priests are supported by contributions from the congregation, (the amount, I could not ascertain [initialled] J.R. Ward).

Habits of the People

The cottages of the peasantry are built of stone and thatched. They have glass windows and in general consist of but 1-storey, which is usually divided into 2 apartments. Very little attention is paid to comfort or cleanliness either in the habitations or persons of the families. Their food consists of potatoes or oaten bread, and sometimes meat and broth. Their dress is varied. There are no remarkable instances of longevity. Early marriages, that is, from 18 to 25 years old, are common among the Roman Catholics. It is said their priests encourage them. The usual number in each family is 5 or 6. They have very little amusement or recreation except attending the fairs in the neighbouring towns.

Emigration

Emigration prevails to a small extent, chiefly to Lower Canada. Some families have lately left the parish for New South Wales and several others have it in contemplation to follow them. A few young men go over to England and Scotland for employment during the harvest.

Parish of Leckpatrick, County Tyrone

Replies to Queries of the North West Society
by George D. Mansfield, 8 October 1821

MEMOIR WRITING

North West of Ireland Agricultural Society Questionnaire.

Copy answers to questions proposed by the North West of Ireland Agricultural Society, by George D. Mansfield Esquire.

Having been favoured with certain statistical queries by the North West of Ireland Agricultural Society, I herewith beg leave to transmit such information as I am capable of affording so far as respects the parish of Leckpatrick in the county of Tyrone and diocese of Derry. [Answers given only, numbered in brackets according to queries].

NATURAL STATE

Locality

(3rd) This parish, of which the Reverend Francis Brownlow is the present incumbent, is situated in the barony of Strabane, between the towns of Strabane and Derry on the eastern bank of the River Foyle. It is about 3 and a half miles in breadth from north to south and about 5 miles in length from east to west.

PRODUCTIVE ECONOMY

Proprietors

(4th) It contains 40 townlands, of which the most noble the Marquis of Abercorn is proprietor of 34, the Lord Bishop of Derry of 2, Mr Sinclair of 2 and a Mr Murray with others of 2 more. Of these, Mr Sinclair is the only resident proprietor. The population is 5,483 by the last return. There are about 5,000 acres in the parish, of which upwards of 2,200 are estimated as being annually under crop. The residue comprises bog, mountain and pasture, which last in the cultivated parts of this district does not exceed the one-fifth part of that in cultivation. Towards the mountains, of course, the proportion is different, the tillage there having probably the same ratio inversely to the pasture.

Mountains, Bogs and Fuel

The mountains stretch along the eastern and southern boundaries of Leckpatrick, and are the principal sources from which the fuel, not only of this parish but also of the towns and neighbourhoods of Strabane and Lifford, are derived, there being no bog of much value or extent contiguous, except in those mountains. Along the banks of the Foyle there is a bog of probably 200 acres in the townlands of Leck and Ballydonaghy, partly belonging to Lord Abercorn, partly to the Bishop of Derry, but being in a low situation and never having been drained, the turf are consequently of the very worst quality. There is the greatest possible difficulty in draining them; and thus what was designed by providence as a blessing to a numerous population is rendered useless and unprofitable by the withholding of a very moderate sum in the expenditure of draining. This bog forms the extreme northern portion of the parish, and as the mountains which yield fuel are in the most distant extremity, the advantage to be derived by converting it from a swamp or a morass into a solid productive bog are both evident and urgent. It is, besides, of very great depth, and rendered firm and compact by draining would afford an inexhaustible supply to the crowded population of the lower part of the parish, to whom, as weavers and manufacturers of linen cloth particularly, an abundance of fuel is indispensable.

Suggestions for Improvement and Use of Fuel

It is the peculiar province of an engineer to ascertain the probable expenses of the improvement, but it cannot be deemed presumption in one who claims no pretensions to skill in that department, nor arrogate any extraordinary share of penetration, to say that there is no expenditure which could judiciously and honestly be made on this bog that would not amply remunerate the proprietor and confer the most extensive advantage on the surrounding peasantry. The property is a joint one and therefore requires co-operation, and as the proprietors are both opulent and, I doubt not, anxious for the improvement and well-being of the country generally, it is humbly presumed that a suggestion which might have escaped their own observation will at least obtain a portion of their attention and lead to such inquiry as shall establish the certainty or fallacy of the opinion now given. The rapid destruction of the peat on our mountains, and the annual increase to the distance of drawing it, render it imperative to adopt such measures as shall diminish this evil where it can be done. An

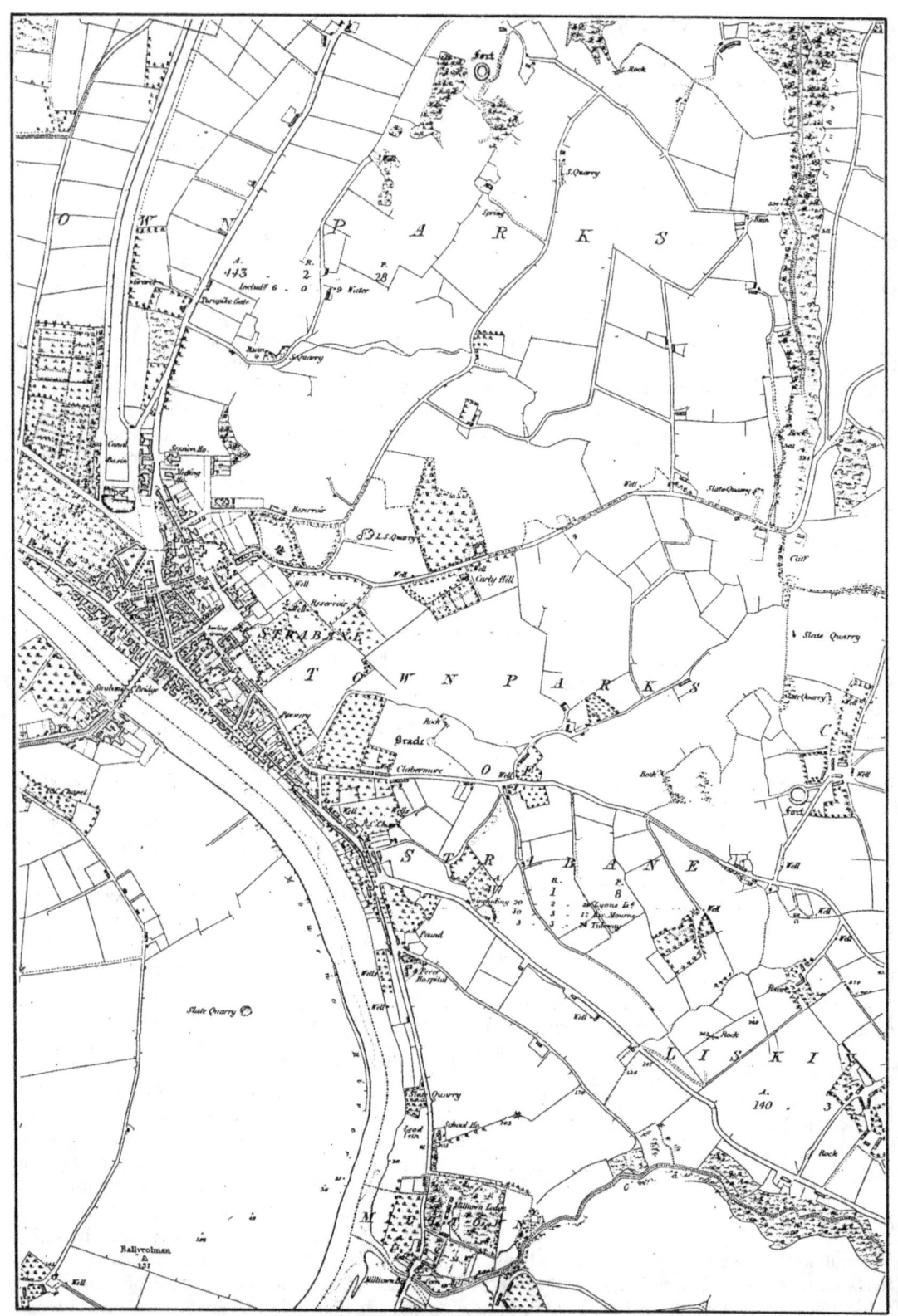

Map of Strabane from the first 6" O.S. maps, 1830s

overflowing population occasions an excessive consumption of fuel, but there being 2 considerable bleach greens in this neighbourhood, one in this parish, the other on the borders of it in Donaghedy <Donaghkiddy> (which also obtains its fuel from our mountains), the rapidity with which bog vanishes is almost beyond credence, and if timely precautions be not used, a calamity will be entailed on this district which no exertion can remove. It is estimated that each of these bleach greens consumes annually as much turf as would supply 100 families, or taken together nearly one-sixth part as much as the entire parish. This may, however, be more than the correct proportion to the whole consumption, but still it proves the necessity of a timely inquiry by the proprietors on this subject, whose property must generally be deteriorated in value in proportion as the tenants are put to greater expense in obtaining their fuel.

Mr Sinclair's Improvements

Whilst I am upon the subject of the fourth query, I shall take occasion to observe that considerable portions have been brought from barren and heathy mountains to a certain state of cultivation and improvement, which, if the advantages be not commensurate with the industry and enterprise that effected it, have at least tended considerably to improve the aspect of our country and to brighten our prospects. Of these, by far the most extensive and the most useful have been made on Mr Sinclair's estate, where many new farms have sprung up in the midst of barren mountains, and comfortable cottages, well-sheltered gardens and quickset hedges are seen where formerly all was one wide waste, the undistinguished abode of the hare and the moor-fowl. However, the prosperity of this new colony is chiefly imputable to the watchful care of the proprietor, whose skill in every department of agriculture enabled him to suggest the most effectual methods of improvement, whilst his liberality induced him to supply in a great measure the means. The woods of Holyhill yielded timber for their houses and farming implements, and its nurseries provided quicks and trees for their gardens and fences, to ask [for] which was as great a source of satisfaction to the donor as to receive it would have been to others. It would afford a good practical lesson to many of our proprietors to visit these newly formed farms. It would suggest, since so much has been done where climate and soil were to be contended with, what might not be done under more favourable circumstances.

Farms and Fencing

(5th) The farms here are in general very limited in extent, many not exceeding 5 acres, some even less; few in the good lands amounting to 20 and not above half a dozen of 30 acres. Mr Sinclair's well cultivated farm of Holyhill and Mr Brownlow's glebe, which he chiefly holds in his own hands, are quite out of this enumeration, being each upwards of 100 acres in extent, exclusive of the plantations.

The enclosures through this parish are generally speaking of an indifferent description, being formed principally of loose stones collected from the tillage lands and put together in an indifferent manner. There are, it is true, some quicksets here and, though the advantage of them is fully acknowledged, yet the spirit for permanent improvement is so little alive that we seldom see any new ditches made with quicks, or at all formed in a durable way. This may in a great measure be ascribed to the narrow limits of the farms, the land being principally in the hands of persons who have little or no capital to embark on the cultivation or improvement of it, and who prefer having their horse or cow tethered on their scanty pasture during the summer months, and during the winter allowing them to range at large over their own and their neighbours' fields, to being at the labour or cost of erecting sufficient fences.

Cultivation and Crops

The manner of cultivation is answerable to the description given of the enclosures. On farms where these are of a better kind, we observe a more improved system of agriculture. The usual routine on the small farms, which constitute the principal part of this district, is planting potatoes generally in the lazy bed way, sowing barley or corn twice, and sometimes thrice after this. A crop of flax follows, which is succeeded by another crop of corn, and by this time the land, being totally exhausted, is left either to recover by lea or, if the stock of the owner be sufficient to enable him to provide manure, it is again potatoed and again undergoes the same exhausting process already described. Our better farmers have adopted the drill method of planting potatoes. They usually lay down at least a part of their potato land with clover or clover and grass seeds. This being used as green feeding in summer increases their stock of manure, keeps their cattle in much better condition, enriches and fertilizes their grounds and improves their crops in the exact proportion that it is practised. The means of improvement therefore are fully evinced, but to have them brought into general practice presents many difficulties viz. small farms, want of fences and want of capital. However, it is to be observed that this system, which experience so strongly recommends, is nevertheless neglected by many who might adopt it, and who, in adhering to their old plans, annually diminish their own returns and progressively deteriorate their soil.

Grazing and Pasture

(6th) There are scarcely any lands here which can exclusively be denominated pasture lands. The scanty portions allotted for this purpose are intermixed with the tillage, and are seldom thus appropriated until they are incapable of yielding any crop. In the River Foyle there are some islands which are almost exclusively used as pasture land, but being subject to the overflowing of the river, they are ill-adapted to any other purpose. The mountains afford a wide range for young cattle during the summer months, which are brought home in the winter and fed on straw or allowed the scanty gleanings of the stubble lands. The lands skirting our mountains, which have not yet been broken in, might be improved considerably by raising fences to afford shelter and covering the heath with lime, which, as that article can be had at a cheap rate, would cost but a moderate sum per acre and would probably be the very best and most efficient method for the improvement of mountain lands; as, when the soil is of an improvable nature, this would at once bring it into good pasture and prepare it for future tillage, and even where the land is of an indifferent quality would effect a considerable change.

NATURAL FEATURES

Mountains

(7th) The mountains are the Owenreagh, Killynaught and Knockivoe. The last, which is the lowest in the chain, is partially cultivated to its summit, and the spots of pasture interspersed which yet remain unsubdued are well suited to the system I have above suggested for the improvement of mountain pasture. Much of Killynaught and Owenreagh are deep bog covered with heath and only useful during the summer months. The banks of the rivulets and the skirts of even these mountains are cultivated; but it can never be a very desirable circumstance to extend mountain improvement. Where it is attempted, it needs much support and direction, and can only attain perfection under the fostering care of a skilful proprietor.

Bogs

(8th) Killynaught, Holyhill and Ballydonaghy are the principal bogs. In Greenlaw and Backfence there are also some portions of low bog, not, however, of the best quality nor of any considerable extent. In answering the fourth query such hints have been thrown out as might prove useful with respect to Ballydonaghy bog. The same are applicable in a great degree to Greenlaw and Backfence bogs, but they have neither the depth nor the extent of the Ballydonaghy bog and are therefore not so deserving of attention. Timber is found in all of these. The low bogs particularly abound with it, fir principally, but I am not enabled to say of what dimensions or quality. It is, however, abundant, and usually cut up for fuel. Its situation is ascertained in summer by the ground immediately above it being free from dew, whilst the ground adjoining is covered with dew. An instrument resembling a spit is there driven into the bog, which ascertains pretty accurately the size and situation of the timber.

Woods

(9th) Our young plantations are almost confined to Mr Sinclair's demesne of Holyhill and the improvements made on the glebe by Mr Brownlow. The former is of considerable extent, containing upwards of 400 acres and, being in a most flourishing condition and disposed with much taste and judgement on beautifully undulating grounds, forms a striking feature in our parish scenery. The woods of Cloghcor and Woodend, the property of Lord Abercorn, are for their extent extremely beautiful, consisting chiefly of oak. The former contains about 30 acres, the latter about 25 acres. There are a number of small orchards in Woodend and Greenlaw, affording apples and plums, few cherries or pears. There is one very indifferent nursery in Woodend.

Trees and Gardens

(10th) The larch grows here most rapidly. The alder is adapted either to moist or exposed situations, and the sycamore and mountain ash are better qualified to bear the violent western gales than any other trees. The farmhouses formerly seldom wanted a garden surrounded by ash trees, but lately little improvement of any kind has been made, and the scattered clumps are daily diminishing for the use of the plough and farmhouse, and no young trees planted in their stead.

.There are many detached spots through this

Parish of Leckpatrick

district, which could with great certainty of success be planted and add most materially to the beauty of the country and the convenience of the inhabitants, particularly on the banks of the Glenmorning river, which are so steep as to be of little value either as pasture or tillage land and where the trees would grow most luxuriantly. Many ravines and mountain dells, which now excite no sensations in the mind of the traveller but of their being a wild and unprofitable waste, if covered with trees would rival the glen of the Downs or the Scalp and attract the admirers of nature in her beautiful mood from the most distant provinces. To effect this must be the work of the proprietor. What a laudable appropriation of the revenues of an extensive estate to bestow a certain portion of its own produce on the beautifying it, which, whilst it excited an interest in the breast of the owner which he could scarcely otherwise acquire, would amply remunerate him for his expenditure.

PRODUCTIVE ECONOMY

Rents and Lord Abercorn's Estates

(11th) The town parks of Strabane are now let at the reduced rent of 5 pounds or 5 guineas per acre. In the interior, 2 guineas is considered a rack rent at present, though a few years since farms on Lord Abercorn's estate at that rent, when offered for sale, yielded large sums as fines to the owners, whilst at present tenants on the very best lands which bear near this rent are unable to stand their ground. However, a liberal reduction is about to take place over the extensive estates of that nobleman in the country, and it is to be hoped that much of the prosperity and comfort which spread itself in former times over his manors, but which has of late fled, will again return, and a tenantry, the most remarkable of any in Ireland for attachment to their landlord and obedience to the laws, be restored to that interest in the soil and that share of independence which their honest industry so well merits. Until this take place, we cannot expect to see much improvement in this part of the country. In proportion to the quality of the soil and the distance from Strabane, which I may call our capital, the rent decreases from 2 guineas to 5s per acre. Mountain land is valued by the number of cattle it is known to feed, and the price of grazing varies with the quantity of stock.

(12th) Mr Sinclair gets 6 guineas an acre for his turf bog, but his tenants are not charged with it. Lord Abercorn's bogs are less convenient to Strabane and consequently have a lower rent. His tenants till lately paid for their bog in proportion to their rents, 1s in the pound.

Improved Farming Techniques

(13th) The Scotch plough has of late years been much used. Drill potatoes are also spreading over the country. Clovers are partially sown by the better description of farmers. Turnips have been long cultivated with much success by Mr Sinclair and Mr Brownlow. Carts have quite superseded the use of the low back car. The value of irrigation has been satisfactorily evinced both at Holyhill and on the glebe. Extensive growers of flax break it with a stone. Winnowing machines and rollers are duly estimated, and in the hands of some besides our gentry, and in short, the happy effects of the good examples set by our solitary resident proprietor and the present incumbent, who display both skill and taste for farming, are daily evinced in the adoption of their principles by their neighbours, which is the strongest encouragement that can be offered to the North West of Ireland Agricultural Society to persevere in their most laudable undertaking.

Fencing

(14th) Our fences need much improvement. The quickset fence is the best fence, least expensive, most ornamental and most permanent.

Employment

(15th) Employment is reasonably abundant here. There are 3 corn mills in this parish, which afford employment to many persons who purchase grain in Strabane market, manufacture it into meal for sale and thus earn a livelihood. Our bleach green engages 40 or 50 hands. A paper mill employs a few, flax mills a few also. Mr Sinclair and Mr Brownlow maintain each a number of labourers. Holyhill mountain affords a good deal of labour in providing turf for Strabane and Lifford and their neighbourhoods, and the proximity of Strabane itself yields employment to some of the Leckpatrick peasantry. Weaving is much followed here, so that perhaps it may be said that this parish has its full share of labour. Spinning linen yarn occupies the women, of late an unprofitable trade, and young boys and girls in industrious families have their share in advancing the staple manufacture of our country, by filling quills and such like employment. The prosperity is not, however, commensurate in many instances with the exertions made, as many of the weavers, not having a sufficient capital to keep their looms going on their own account, are obliged either to obtain yarn on credit at an advanced price, or to work for others at the rate of 1s for each penny that the web sells for per yard; which, since the reduction in the price of linen cloth, leaves them little for their labour in comparison of what they might earn were they able to purchase yarn, as a web sold for 13d a yard pays the weaver but so many shillings for weaving. During winter, labourers here, as in most places, are most easily had.

(16th) Farmers pay labourers living in their houses from 3 to 4 guineas a year. Daily labourers get generally 1s per diem piece work. It is impossible to state the exact value of [blank].

Crops

(17th) The introduction or rather the extension of green crops is perhaps the most necessary and useful improvement that could be suggested for this parish. The soil is peculiarly adapted for turnips and clover, being of a dry gravelly nature, ill-suited for permanent pasture, being inclined to fog where more than 2 or 3 years lea, and requiring the aid of these crops, both as food for the cattle and as a means of fertilizing a soil exhausted by too frequent tilling. A want of meadow is a further necessity for the growing of clover and turnips, and were all the reasons which appear for this change in our husbandry to be given, they would be multiplied to infinity. Suffice it to say that I conceive we never can expect to see agriculture attended with much profit here, the cattle well fed or abundant crops raised, until each farmer grows his patch of turnips in proportion to the extent of his holding, and lays down his potato land regularly with clover.

(18th) The best of our farmers sow artificial grasses. The rye grass and timothy are the most esteemed; the former is adapted to dry lands, the latter to low grounds that admit of irrigation.

Drains

(19th) The greater part of this parish is very dry, not requiring much draining, but in many instances that it would prove useful, it is very insufficiently executed. Surface drains are the most general.

Manure

(20th) Composts of bog and clay, where the bog can be had, mixed with lime is used as manure, and on our dry hills affords good potatoes, but do not enrich the soil much for future crops. Clay has been burned by Mr Sinclair. In lands having a certain portion of moss, it is usual to dig a furrow out of each ridge, the sods of which are burned for manure. Clay requires to be burned after the manner of brick kilns, the sods barely being placed in heaps. Ashes are particularly good for turnip crops and grasslands. Lime is useful for all soils and is used very generally by all industrious farmers.

Irrigation

(21st) Mr Sinclair and Mr Brownlow have watered their meadows with great success. Any other irrigation is imperfect and but partial.

Dairies

(22nd) No dairies here, but if established and the necessary care and attention paid to the improvement of the stock and the providing different food for the cattle, there is little doubt of their proving successful. The great population would afford a ready market for the milk and butter [which] bear at present the best price of any agricultural produce.

Oxen

(23rd) Few oxen have been used in husbandry, and these only by Mr Sinclair: it would seem the description of cattle best suited to small farms, as being most easily fed; but the Irishman likes to have his horse to ride as well as to work.

Spade Husbandry

(24th) Spade husbandry is only practised in wet lands and in the cultivation of potatoes.

Crops

(25th) Barley, oats, wheat. I have seen rye, but it is a scarce crop. As to price, the Strabane market, which is our standard, is generally as high as any in Ireland.

Land Measurement

(26th) On Lord Abercorn's estate the plantation acre is given; the bishop lands, glebe and all others have the Cunningham or Scotch measure.

Livestock

(27th) The general description of stock here is indifferent: the scanty pastures do not allow of large kinds. Of late, the Ayrshire breed has been introduced and appears well suited to the soil.

(28th) The young cattle reared in the cultivated lands are sent in summer to graze on the mountain pasture.

(29th) Except in the mountains there are few sheep: the narrow bounds and bad fences form a strong objection to the introduction of that stock. Those we have are of a small size, but well adapted to the soil they are fed on.

(30th) The farming horses are of a diminutive size, what may be termed hacknies. There are few, if any, good horses bred in this parish, but under the present arrangement of farms little improvement can be expected. The number of them is perhaps the greatest cause of complaint, as every landholder deems a horse indispensable, and thus an expensive and unproductive stock consumes a vast proportion of the produce.

(31st) The swinish multitude are of various descriptions, and though few of the most improved breeds, yet many very excellent. They are of the middle size, long-eared.

(32nd) I find it impossible to give an exact answer to this query, but the general description of the parish, the appropriation of the soil may assist in forming a tolerably correct view of both the nature and number of the stock. Before any material improvement can be effected in either the number or quality of the stock, the system of cultivation must in a great degree be changed, additional and better food must be obtained, to effect which the introduction of clover and green crops is indispensable. To bring this about, fences are required, additional capital must be brought into action both to raise the crops and afterwards to obtain cattle to consume them.

(33rd) I cannot, generally speaking, state any [improvements in stock].

Rivers and Fish

(34th) The Foyle forms the western boundary of the parish, the Burndanet the northern, the Glenmorning running from east to west intersects it. It has Moorlough, a mountain lake, on its southern limb and Lough Neagh on its western. The Foyle affords excellent salmon and sea trout, the Burndanet bog trout, Moorlough bog trout and Lough Neagh eels.

Minerals and Mines

(35th) I know of no mines ever having been worked here. Iron displays itself in many of our mountain streams.

(36th) There are limestone quarries in Holyhill and Glenmorning, situations peculiarly well adapted for the improvement of the surrounding soil. There are quarries of stone in various places, but not deserving particular description. There can be no export of them from this.

(37th) The limestone is of a blue colour, hard, burned in arched kilns and sometimes in what is termed pot kilns. It is broken into small portions and put into the kilns in alternate layers with turf. It is of a reasonably good quality generally, though not of the best. The present price is from 10d to 1s per barrel.

(38th) No coal mines here.

(39th) No mineral springs here.

(40th) Marl has been found on the glebe of an argillaceous nature. It has yet been little used, but its existence is ascertained.

SOCIAL AND PRODUCTIVE ECONOMY

Habits of the People

(41st) The inhabitants are remarkable for good order, temperate habits and friendly dispositions. The upper class of farmers live comfortably and display a taste for decency in the interior of their houses. The outside is generally less attended to. The more humble present various shades for description, many of those also maintaining a decent appearance whilst some of them have everything indicative of poverty. A very great improvement might be effected in the dwellings of the poor at a moderate expense. Most of those who are not themselves landholders rent their cabins under the condition of having them kept in order by the farmer from whom they hold.

A desire of raising an income induces farmers in situations favourable to cottiers (that is near bogs and water, as these cottiers are in general weavers) to multiply cabins to such an extent as entirely precludes the possibility of the landlord fulfilling his part of the agreement. All the straw on the farm would not in many instances be sufficient to thatch the cottiers' houses. For this there are many other uses, and of course the poor cottier must bear a share of the inconvenience and be well satisfied with a half-thatched house. As to lime inside or out on these farmed out abodes, it is never thought of, and by this means our country hamlets generally present a most impoverished appearance. This evil might be obviated by the lord of the soil withholding turf bog from every cabin that was not kept in tenantable repair.

Turf is the greatest object with these people in taking such habitations. The landholder obtains his rent for the hut by being able to accommodate it with bog and, fulfilling this part of the contract at the expense of the proprietor of the soil, he is little anxious about any other conditions promised by him. This is a crying evil and demands immediate interference.

Occupations of the People

[42nd] Habits of industry prevail very generally. Without a reasonable share of exertion, existence would be impossible here. Weaving occupies probably one-half of the male population. In the spring and harvest these hands are applied to the labours of agriculture, and when employment is withdrawn from that source they return to their looms. In proportion to their success in life they generally extend their comforts. Those who become independent like to have their families well dressed and comfortable, and usually give evidence of their prosperity by the smartness of their appearance. A greater taste for dress displays itself amongst the lower classes than for domestic comforts. More money is expended on their backs than on their dwellings. The one requires regular care, attention and steady habits of order, which as yet have made but a moderate progress here, so far as relates to domestic arrangements, whilst the Saturday night's labour cuts a great figure on the Sunday morning. The replies to these last queries embrace a general description of both farmers and cottiers, the last most particularly as being the most numerous.

Fuel

(43rd) Turf forms the exclusive fuel of this parish. It is reasonably abundant and consequently cheap. From 2 to 3 pounds is the average value of turf by the hundred on Lord Abercorn's mountains, the hundred consisting of 240 barrels each 3 cubic feet. On Mr Sinclair's bog, being nearer to Strabane, it is dearer.

Food

(44th) Meal is much used here, potatoes of course. The farmers have milk and butter; little of the latter is sent to market from this parish. Those who hold 8 or 10 acres of good land usually kill a pig or two and buy a cow or part of a cow at November, particularly if they have a loom or two at work, but the consumption of turf amongst the farmers is sadly diminished of late years, nor do we discern any prospect of amendment.

Farmers and Weavers

(45th) Here we can scarcely distinguish between the farmers and manufacturers. They are a mixed race, participating in the nature of both and resembling each other in habits and enjoyments. The manufacturer, by which I mean the weaver, that can employ himself with his own capital is generally as well off as the farmer and lives as well. The farmer seldom trusts altogether to the profits of his land, but usually calls in the aid of the loom.

Labourers and Poor

(46th) The poor and labourers live on meal and potatoes. Milk with them is very scarce, butcher's meat quite a rarity, herrings and salt delicacies. The weaver who has not capital to employ himself but trusts to others for work, is worse off than the labourer. The profits of his trade are small, his employment uncertain, his health often indifferent and his condition, upon the whole, such as needs amelioration. In all mention of poor, it is to be understood that only the industrious resident poor are meant, not itinerants or beggars.

Education

(47th) A very general wish for education does prevail, and as far as the means of the people allow, education has spread. Poverty appears the only barrier to it. Popular opinion is with it. A spirit of inquiry is abroad. The Scriptures are in the hands of most people. Their very pursuits render a certain degree of education necessary: buying and selling cloth and yarn constantly, a knowledge of arithmetic is required, and a weaver can calculate his 7d 3 farthings or his 15d 3 farthings a day for his 52 or his 102 yards as accurately as the merchant who purchases it. The upper class of farmers are particularly intelligent. The learned languages are little studied, except by those designed for the learned professions, so that the description of education is pretty nearly alike. It is the extension of it which constitutes the difference.

(48th) The schools here only teach writing, arithmetic and English, the charge for which is from 7s to 2s per quarter according to the progress of the scholar and the acquirements of the teacher. Mr Sinclair has established a school on the foundation of the London Hibernian Society on his estate. Mr Brownlow gives a salary to the parish schoolmaster. The other schools, which are 5 or 6 in number, derive their entire support from the pupils, which in some instances is a very precarious one. A school on the foundation of Erasmus Smith was about to be erected on the glebe a few years since, but the grant by some mismanagement was withdrawn and has never been renewed, and

Parish of Leckpatrick

perhaps there are few situations better suited or more in need of such an establishment than this parish.

(49th) Habits of decency and order are observable amongst the children of the poor who are educated, foreign from those who are uneducated. The one is the rational accountable being, the other the idle mischievous and inconsiderate creature who, from want of proper employment, is constantly engaged in either what is useless or wicked.

Diseases

(50th) This is a most healthy district. A dry soil and a fine climate contribute to the salubrity of the inhabitants. Rheumatism is the prevailing disease, occasioned partly by damp ill-thatched houses amongst the poor and amongst the weavers, who suffer mostly from this cause from the looms being sunk in the ground and requiring a certain degree of dampness to make the yarn work properly.

Savings Bank

(51st) We have no friendly societies. A savings bank has been lately established in Strabane, the advantages resulting from which are yet but partially felt. However, it is to be hoped that as its principles are better understood the labouring classes will avail themselves of its benevolent intention. There is no institution more likely to improve good habits and stimulate industry than this. Independence is the best foundation for moral principle, and to obtain independence by our own exertions is the most laudable and useful exertion of our ambition. This country is particularly in need of a savings bank. When provisions are cheap and the linen trade productive, all persons engaged in it have something to lay up. The difficulty of disposing of this safely and to advantage makes them less frugal and money is often squandered which probably the succeeding year would have greatly needed.

Ballymagorry Village

(52nd) Ballymagorry, an inconsiderable village, having 2 fairs and no market, is the principal town, but this parish enjoys the advantage of having Strabane immediately on its frontier.

PRODUCTIVE ECONOMY

Remarks about Industry

(53rd) The inhabitants of Leckpatrick are well qualified for being benefitted by any exertions which may be used for the improvement of their condition in any way. They are a sensible tractable race of people, capable of receiving instruction and willing to receive it. For the most part they are very deficient in the science of agriculture, and it will require considerable exertion and some time to effect any material improvement. New fences are to be erected. Farms are, whenever this can, to be enlarged, green crops and clover to be introduced. Farmhouses also need much improvement, farming implements are yet imperfect and what is more to be lamented, all these complicated ills generally attach to the poorest of our farmers, who require something more than precept to lead them into the right way and upon whom their present methods of farming must for ever entail poverty. I think it may safely be stated that amongst the lower class of farmers more than one-half of the corn ground fails of paying the expense of seed, labour and rent.

(54th) I need scarcely mention Mr Sinclair and Mr Brownlow, Mr Andrew Austin, Milltown, Mr Robert McCrea, Leck and Mr James McCrea, Farmhill, [who] are all active intelligent farmers.

Linen Manufactory

(55th) The linen is our only manufacture. It appears to hold its ground, notwithstanding that times have been rather unfavourable latterly. The weaver with his own capital can make good wages, but if dependent upon others for employment, is ill-paid. However, an excessive population must have recourse to every means of employment. The spinner of late years is ill-paid, as shall appear hereafter.

(56th) We have 1 bleach green, which can finish from 8 to 10,000 pieces of linen annually.

Preparation of Flax

(57th) The flax is generally sown after corn, usually the second crop of corn after potatoes. The ground undergoes 2 and sometimes 3 ploughings. It is commonly hinted and shovelled. A considerable quantity is sold for export in Strabane and Derry, though much is also spun at home. Of late, little flax has been saved.

(58th) Fire is used in drying flax. Extensive growers break it with a stone, turned by a horse, as in a bark mill: almost invariably it is scutched at the mill.

Linen Yarn

(59th) Warp yarn is spun from 2 hanks, 8 cuts to 3 hanks for the pound; wefts from spangle to 5 hank yarns. The greater part of this latter, however, is bought in the Letterkenny market. The coarser kind is principally spun here.

(60th) The fine yarn averages 2s 7d a spangle, the coarse 2s 2d. A hank is considered the labour of a day, which at once shows the wages, allowing 8d ha'penny per pound, the present price of clean flax.

(61st) Most of the spinners purchase their flax.

Spinning Wheels

(62nd) The double wheel has made its way here; two or three of our most respectable farmers' daughters have got them, but there does not appear a general wish to adopt them or a conviction of their being better than the common wheel. I can, however, only give the opinion of those I have conversed with on the subject, and, as in all matters connected with any new improvement, it admits of a diversity of opinion.

Preparation for Weaving

(63rd) The manufacturer is obliged to prepare the yarn for the loom after purchasing it, which occasions considerable loss of time and costs 2s 2d for each web besides the fire for boiling, the labour of bleaching and a scald.

(64th) No yarn greens here, but from what is reported of such establishments elsewhere, there is every reason for thinking they would prove useful.

(65th) The Coleraine is the description of linen made here, price from 1s to 1s 4d per yard, Strabane, the principal market. The fine webs go to Derry.

Woollen Manufacture

(66th) In answering this and the 4 following queries, we have to regret that so little remains for us to say. The woollen manufacture can scarcely be said to exist here, beyond the making of a few stockings for home consumption. The yarn for these is spun on the small wheel and the whole process conducted on the worst principles. There can be no doubt but the introduction of wool spinning would benefit this country. The wages earned elsewhere by it far exceeds that our spinners of linen yarn can earn. Were our peasants even to make their own clothes <cloths>, they would find the advantage of it. One suit made at home would wear as long as two bought in the shops, and it would be obtained more easily as their own labour would constitute the principal part of the expenditure. I conceive measures should be adapted for its introduction. The sheep are never shorn more than once in the year.

Cotton Manufacture

(71st and 72nd) There is no cotton manufacture here.

Kelp

(73rd, 74th and 75th) No kelp.

Fisheries

The answers on this subject may be compressed under 1 head. Our only fishery is the salmon in the Foyle, in which but a few small boats are employed and the produce of which is disposed of in the Strabane market and [sold ?] to carriers. It is not an object which can well be brought under the consideration of the public.

Memoir Writing

Memoir Writing

In answering these queries, it has been my wish to confine myself as much as possible to the questions asked and to adapt the answers more to the general situation of things and persons than to particulars. A more pleasing picture might have been delineated had a different plan been pursued, but knowing that the object of the North West of Ireland Agricultural Society was to stimulate to industry and promote improvement where indolence and mismanagement prevailed, I have endeavoured to give a correct though hasty outline of the habits and customs of this small district, which probably for its extent affords as promising a field for the benevolent intentions of an enlightened society to commence their labours in as any other. Any further communication I can at all be useful in making, I shall be most ready to give. I have the honour to be, Sir, your very obedient humble servant, George D. Mansfield, 8th October 1821. Letter containing answers to queries proposed by the North West of Ireland Agricultural Society, and addressed to W. Marshall Esquire.

Parish of Longfield (West), County Tyrone

Draft Memoir, with Letter to J.R. Ward

Natural Features

Hills

The northern, southern and western parts of this parish are very mountainous and wild. The principal hills are Dooish, Carrick-a-stoken and Bin. The first of these is 1,119 feet above the level of the sea, the second is 909 feet and the third 1,097 feet. They are all connected with each other and form the termination of the Donegal mountains. The only general name I could find they are known by is that of the Longfield hills.

Glens

There are several picturesque and wild glens in this parish. The principal ones are Carrick-a-ness, which is situated 2 miles to the west of the town of Drumquin and which contains no less than 4 small waterfalls within the space of 200 yards, the total fall of the water in that space being 50 feet.

The other glen is situated 3 and a half miles to the west of Drumquin and is called Slevin glen. In it there are 2 waterfalls, which, combined with a ruined bridge and the wildness of the glen, have a very picturesque effect.

Rivers

The streams of any note in this parish are the Fairy water and the Drumquin water. The Fairy water forms the boundary of the parish on the north eastern side for 4 miles, and as far as regards this part of it runs through very flat bog. It flows south east and averages from 30 to 40 feet in breadth. The depth in some parts is considerable, owing to its flowing through a flat boggy country. It rises in the adjacent parish of the Skirts of Ardstraw. It is not useful for water power. There are no falls or rapids on it; the fall in this parish is 10 feet in a mile. It is subject to floods which soon subside; they do no harm. This river impedes communication and flows over a gravelly bed. Its banks in this parish are boggy and uncultivated.

The Drumquin water takes its rise in the Loughs Lee and Bradan. Its length in the parish is 7 miles when it joins the Fairy water. The source of this water is nearly 1,000 feet above the level of the sea. Its branches abound in small waterfalls. By the time it joins the Fairy water its breadth is nearly 40 feet. At this part its depth is considerable, in consequence of the ground being very level. The general direction of this stream is north east, it is not liable to overflow, its bed is rocky. For account of the falls, see Natural Features.

Springs

The parish is well supplied with water from springs. There is, if anything, too much water. There are no chalybeate wells.

Lakes and Tradition

The principal lakes in this parish are Lough Bradan, Lough Lee and Lough Corr. Lough Bradan contains 50 acres of water, is 636 feet above the level of the sea [and] is situated in the south west part of the parish. Its depth is unknown. Its greatest length is 35 chains and breadth 19 chains. The shores of it are very soft and boggy and it is surrounded by hills. It contains some large black trout. I met with a country man who told me that when he and another man were on the shore one day fishing, they perceived an animal about the size of a sheep swimming towards them; but they not relishing such suspicious company took to their heels and saw no more of it. No other persons have seen this stranger, but the lough has the reputation of containing wild horses, as has also Lough Lee, which is situated on the north east boundary of the parish. Its length is half an English mile and its breadth 14 chains. Its shores are rocky, and there is a fine white sand procured from it which is used for sharpening scythes and for scouring. Only the half of the Lough Lee is in West Longfield parish. The other half is in the parish of the Skirts of Urney and Ardstraw. The part which is in this parish consists of 24 and a half acres. Lough Lee is situated at the great height of 964 feet above the level of the sea. Like Lough Bradan it is nearly surrounded by hills.

Lough Anagh is situated about a mile to the south of Lough Bradan. It contains 17 acres 1 rood 20 perches. It is 18 chains long and 14 chains broad and is 500 feet above the level of the sea. The depth of none of the above lakes is known.

Lough Lack is situated in the west of the parish, the boundary running through the centre. It contains 45 acres 1 rood 28 perches and is 750 feet above the level of the sea.

Woods

Meencargagh wood is the remains of a large tract which existed in this parish about 60 years since.

It is situated in Meencargagh townland and is in extent about 40 acres. The trees (which are small) principally consist of birch and holly, with a few oak and ash.

Bogs

All the mountains (or at least the greater part) in this parish are covered with bog, and there is also a great quantity of bog in the flat lands in the north eastern part. There is but little timber found in the bogs. It is principally oak and appears to have been blown down, as all the trunks [are] horizontally laid in a south eastern direction, with the roots to the north west. The prevailing and most violent winds are from the north west.

The depth of the bogs vary from 2 to probably 20 feet. In the neighbourhood of Lough Bradan there is a large flow bog (called by the peasantry a "scraw") which is very dangerous, as the turf which forms the crust of it is apt to break through on any person passing over it. Cattle are sometimes lost in this bog. In the bogs in the lower part of the parish there are islands of hard ground. They are all cultivated if they are capable of bearing crops.

Climate

In consequence of the hilly nature of this parish, the climate is very moist, both in the high and lowlands.

Modern Topography

Gentlemen's Residence

West Longfield Glebe House, the residence of the Reverend Gilbert King, is the only gentleman's residence in the parish. It is situated three-quarters of a mile to the west of the town of Drumquin. There is nothing remarkable in its appearance. It is a plain but large whitewashed building of an oblong form, with a good quantum of fir trees about it.

Social Economy

Local Government

Mr King (the Reverend Gilbert King, see above) is the only magistrate in West Longfield. He is not stipendiary, is firm and respected by the people. The police both of the revenue and constabulary for this parish, are stationed in the town of Drumquin (vide East Longfield). There are not any petty sessions, the inhabitants generally attending those of the town of Omagh. There are no legal disputes about rights of land. Now and then outrages occur, such as burning turf stacks and waylaying and beating persons at night, but nothing of a more serious character. They are, however, perhaps rather on the increase. Illicit distillation was carried on to a large extent a few years ago, but the revenue police have now fairly hunted it away.

Modern Topography

Mills

The following are the mills in the parish [table]: Drumowen, breast wheel, 14 feet by 1 foot 8 inches, corn mill, belongs to James Johnston.

Coolavannagh, breast wheel, 12 feet by 1 foot 6 inches, corn mill, belongs to Robert Brodley.

Communications

The only road of consequence passing through the parish is the road from Londonderry to Enniskillen, and which runs through Drumquin. Its length in the parish is 8 miles, its average breadth 27 feet. It is an excellent road. All the rest of the roads in the parish are execrable. 20 years ago there were not 4 carts in the whole parish.

There is a very bad road leading from Drumquin to Irvinestown. At one part it rises to the height of 900 feet (or nearly so) above the level of the sea.

Social Economy

Schools

[Table contains the following headings: name, situation and description, when established, income and expenditure, physical, intellectual and moral education, number of pupils subdivided by age, sex and religion, name and religious persuasion of master or mistress].

London Hibernian Society school, 1 mile to the west of Drumquin, established 1825; income: Reverend G. King give 3 guineas per annum and a dwelling house, from pupils 1s a quarter; physical education: rod; intellectual education: Dublin Society books, testaments; moral education: a Sunday school held; number of pupils: 80 males, 40 females, 120 total pupils, 80 Protestants, 40 Roman Catholics; master John Rogers, Presbyterian.

Bomacatall, on the roadside between Drumquin and Castlederg, a neat cottage 22 feet by 14 feet, established 1817; income: from the London Hibernian Society 12 pounds 12s per annum, from pupils 4 pounds per annum; expenditure none; physical education: not understood; intellectual education: books furnished by the Sunday School Society; moral education: the Reverend G. King,

Parish of Longfield (West)

rector, visits for the purpose of hearing catechism; the Bible is mostly read; number of pupils: males, 24 under 10 years of age, 38 from 10 to 15, 10 above 15, 72 total males; females, 16 under 10 years of age, 32 from 10 to 15, 3 above 15, 51 total females; 123 total number of pupils, 50 Protestants, 40 Presbyterians, 33 Roman Catholics; master Samuel Phillips, Protestant.

Friendly Society

There is a society called the Friendly Society in this parish, from which the poor receive a great deal of assistance.

Habits of the People

The dress worn by the inhabitants differs in no respect from that of the surrounding parishes, and there are no remarkable peculiarities in it. Their diet consists principally of potatoes and porridge made of oatmeal, and sometimes their dinner is varied by the addition of a little bacon and greens, or oatmeal cake. Their manners are generally civil and obliging. They complain much of the short leases and high rents, and with justice, if we may judge from the squalid and poverty-stricken appearance of many of them. The farms average about 10 acres, the rent 1 pound an acre.

MODERN TOPOGRAPHY

General Appearance and Scenery

The general appearance of West Longfield in the western and southern parts is very wild, and there is little wanting but trees to render it highly picturesque. Indeed there is a great scarcity of wood in the whole parish, with the exception of the plantations at the Glebe House and Meencargagh wood. The eastern part of the parish partakes of that hillocky appearance which pervades the whole of the lowlands of Tyrone.

PRODUCTIVE ECONOMY

Crops

Neither barley nor wheat are grown in this parish. Oats are sown in March and April and cut in September. Potatoes are put down in May and taken up in November. Hay is cut in August. Crops are rather worse than the surrounding parishes.

MODERN TOPOGRAPHY

Towns

There is no town in this parish, but on the western boundary of it, in the parish of East Longfield, lies the village of Drumquin, for account of which see parish of East Longfield.

Church

West Longfield parish church is situated 1 mile to the west of the town of Drumquin. The rector is the Reverend Gilbert King. The average attendance is 200 persons and the total congregation 1,128 persons. The building is very small and plain. It has no steeple [and] is 65 feet long and [blank] feet broad. It was repaired about 12 years ago at a cost of 20 pounds. The church will accommodate 300 persons. The Dissenters attend divine worship in the parish of East Longfield.

Roman Catholic Chapel

A Roman Catholic chapel, situated in Dooish townland, is a neat stone building, roughcast and whitewashed. It was built in 1831; the expense of 800 pounds was defrayed by voluntary subscriptions. The average attendance on each Sunday is from 1,000 to 1,200 persons. [Insert] Note concerning Roman Catholic chapel: The congregation amounting to so great an average as 1,200 persons is accounted for by the fact that this chapel is attended by the Roman Catholic population of both East and West Longfield parishes.

SOCIAL ECONOMY

Poor

The only provision for the poor is the money that is collected in church on Sundays. This money is distributed at Easter and amounts to 3s or 4s a head.

Religion and Character of the People

Three-fourths of the inhabitants are Catholics. The remainder are for the most part Episcopalians. There are a few Presbyterians. The people in this parish are very civil and obliging, whereas if you proceed 4 miles northwards you will meet with a very uncouth race. The former are mostly Catholics, the latter Presbyterians. The former are, however, very often dishonest and insincere, the latter on the contrary are mostly upright men. Both parties are very superstitious.

Poems

Regarding poems, there is a peculiarity worthy of note here. The country people have often 2 versions for most of the popular songs, for instance Scott's poem of "Young Lochinvar" is metamorphosed into some abominable doggerel called "Green Sleeves!" I need hardly add that with them the doggerel is the favourite, and in many cases entirely supersedes the original.

Emigration

Emigration prevails here with both old and young. Spring is the season chosen.

Letter concerning Roman Catholic Chapel

[On cover] J.Rodrigo Ward Esquire, Post Office, Drumquin.

Sir, The chapel of Longfield was built in the year 1831. As it was built before I came to the parish, and as the work was not done by contract, I am not certain as to its cost. People, however, tell me that the expenses amounted to upwards of 800 pounds, paid by voluntary subscription. The average attendance at morning mass is 200, at the 12 o'clock mass from 10 to 1,200. The chapel is for the accommodation of the Catholics of both the Longfields. The Catholic population of West Longfield is 2,843. I have the honour to remain, Sir, your humble servant, Francis McHugh.

Parish of Longfield (East)

Parish of Longfield (East), County Tyrone

Statistical Report by Lieutenant William Lancey, 20th November 1834

NATURAL STATE

Situation and Extent

The parish of East Longfield is situated in the barony of Omagh, county Tyrone and diocese of Derry. It is surrounded by West Longfield, Ardstraw, Drumragh and Dromore. It contains 9,716 statute acres and lies 3 and a half miles west of Omagh and 4 south west of Newtownstewart, which are the principal outlets for its produce.

NATURAL FEATURES

General Appearance

Its general appearance is unpromising. The mountain of Corridinna towards the south, tracts of bog in the north, with numerous patches of rough stoney ground in various places, render East Longfield the least fertile parish in my part of Tyrone. In passing through it from Omagh to Drumquin, the best parts of it are crossed, but as a great deal of it lies on sandstone beds, vegetation does not flourish to any extent.

Hills

Corridinna is the only high ground in the parish.

Rivers

The Fairy water, dividing it from Ardstraw, is the chief stream, and a small river running through Drumquin separates it from West Longfield.

Loughs

There are 2 loughs in Claraghmore connected by a small drain.

MODERN TOPOGRAPHY

Principal Buildings: Parish Church

The parish church is a modern building erected in 1803, and on the direction of the Reverend F. Gauldsbury at an expense of 500 pounds. It has no gallery and is capable of holding 170 persons. A bell was placed in its tower in 1833.

Meeting House

A meeting house stands in the village of Drumquin, belonging to the Synod of Ulster.

Roman Catholic Chapel

A Roman Catholic chapel was erected in 1831 under the superintendence of priests Starrs and McAleer, at a probable cost of 600 pounds. It is not fitted up with galleries and can at present hold 800 persons.

Glebe House

The Glebe House was built by the Reverend Francis Gauldsbury in 1801 and cost 950 pounds. It is well situated in the best land in the parish and commands an interesting view.

Gentlemen's Seats

Drumrawn Lodge was erected by Mr James Boyle in the year 1808 at about 160 pounds expense. It is scarcely better than a farmhouse.

Burn's Folly was built in 1779 and cost Mr Robert Sproul about 350 pounds. A new range of offices was added in 1832 by the present proprietor, Mr Edward Sproul, which cost 200 pounds.

Village of Drumquin

The village of Drumquin is partly in East and partly in West Longfield. It is a poor-looking place, the houses mean and out of repair. It has a weekly market on Thursdays and a daily foot post, but has no trade to enrich it. Quarterly cattle fairs, to which English dealers resort, are the principal means of circulating money in Drumquin.

Farmhouses

There are a few good farmhouses and a number of poor cabins in the parish. They are built of stone, are all thatched and usually whitewashed.

SOCIAL ECONOMY

Religion

The inhabitants are generally poor, but a few possess independence. They are in a lamentable state of ignorance respecting religion. No parish has been more neglected by its ministers. Until lately part of the parish church has been used for a barn, and divine service very irregularly performed. The Presbyterians are little better taught than those of the Established Church. The Protestant places of worship and the Bible are much neglected in East Longfield.

Dress and Food

Their dress is indifferent and their food potatoes, meal, water and milk. No efforts appear to be made to improve them. Few migrate for harvest. The habits of the poor people respecting their houses are similar to all the adjacent parishes: dunghill at the doors, broken windows stuffed with straw, pigs, chickens and cows huddled together, the whole enveloped in smoke, are the chief characteristics of the cabins in East Longfield.

Schools

There are 4 schools situated in Drumnaforke, Dressog, Garvaghullion and Glebe, 3 of which are supported by the Kildare Street Association. These educate about 230 children. The sexes as usual sit together and the teachers do not reside on the premises. The terms of education are not known, but the usual rate in the neighbouring parishes is 2s 6d a quarter.

Dispensary

A dispensary common to the 2 parishes of Longfield is situated in the village of Drumquin. It is supported by annual voluntary subscription of about 33 pounds, with a presentment from the grand jury of 30 pounds. The number of patients amount on an average to 540, and the usual diseases are affections of the stomach proceeding chiefly from poverty of food, and rheumatism arising from wet damp cabins and want of proper clothing.

PRODUCTIVE ECONOMY

Farms

The land is generally let by the [?] take, in portions varying from 5 to 70 acres, but when let by the acre the rates vary from 5s to 30s, the average being 21s an acre. The principal crops consist of potatoes, corn, barley and flax. A little wheat is sown on the best lands. Oats in Claraghmore produce about 80 stones the English acre, flax from 2 to 4 pounds, potatoes 5 to 7 pounds and butter 2 pounds a firkin. A few iron ploughs are in use in the parish.

Manure

There is limestone in the Glebe, Magherny and 2 small bad quarries in Claraghmore, but the principal supply is obtained from Liggat's quarry in West Longfield, where it can be purchased at 5d a load. This mixed with farmyard compost forms their chief manure.

Cattle and Horses

Cattle are grazed in the mountain of Corridinna, but they are not celebrated for being of superior quality. Farmers named Nidderry have grazing farms and purchase and rear young cattle. If they do not sell them advantageously on the spot, they take them to England. Sometimes their drove amounts to 150 head. Mr Davis of Unchenagh also feeds young stock to some extent, and those who cannot stock their lands feed for others at the rate of 8s 4d a head for the summer. The prices of cattle are much the same here as at Omagh, varying from 3 pounds to 7 pounds. The horses in East Longfield are not better than the neighbouring parishes. There is no good breed around Omagh. All who require superior cattle go to the markets of Moy or Enniskillen. The general prices of horses in the parish run from 4 pounds to 12 pounds.

Sheep and Pigs

Sheep are not grazed in large numbers, but the common country kind can always be purchased at rates varying from 5 to 25s according to the quality. Pigs are plentiful and realize from 10 to 60s apiece.

Fish and Game

The fish are salmon, pike and trout; the game grouse, hares, snipe and partridge.

Fruit

There are 5 small orchards in East Longfield, 2 at Burn's Folly, 1 at the Glebe and 2 young ones in Legphressy. Common fruit is, however, to be obtained in the Omagh market at a very cheap rate during the season.

Mills and Manufacture

There are no mills in the parish. Linen cloth is the chief manufacture. It is made in the townlands of Coolkeeragh, Drumbarley, Dressog and Drumhonish, Legphressy, Mogherenny, Segully and Unchenagh, but not to any extent. The wages of the journeyman are much the same here as elsewhere, as they are regulated by the Omagh, Newtownstewart and Strabane markets. They earn from 12s to 20s in 10 days and they are generally better paid than those who grow the flax. Farm servants are hired at 3 pounds the half year and diet, day

Parish of Longfield (East)

labourers from 8d to 12d and women from 6d to 8d in summer.

MODERN TOPOGRAPHY

Roads

The leading crossroads which traverse this parish are from Omagh and Dromore and Fintona to Drumquin and are in tolerable repair. Some of the country roads are sufficiently bad, but those mentioned above are the only throughfares. Those principally repaired with freestone are usually dry.

NATURAL FEATURES

Woods and Plantations

There are the remains of a natural wood in Claraghmore, but it contains no timber, and there are 5 acres of good firs in Unchenagh, the property of Sir Robert Ferguson, and some planting at Drumrawn Lodge and Burn's Folly.

Fuel

Turf and bog wood are the only materials used as fuel in East Longfield. The former is plentiful, especially in Corridinna and the banks of the Fairy water.

Rocks

Gneiss, talc slate, mountain limestone, clay and micaceous sandstone are found in East Longfield. All abound, except limestone which is rather scarce. A basaltic dyke with crystals of felspar traverses the south end of the parish and runs to the north west through Dooish, and the south east through Drumragh and Donacavey parishes.

ANCIENT TOPOGRAPHY

Church

The ruins of an old church exist in Magherenny a little south of the mearing of the Glebe. Nothing remains but the trace of the walls. It stands in an old enclosure formerly used as a burial ground. There are no other vestiges of antiquity in East Longfield known to me. [Signed] William Lancey, Lieutenant Royal Engineers, 20th March 1834.

Parish of Longfield (Lower), County Tyrone

Replies to Queries of North West Society by Reverend Gilbert King, 3 September 1823

Natural Features

Situation and Description

Name of the parish is Lower Longfield, names [blank]. The soil is of a mixed nature: limestone, heavy clay and moory. There is a large tract of improvable mountain in this parish. There are 2 small rivers called the Black water and Fairy water. There are a few small lakes of no consequence. There are not many plantations. The parish is 25 miles from the sea coast.

Minerals

Section 2. There are coal mines, but I never heard of minerals. There are particularly fine limestone quarries, as also freestone and whin quarries.

Modern Topography

General Appearance

Section 3. We have neither modern buildings, towns, nor gentlemen's seats. The scenery is in parts romantic and picturesque, the roads are numerous but indifferent.

Ancient Topography

Castle and Church

Section 4. There is a ruin of an old castle called Kirlish. There is a parish church.

Social Economy

Habits of the People

Section 5. The principal food of the inhabitants is meal and potatoes. The better kinds of farmers eat flesh meat occasionally. The fuel is turf and bog fir. The poorer description of people are subject to stomach complaints proceeding from indigestion and bad quality of food, and the elderly people complain much of rheumatism.

Character and Customs of the People

Section 6. The inhabitants are naturally sharp and cunning, but for want of stimulus they become sloathful and listless. They all speak English, but [in] the mountain districts Irish is a good deal spoken. Their manners, from not having had much intercourse with the upper classes, are short and blunt. Those who belong to the Established Church bring their children to be christened in the church. The Presbyterian minister, I believe, generally goes to their houses, as does also the Roman Catholic priest. The custom of wakes is strictly practised in general. Funerals are numerously attended. There is nothing particular in their marriages.

Education

Section 7. There will soon be 7 excellent schoolhouses, and well attended by masters and children. The children are employed a good deal in winding quills for weavers, and in summer in herding, a most idle pernicious habit. These books have been supplied chiefly by the Kildare Place, Hibernian and Sunday School Societies.

Religion

Section 8. The religious establishment consists of the Church of England, Presbyterian and Roman Catholic. There is a church and a Catholic chapel in this parish. The meeting house is in the adjoining one. There is a probability that the tithe composition acts will come into operation here.

Productive Economy

Agriculture

Section 9. They have a very [blank] mode of agriculture. They use a great deal of manual labour, often digging the ground for the seed and trenching in the corn. Their usual mode of cropping is first potatoes, then flax, then 2 crops of oats, then "let out to rest", by which means the land is completely impoverished and casts up weeds. The houses are of a small indifferent description, cows the same. Sheep numerous, but small and bad quality. Pigs are of a middling quality. There is a monthly fair at the village of Drumquin, where there is also a very indifferent weekly market. The average rate of wages in spring and harvest is about 1s per day.

Trade

Section 10. The only trade here is the linen trade.
Section 11: blank.

Parish of Longfield (Lower)

SOCIAL ECONOMY

Improvements

Section 12. It is superfluous attempting to suggest every particular means for improving the condition of the poor. Here the whole system is a bad one and requires a radical reformation. Sir, I request you will have the goodness to submit the above remarks upon the state of this part of the country to the corresponding committee of the North West Society of Ireland. I hope they will be in time to be of any use in throwing even a glimmer of light upon the interesting subject they are engaged in, and wishing them every success in their patriotic labours. I have the honour <honor> to be Sir, your obedient servant, Gilbert King, rector, Lower Longfield. September 3 1823, Longfield Glebe, Omagh.

Parish of Skirts of Urney and Ardstraw, County Tyrone

Memoir by J. Rodrigo Ward, 1836

NATURAL FEATURES

Hills

The northern and southern parts of the parish are of a mountain character. The latter is the most elevated, the principal points being the Bin, 1097 feet, and Scraghy, 1,117 feet above the sea. The northern parts vary from 400 to 600 feet in height and fall gradually towards the Derg river, where the altitudes are from 165 to 140 feet. Between the Derg river and the Fairy water there is a range of cultivated hills, the principal of which are Garvetagh, Ardbane and Silver hill. The first is 628 feet, the second 589 feet and the latter 426 feet above the sea. The valley through which the Derg river runs is well cultivated and fertile. The Fairy water runs through a flat valley varying from 320 to 250 feet above the sea. The country rises rapidly on the southern side of the Bin and Scraghy mountains, those parts which are near the river being partly cultivated, but the coldness and rocky state of the ground scarce repay the farmer for his trouble. Within the memory of several of the inhabitants, all the lower part was uncultivated and there were but few houses except those in which herds lived.

Lakes

16 acres 1 rood of Lough Lee are in this parish, for particulars of which see Memoir of West Longfield parish.

Rivers

The Derg river flows through the north centre of the parish from west to east. Its breadth in it averages from 130 to 170 feet, and its depth from 1 to 10 feet. It takes its rise in the county Donegal. It is useful for drainage and water power. There are no falls or rapids in the parish. The average fall is not more than 10 feet in a mile. It is subject to floods which soon subside; they do no damage. The river impedes communication, its bed is gravelly, its banks are well cultivated but uninteresting.

The Fairy water rises in the south west of the parish in the townland of Binawooda, flows east and joins the south east boundary, along which it runs for 2 and a half miles. It averages in breadth from 10 to 20 feet and is very shallow. It is usefully situated for drainage and water power. There is a considerable fall on it from its source for the first mile, about 450 feet, forming in wet weather very pretty cascades. After that until it leaves the parish the fall is not more than 15 feet in a mile. The floods in this part of the river are very considerable. They occur mostly in November and April. The source of the Fairy water is 650 feet above the sea. It falls into the [blank] river, three-quarters of a mile north of Omagh, 15 miles from its source. The parish is well supplied with water from springs and rivulets. There are no mineral or hot springs.

Bogs

The mountains in the north and south of the parish are all boggy, and from them the inhabitants get their fuel. There is very little timber found in them. They average from 400 to 1,000 feet above the sea. The depth of the turf is from 3 to 10 feet. In the north west corner of the parish there is a large flow bog. Woods: none.

Climate and Crops

The climate of this parish is moist, and the valleys through which the Derg and Fairy rivers run are subject to dense fogs. The principal crops are oats, flax and potatoes. Oats are sown in May and cut in the beginning of September. Flax is sown in April and May and pulled in August and September. Potatoes are planted in May and dug in October and November. The mountains on the southern part are, from the coldness of the ground, a fortnight behind the central parts of the parish.

MODERN TOPOGRAPHY

Town of Castlederg

Castlederg, more generally called Derg or Dergbridge by the surrounding inhabitants, is 110 English miles by the mail road from Dublin, in about 54 degrees 40 minutes north latitude and 7 degrees 30 minutes west longitude. It runs nearly at right angles with the Derg river and is situated on the north side of it. The town consists of 1 street 360 yards in length and is well situated for retail trade. There is but little picturesque beauty in the surrounding country, which is in general fertile and well cultivated. There is an old castle in ruins on the west side of the town. It has been a square building with small square towers at each corner.

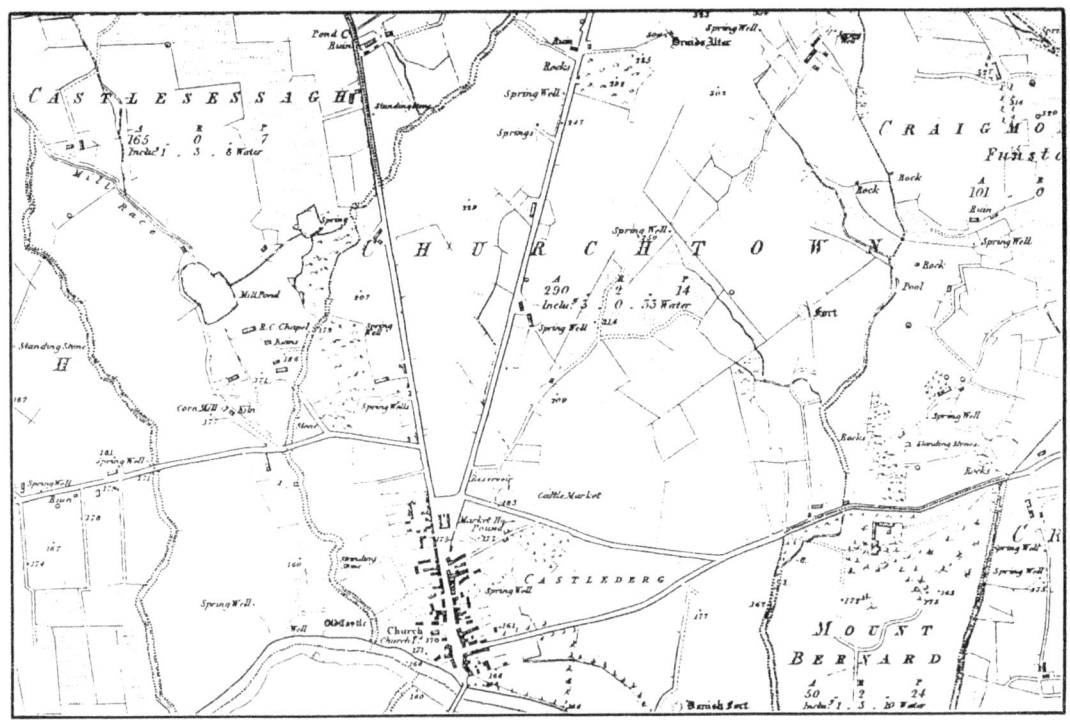

Map of Castlederg from the first 6" O.S. maps, 1830s

A few naked walls well loopholed are all that now stand of it.

Buildings in Castlederg

The only church in the parish is situated in the town. It is a plain stone building with a square tower and low steeple. It was rebuilt in 1735. The cost, which was paid by subscription, is not known. The body of the church is 56 feet long and 28 feet broad, and is neatly fitted up with pews, affording accommodation for 260 persons. The average attendance is 220.

The market place with a court house and police barrack attached to it was built in 1828 and cost 300 pounds, which was defrayed by Sir Robert Ferguson. The architect was Mr George Hagherty of Londonderry. There is but 1 street of any consideration in the town. There are 8 houses of 1-storey, 48 of 2 and 14 of 3-storeys; 33 of those are thatched, the remainder are slated. They have a neat and clean appearance. The town is supplied with water by means of pipes from a reservoir situated near the north end of it. This means of supply commenced in 1829 and cost 170 pounds, of which Sir Robert Ferguson paid 85 pounds. The remainder was paid by the inhabitants.

SOCIAL AND PRODUCTIVE ECONOMY

Fairs

On the first Friday in every month a fair is held, every other Friday being market day. The traffic on market day consists of grain, butter, eggs and soft goods; on fair days of cattle, horses, pigs and sheep. Sir R. Ferguson has given a large piece of ground free of toll for a cattle and pig market, and enclosed the same with a stone wall at his own expense.

Transport

Cars are to be had for hire in the town, the post car between it and Strabane being the only regular public conveyance. In summer it leaves Castlederg at 8 a.m. and returns at 4 p.m., in winter at 9 a.m. and 5 p.m. The town has been much improved in the last 10 years, and is still improving under a good landlord who does all he can for its good. For particulars of the dispensary, see [dispensary].

Table of Occupations

Apothecary 1, bakers 2, dyer 1, grocers 8, grocers and spirit dealers 6, grocers and general dealers 5, grocers and haberdashers 1, milliners 2, nailers 1, reed makers 3, shoemakers 2, smiths 1, spirit dealers 14, surgeons 2, tailors 2.

MODERN TOPOGRAPHY

Roman Catholic Chapels

Beside those public buildings which are mentioned as situated in Castlederg, there are 5 places of worship in the parish, viz. a Roman Catholic chapel situated in Castlesessagh townland. It was built about the year 1790. The expenses of the original building and subsequent addition are supposed to have amounted to 200 pounds. This sum was defrayed by the late Mr Gilly McHugh of Castlederg, who was afterwards remunerated by voluntary subscriptions. The length of the chapel is 80 feet and breadth 25 feet. It will accommodate about 500 persons. The average attendance is more than the chapel will accommodate.

A Roman Catholic chapel, situated in Carncorran Glebe, is a neat stone building 56 feet long and 24 broad. It was rebuilt in 1831 at an expense of [blank] pounds, which was defrayed by general subscription. It will accommodate 370 persons; the average attendance is 350.

Seceders Meeting House

A Seceders meeting house situated in Bridgetown is a plain stone building 36 feet long and 24 broad. It was erected in 1793. The cost, about 300 pounds, was defrayed by the congregation. It will accommodate 330 persons; the average attendance is 300 persons. It is styled Castlederg or Ballylennan meeting house.

Presbyterian Meeting House

Garvetagh Presbyterian meeting house, situated in Garvetagh townland close to the road between Drumquin and Castlederg, is a plain stone building 36 feet long and 28 broad. [It] is neatly fitted up with pews, affording accommodation for 350 persons. The average attendance is 180. The meeting house was built in 1792 and cost 450 pounds, raised by voluntary subscriptions.

Methodist Meeting House

A Methodist meeting house in Lisleen townland is a roughcast stone building 54 feet long and 24 broad. It was built in 1789; the cost is not known. It will accommodate 230 persons; the average attendance is 200.

Gentlemen's Seats

Mount Bernard, the residence of the Reverend Archibald Hamilton, rector of the parish, is situated about half a mile east of Castlederg near the Strabane road. The house was built in 1793 at an expense of 500 pounds, of which 150 pounds was granted by the Board of First Fruits. The remainder was defrayed by the incumbent.

Bleach Green and Mills

In Spa Mount townland there is a bleach green. The extent of it is varied according to the quantity of linen in progress.

[Table of mills contains the following headings: name of townland where situated, type of mill, dimensions and type of wheel].

Ballylennan, corn mill, 12 feet by 1 foot 10 inches, undershot.

Binawooda, corn mill, 12 feet by 2 feet, undershot.

Castlesessagh, corn mill, 12 feet by 1 foot 10 inches, undershot.

Coolnacrunaght, corn mill, 14 feet by 2 feet 3 inches, undershot.

Golan Sproul, corn mill, 12 feet by 1 foot 6 inches, undershot.

Spa Mount, beetling <beating> mill, 17 feet by 5 feet 6 inches, breast.

Spa Mount, beetling mill, 14 feet by 2 feet 10 inches, breast.

Spa Mount, washing and rubbing mill, 14 feet by 5 feet 6 inches, breast.

Communications

The parish is well intersected with roads, branching from Castlederg in all directions. The mail car road between Strabane and Castlederg traverses the parish north east for 1 and a half miles. Its average breadth is 28 feet. It is a well laid out road and in good repair.

The Castlefin road traverses from Castlederg almost due north for 3 miles, its breadth being 27 feet. It is in good repair.

The Castlederg and Drumquin road traverses the parish south east by south for 3 and a half miles. Its average breadth is 27 feet. This road is very hilly, but in tolerable repair.

The main road between Castlederg and Killeter and Donegal traverses south west for 2 miles and its breadth is 28 feet. It is well laid out and in good repair.

All the above roads were made at the expense of the barony and county, besides which there are a great quantity of useful by-roads in good repair.

Parish of Skirts of Urney and Ardstraw

Bridges

Castlederg bridge, at present building, is 168 feet long and the roadway will be 30 feet broad. It is to consist of 4 arches. At present only the piers are finished. [Insert note: the old bridge was taken down on account of its being too narrow and steep on each side. One of the stones taken out of it is said to have the year 1613 marked on it, but I could not find the stone]. The architect has contracted to build it for 700 pounds, of which Sir Robert Ferguson pays 100 pounds. The remainder is to be paid in 6 instalments by the county.

Clare bridge, on the road between Drumquin and Castlederg, crosses the Fairy water about half-way between them. It is 50 feet long and 22 broad and consists of 3 arches. The date and cost of building are not known.

General Appearance and Scenery

This parish is a transversal strip of the wide valley through which runs the river formed by the junction of the Glendergan, Mourne-Beg and Derg rivers, the latter of which, being the most considerable, gives its name to the combined stream. This valley has a fine open appearance and is neither uncultivated nor unfertile, but from the great want of trees has, especially in winter, a peculiarly bleak and cold character of scenery. This effect is very much increased by the aspect of the distant mountains higher up this long valley, some in the neighbouring parishes of Termonamongan, some far to the east in Donegal, which are very lofty, wholly uncultivated and barren, and in winter almost always covered with snow.

The valley runs from east to west, and in the latter direction the mountains Bessy Bell and Mary Grey, with the wild high tops above Newtownstewart and Gortin, present an unvaried panorama of desolate and bleak scenery. It is rather a striking point in this landscape, that looking east on a bright day the River Derg in its various windings breaks shining on the eye, is lost and reappears in several places, with a pleasing effect, enabling one to trace the exact course of its waters independently of the guidance afforded by the features of the ground. The mass of ground called the Bin Rock, which forms the southern boundary of the parish, is a huge black-looking frowning wall of barren ground. At the very summit of it is [a] large lake of a singularly wild appearance.

SOCIAL ECONOMY

Local Government

The Reverend Archibald Hamilton, rector, is the only magistrate residing in the parish. He is firm and much respected by the people? There are 4 of the constabulary police stationed in Castlederg. Military were formerly stationed here, but there has been none for the last 7 years. Petty <petit> sessions are held in Castlederg on every other Saturday; 2 magistrates are generally in attendance. [Insert note: these magistrates are the Reverend Archibald Hamilton, residence Mount Bernard, and James Anderson Esquire, residence Lisnacloon, parish of Termonamongan <Tarmonagmongan>]. Outrages are greatly diminished. Illicit distilling was formerly carried on to a great extent, but it is now diminished (but a few stills are at work on the mountain districts and some of them make excellent whiskey).

Dispensary

The dispensary for this and part of the surrounding parishes is situated in Castlederg. It was established in 1823 and is supported by subscriptions and grant from the county. The medical officer's salary is 60 pounds per annum, and medicine is supplied by contract for 24 pounds per annum. House rent costs nothing, and the only additional expense, from 3 to 4 pounds a year, is expended in fuel and stationery. For the above expenditures, the grants of the grand jury amount to 50 pounds per annum. The remainder is made up by subscriptions.

Table of Diseases

Table of diseases treated at the above mentioned dispensary from the 1st January to 31st December 1836: rheumatism 115, dyspepsia 262, wounds 35, pneumonia 27, skin diseases 167, contusions and sprains 34, quinsy and sore throats 16, catarrh and colds 67, constipations 34, diarrhoea 33, fever 199, stricture 1, infantile [? remedies] 22, boils and abcesses 36, toothache 22, porrigo 29, ulcers 23, consumption 5, intoxication 1, retention of urine and diseases of bladder 14, diabetes 2, haemoptysis 5, scrofula 7, opthalmia 36, cataracts 3, burns 27, ruptures 6, whitlow 2, dropsy 12, diseases of ovary 2, fractures 13, prolapsus ani 3, haemorroids 9, plurisy 5, smallpox 3, hydrocephalis 1, colic 5, diseases of womb 24, inflammation of bowels 3, dysentery 21, asthma 8, polypus of ear 1, neuralgia 1, hysteria 16, worms 20, epilepsey 3, whooping <hooping> cough 9, otitis and otorrhoea 8, tabes mesenterica 1, syphilis 1, ague 1, caries 3, mebra 1, measles 1, cholera sporadic 3, aphtha and [? dorthous] 7, jaundice 1, erysipelas 6, mumps 3, total 1,407.

NB From the extent of the district (about 15 miles long and 12 broad), with many other causes, it is impossible to give the results with any degree of accuracy. John Motherell M.D., surgeon to the Castlederg and Killeter dispensary.

Schools

[Table contains the following headings: name, situation and description, when established, income and expenditure, physical, intellectual and moral education, number of pupils subdivided by age, sex and religion, name and religious persuasion of master or mistress. No expenditure or physical education].

Castlederg national school, Castlederg, established 1822; income: patronage 2 pounds per annum, from pupils 1s 6d each per quarter; intellectual education: books of all kinds furnished by the National Board; moral education: Scriptures are read and catechisms heard by the master; number of pupils: males, 32 under 10 years of age, 26 from 10 to 15, 1 above 15, 59 total males; females, 7 under 10 years of age, 6 from 10 to 15, 13 total females; 72 total number of pupils, 15 Protestants, 30 Presbyterians, 27 Roman Catholics; master Alexander Eglington, Protestant.

Crawfordstown day school, a small cottage in the townland of Coolnacranaght, established 1833; income: supported by the pupils, 1s 6d per quarter; intellectual education: general school books; moral education: the Scriptures are read and all kinds of catechisms taught; number of pupils: males, 24 under 10 years of age, 15 from 10 to 15, 39 total males; females, 15 under 10 years of age, 10 from 10 to 15, 25 total females; 64 total number of pupils, 9 Protestants, 23 Presbyterians, 21 Roman Catholics, 11 other denominations; master Robert Caldwell, Roman Catholic.

Garraghan national school, a small cottage on the roadside between Castlederg and Kesh about 2 miles from the former, established June 1833, income: from National Board 8 pounds per annum, from pupils 16 pounds per annum; intellectual education: books furnished by the National Board; moral education: visited by the Reverend Archibald Hamilton, the Scriptures and scripture lessons read, catechisms taught; number of pupils: males, 18 under 10 years of age, 8 from 10 to 15, 26 total males; females, 38 under 10 years of age, 7 from 10 to 15, 45 total females; 71 total number of pupils, 13 Protestants, 53 Presbyterians, 5 Roman Catholics; master Patrick Monaghan, Roman Catholic.

Freughlough, situated on the roadside leading from Castlederg to Castlefin, one mile from the former, established June 1833; income: from Mr J. Lloyd of Dungannon 2 pounds per annum, from pupils 1s 6d to 3s per quarter each; intellectual education: general; moral education: Scriptures are read and catechisms taught; number of pupils: males, 29 under 10 years of age, 8 from 10 to 15, 2 above 15, 39 total males; females, 15 under 10 years of age, 4 from 10 to 15, 19 total females; 58 total number of pupils, 4 Protestants, 44 Presbyterians, 10 Roman Catholics; master Joseph Clegg, Presbyterian.

Mount Bernard national school, a small cottage near the Glebe House, established 1831, income: from National Board 5 pounds per annum, from pupils 1s 10d per quarter; intellectual education: general; moral education: visited by the Reverend Archibald Hamilton, catechisms heard and Scriptures read; number of pupils: males, 11 under 10 years of age, 1 from 10 to 15, 12 total males; females, 10 under 10 years of age, 5 from 10 to 15, 1 above 15, 15 total females; 28 total number of pupils, 12 Protestants, 10 Presbyterians, 6 Roman Catholics; mistress Eliza McDart, Protestant.

Clare school, a neat cottage in Upper Clare; [insert footnote: this school is at present closed for want of understanding between the master and a Methodist parson in the neighbourhood].

Kilclean national school, a small cottage on [?] Winkle hill; closed at present, master in Dublin receiving education.

The schools in this parish are generally well attended and the people appear to be anxious that their children should have as much education as possible.

Poor

There are no charitable institutions in the parish.

Religion

The proportions of population in religious persuasions are 1,200 Roman Catholics to 1,500 Protestants, in which last are included all the different sects of Presbyterians.

Habits of the People

The cottages of the peasantry are generally built of stone and slated or thatched. The latter is the most prevailing. They have all glass windows and are generally of but 1-storey, which is divided into 2 or 3 apartments. Very little attention is paid either to comfort or cleanliness by the inhabitants, who generally have their manure heaps [underlined] in front of the door. Their food is potatoes, stirabout, flummery, oaten bread and sometimes a little fresh meat and broth. A particular kind of bread called boxty is often eaten. It is made with potatoes and potato starch. Turf is their only fuel. Their dress is varied. The usual number in a family is 6. Early marriages are common, that is from 18 to 25 years. They have very little amusement or recreation. At Christmas the young men amuse themselves shooting at a target for geese and whiskey. They have nothing remarkable in their costume.

Emigration

Emigration prevails to a small extent. The spring is the favourite time. They mostly take shipping in Londonderry for America and at Belfast for Van Dieman's Land. There are several men in the parish who have returned from America, not from any dislike to it but that they thought long for Old Ireland. Those emigrants who stay in America send encouraging letters to their friends in this parish to go out as soon as possible.

Memoir Writing

Letter concerning Chapel

Lisdoo, December 30th, 1835. Sir, I was honoured <honored> by a communication from you on Sunday morning last. After diligent enquiry, I have been enabled to give the subjoined answers to queries proposed by you relative to the chapel in Churchtown near Castlederg. I have the honour to be, Sir, your most humble and obedient servant, Hugh Nugent.

1st, Castlederg was built about the year 1790. 2nd, the expenses of the original building and subsequent addition are supposed to be about 200 pounds. They were defrayed, in the first instance, principally by the late Mr Gilly McHugh of Castlederg, who was afterwards remunerated by the voluntary subscriptions of the people and collections at the chapel door. 3rd, there were 558 persons in attendance on last Sunday (there was not sufficient accommodation for that number). The attendance of last Sunday may, I think, be fairly taken as the average attendance of the winter season. Of course, a much larger number attend in the summer, and consequently in that season a greater number of persons are obliged to remain outside during divine service.

Letter concerning Meeting House

Castlederg, 13th January 1836. Sir, you will excuse my not replying to your last sooner as I was not at home when it reached this. The date of the building of the present meeting house is 1792, the cost about 450 pounds, raised by voluntary subscription. It will accommodate 350 persons and the average attendance is 180. Since 1825, 198 pounds 7s have been expended in increasing the accommodation and repairing the house, raised also by subscription. Your [? obedient humble servant], James Adams, [to] J.R. Ward Esquire.

Parish of Termonamongan <Tarmonamongan>, County Tyrone

Memoir by J.R. Ward, [?] October 1835

NATURAL FEATURES

Hills

[Note on cover: received from Captain Leach R.E., August 1851]. The hills of this parish are high, barren and gloomy. They may be divided into 3 great masses or ridges: the highest and most considerable between the Mourne-Beg and Glendergan rivers, the next between the Glendergan and Derg rivers, though this is rather a great wedge than a ridge, and lastly all the high mass of ground south of the Derg river. The highest point of ground in the parish, which is the utmost east corner of parish and county, is 1,212 feet above the level of the sea; the lowest, where the Derg river flows out at the west end, about 170 feet above the same. Nearly the whole surface of this parish is composed of huge mountain features, whose forms are remarkably massive, solid and compact. There are very few broken chains or turning twisting ridges and tails of features. Rock, generally a species of sandy freestone, breaks out frequently in these mountains. It is said that some veins of coal had been slightly traced in some parts of them.

The country people cut millstones out of these rocks, which they fashion out on the mountain, and when finished, putting a great pole through the hole in the centre, they assemble their friends and roll the stones by main force down to the roads, guiding the impetus by the above mentioned pole. There are a great many small lakes in the tops of these mountains, and indeed their general surface is of a very moist tendency. In winter all the tops are nearly impassible bogs. Chalybeate springs are to be found occasionally.

Lakes and Fish

Small lakes abound in the mountains of this parish. They are not very deep, have sometimes gravelly bottoms, and almost all contain fine trout, which are very much fished for in spring and summer.

Rivers

The Rivers Derg, Glendergan and Mourne-Beg run through this parish from east to west. The three join in the parish and leave it in one broad river, which retains the name of the Derg river. The Derg river takes its rise in Lough Derg, about 1 furlong from the boundary in the county of Donegal. It is so narrow at its first exit from the lake that it can easily be stepped across, but after flowing through a broken rocky channel for about a mile it becomes by means of its tributary streams, deep, broad and rapid. Its banks are generally smooth and flat, its bed rocky and its windings frequent but not considerable. The greatest breadth it attains in the parish is between 30 and 40 yards. It contains trout, salmon and some pike.

The overflowings of this river are in some parts so great and have been productive of so much damage, that the proprietors on its banks have been obliged to build strong embankments at a great expense to keep out the water. For the Glendergan and Mourne-Beg rivers the same general description may suffice, except that their beds are more rocky, shallower, of quicker slope and less breadth. They also rise in Donegal and flow in a westerly direction to meet the Derg. They also contain fish.

Bogs

Almost all the high ground in this parish is one general surface of wet slushy bog. A great deal of turf is cut, but is not very valuable from the great distance to a market.

Woods

No ancient [woods], unless a few stunted remains of brushwood may be so called, which still fringe some of the narrow ravines. Sir Robert Ferguson, the principal proprietor in the parish, has made great exertions to spread new plantations, which are thriving well. They are principally of fir.

Climate

The climate of this parish is, as might naturally be expected from the nature of its surface, cold, damp and chilling to vegetation. Crops, flowers and leaves of the trees are all backward here. It rains incessantly in winter and the early months of spring, and snow is retained a long time on the high mountain tops.

Crops

Oats, flax, potatoes and a few fields of [blank] in the low ground are the principal, indeed only,

Parish of Termonamongan

crops. These mountains are generally a fortnight behindhand in the seasons for reaping and gathering.

Modern Topography

Killeter: Locality

Killeter, a small village situated in the townland of Crilly Hill on the road between Castlederg and Pettigoe, 4 miles from the former. There are no public buildings in the village, which is composed of 12 thatched houses, 4 of 1-storey and 8 of 2-storeys.

Productive Economy

Fairs

There are no markets, but fairs are held on the 21st of every month and are tolerably well attended. The traffic is in cattle, pigs, sheep and linen yarn. No tolls are paid and premiums are awarded to the persons who make the greatest purchases. These premiums amount to 2 pounds each fair day and are awarded as follows: to the greatest purchaser of cattle 10s, to the next greatest purchaser of cattle 10s, to the greatest purchaser of yarn 10s, to the next greatest purchaser of yarn 5s, to the greatest purchaser of pigs 5s. Henry Smith Esquire, landlord of the town, gives 10 pounds per annum towards the amount of money laid out in these premiums, and the remainder is made up by subscriptions among the inhabitants.

Table of Occupations

Grocer and spirit dealer 1, spirit sellers 2, farmers 3, tailors 1.

Modern Topography

Public Buildings: Parish Church

The parish church is situated in the townland of Speerholme. It was built in 1821 and cost 800 pounds, which was defrayed by a loan of 600 pounds from the Board of First Fruits and subscriptions. It is a neat rectangular building 60 feet long and 30 broad. The inside is neatly fitted up with pews, affording accommodation for 350 persons, but as the attendance in summer is much greater than this accommodation, it is intended to enlarge the church or to erect a gallery.

Presbyterian Meeting House

A Presbyterian meeting house, situated in Magheranageeragh townland, was erected between 40 and 50 years ago. The exact time or the cost of building cannot be ascertained. It is a plain rectangular stone building 60 feet long and 25 feet broad, and will accommodate 200 persons. The average attendance is 120.

Roman Catholic Chapel

A Roman Catholic chapel, situated in Aghyaran townland; it was built in 1799 and the cost, which cannot be correctly ascertained, was defrayed by the parishioners. It is a plain thatched building 120 feet long and 24 broad, affording accommodation for 900 persons. The average attendance is from 700 to 1,000.

For the better convenience of the Roman Catholics living in the southern parts of the parish, mass is held in a small glen in Aghalougher townland, at which place there is no chapel but a small shed for an altar.

Gentlemen's Seats

Derg Lodge, a shooting-box of Sir Robert Ferguson Bart, is situated in Aghyaran townland.

The Reverend George Knox, rector of the parish, intends to build a Glebe House. At present he resides in a house in Woodside townland, the private property of the late rector of the parish.

Lisnacloon, the residence of James Anderson Esquire (land agent to Sir Robert Ferguson), is situated in Lisnacloon townland.

Mills

[Table contains the following headings: name of townland where situated, nature of mill, dimensions and type of wheel].

Lisnacloon, flax mill, 1 foot 10 inches by 12 feet, undershot.

Mourne-Beg, flax mill, 2 feet by 12 feet, undershot.

Mourne-Beg, corn mill, 2 feet 10 inches by 12 feet, undershot.

Speerholme, corn mill, 1 foot 9 inches by 12 feet 3 inches, undershot.

Commmunications

This parish, though of very large extent, has very few roads. 7 miles of the road from Pettigoe to Castlederg are contained in the bounds. It is a very hilly, almost impassible, broken road, carried straight from end to end, in utter defiance of all the mountains that happened to interfere with the line.

6 miles of the road from Kesh to Castlederg, much better.

9 miles and a half of the road from Donegal to Castlederg, very good and firm, though in some parts very steep and hilly.

About 2 miles of a crossroad from Killeter to Killygordon, steep and bad, and 6 miles of road from Killeter to Ballybofey, which is rather better.

Social Economy

Local Government

James Anderson Esquire is the only magistrate residing in the parish. He resides in Lisnacloon townland. He is firm and respected by the people. An officer, a sergeant <serjeant> and 11 privates of the revenue police are usually stationed in the parish. The barracks is in the townland of Magheranageeragh. The nearest constabulary force is stationed in Castlederg, where petty <petit> sessions are held (for particulars see Memoir of the parish of Skirts). Illicit distilling was formerly carried on to a great extent, but it is greatly diminished owing to the great exertions of Lieutenant Hunt and his party of revenue police. About 10 years back it is said there were upwards of 60 private stills in the parish: at present there are not 2.

Dispensary

The dispensary of this parish is in connection with the Castlederg dispensary; for particulars, see parish of Skirts.

Schools

The schools in the parish are well attended. The people are anxious that their children should obtain information, but are loath to pay too high a price to the teachers, who complain. As will be perceived by the table, the clergy take no notice of these schools. The present rector is very much against the National Board, and for this reason will not visit them. The former rector was the means of getting most of the schools under the National Board.

Table of Schools

[Table contains the following headings: name, situation and description, when established, income and expenditure, physical, intellectual and moral education, number of pupils subdivided by age, sex and religion, name and religious persuasion of master and mistress].

Aghnahoo national school, a small cottage in Aghnahoo townland, established June 1833, income: from the National Board 8 pounds per annum, from Sir James Strong 3 pounds per annum, from pupils 1s each per quarter; intellectual eduction: books for general education furnished by the National Board; moral education: catechisms taught by the master on Saturday; number of pupils: males, 27 under 10 years of age, 10 from 10 to 15, 37 total males; females, 8 under 10 years of age, 2 from 10 to 15, 10 total females; 37 total number of pupils, 32 Protestants, 5 Presbyterians; master John Brian, Protestant.

Altamullan national school, a slated cottage in Altamullan townland, established 1823, income: from National Board 8 pounds per annum, from Sir Robert Ferguson Bart, 2 pounds per annum, from pupils 1s each per quarter; intellectual education: books for general education furnished by the National Board; moral education: catechisms taught by the master on Saturday; number of pupils: males, 18 under 10 years of age, 32 from 10 to 15, 6 above 15, 56 total males; females, 15 under 10 years of age, 19 from 10 to 15, 34 total females; 90 total number of pupils, 37 Protestants, 31 Presbyterians, 22 Roman Catholics; master William Keatly, Protestant.

Carncoghan national school, a slated cottage in Carncoghan townland, established August 1834; income: from National Board 8 pounds per annum, from pupils from 1s to 2s per quarter each; intellectual education: books for general education furnished by the National Board; moral education: catechisms taught by the master on Saturday; number of pupils: males, 25 under 10 years of age, 15 from 10 to 15, 2 above 15, 42 total males; females, 9 under 10 years of age, 10 from 10 to 15, 19 total females; 61 total number of pupils, 2 Protestants, 3 Presbyterians, 56 Roman Catholics; master Owen Flagherty, Roman Catholic.

Killeter national school, a 2-storey house near the parish church, under the Kildare Street Society in 1828, under present board March 1833; income: from National Board 8 pounds per annum, from Sir R.A. Ferguson 2 pounds, from Henry Smith Esquire 1 pound 1s per annum, from pupils from 1s to 2s 6d per quarter each; intellectual education: books for general education furnished by the National Board, moral education: catechisms taught by the master on Saturday; number of pupils: males, 12 under 10 years of age, 23 from 10 to 15, 5 above 15, 40 total males; females, 16 under 10 years of age, 14 from 10 to 15, 30 total females; 70 total number of pupils, 21 Protestants, 14 Presbyterians, 35 Roman Catholics, [sic] 70 other denominations; master William Dogherty, Presbyterian.

Lisnacloon national school, a slated cottage in

Parish of Termonamongan

Lisnacloon townland; intellectual education: books for general education furnished by the National Board; moral education: catechisms taught by the master on Saturdays.

Magherakeel national school, a cottage in Magherakeel townland near the old church, established May 1832; income: from National Board 8 pounds, from Henry Smith Esquire 7 pounds 1s, from pupils from 1s to 4s per quarter each; intellectual instruction: books for general education furnished by the National Board; moral education: catechisms taught by the master on Saturday; number of pupils: males, 19 under 10 years of age, 26 from 10 to 15, 5 above 15, 50 total males; females, 11 under 10 years of age, 7 from 10 to 15, 18 total females; 68 total number of pupils, 15 Protestants, 17 Presbyterians, 36 Roman Catholics; master William Manley, Protestant.

Magherakeel national school, a wretched hovel in Laghtmorris townland, established November 1834; income from pupils 1s to 2s 6d per quarter each; intellectual education: *Universal spelling book* and Testament; moral education: catechisms of all kinds taught; number of pupils: males, 15 under 10 years of age, 28 from 10 to 15, 1 above 15, 44 total males; females, 8 under 10 years of age, 4 from 10 to 15, 12 total females; 56 total number of pupils, 2 Protestants, 2 Presbyterians, 52 Roman Catholics; master Simon Rogers, Roman Catholic.

Memoir Writing

[Tracing of part of [map] Sheet 50, with a new road between Trillick and Dromore sketched in red. J.R. Ward, 19 October 1835].

Poor

No charitable institutions.

Religion

The religious persuasions in the parish are Protestant, Roman Catholic and Presbyterian. The proportions are Presbyterian 1, Protestant 2 and Roman Catholic 4. The Roman Catholics generally occupy the mountainous parts of the parish, while the Protestants with very few exceptions dwell in the valley around their church. The rector is supported by tithes and glebe lands, the Presbyterian minister by subscriptions and regium donum and the Roman Catholic priest by contributions from his congregations.

Habits of the People

Habits of the people are the same as those of the parish of the Skirts of Urney and Ardstraw.

Emigration

Emigration prevails to some extent, generally in spring, for America.

Miscellaneous Papers, County Tyrone

Extracts from Annals of Ireland [by John O'Donovan ?]

ANCIENT HISTORY

Twelfth Century Annals

1177: Niall, the son of MacLoughlin, was slain by Muinter Branain at Dal mBuinne. Hugh O'Neill, nicknamed Macaomh Tainliase, who had been for some time Lord of Tyrone and heir presumptive to the throne of Ireland, was slain by Melaghlin O'Loghlin and Ardgal O'Louglin, but Ardgall himself fell by the hand of O'Neill on the spot.

1181: Donnell, the son of Hugh McLoughlin and the Kenel Eagan of Tullyhoge, defeated the Ulidians McDonlevy and O'Flynn.

1182: Donnell, the son of Hugh O'Loughlin, marched with an army to Dunbo in Dalriada, and engaged the English there; but was defeated with the loss of Randal O'Breslen and Gilchriest O'Kane.

1186: Maelseaghlin, the son of Mortagh O'Loughlin, was slain by the English.

1186: Donnell, the son of Hugh O'Loughlin, was deposed, and Rory O'Flaherty was elected by some of the Kenel Eogan of Tullyhoge. Con O'Breslen, chief of Fanad, was slain by the son of MacLoughlin and a party of the Kenel Eagan, in consequence of which Inishowen was plundered.

1187: Rory O'Flaherty, Lord of Kenel Owen, slain.

1188: Donnell, the son of Hugh O'Loughlin, Lord of Aileagh and heir to the throne of Ireland, fought and defeated the English in Tirone, but was himself slain.

1189: Donnell, the son of Mortagh McLoughlin, was slain by the English of Dalaradia.

1196: Mortagh, the son of Mortogh (i.e. King) O'Loughlin, Lord of Tyrone, heir presumptive to the throne of Ireland, tamer of the valour <valor> and achievements of Leth-con, destroyer of the towns and castles of the English, founder of churches and sanctuaries, was killed by Donogh, the son of Blosga O'Kane, at the instigation of the Kenel Owen, who had pledged themselves before the 3 shrines and the canons of St Patrick to be loyal to him. His body was carried to Derry and there interred with honour and veneration.

1198-1199: Hugh O'Neill, Lord of Tirone.

Thirteenth Century Annals

1200: Hugh O'Neill was deposed by the Kenel Owen and Connor O'Loughin was elected in his place. He was killed in the same year by the Kenel Connell.

1201: Magnus, the son of Dermot O'Loughlin, was slain by Mortagh O'Neill, and Mortagh was slain in revenge of his death.

1203: Dermot, the son of Mortagh O'Loughlin, plundered the shrine of Columbkille (Ballynascreen) in Tyrone, but was attacked and slain.

1208, 1211, 1212, 1221: Hugh O'Neill, Lord of Tyrone, died with a noble character 1230.

1213: O'Kane and Fir-na-Craoibhe came to Derry to storm the house of the sons of McLoughlin. The prior interposed and was killed.

1232: Donnell O'Loughlin, Lord of Tyrone, at the head of a numerous army, composed of the English and Irish, made an incursion into Tirconnell and plundered an extensive portion of Fanad, carrying away the hostages of Donnell O'Boyle and O'Taichid.

1234: Donnell, the son of Hugh O'Neill, Lord of Tyrone and heir presumptive to the throne of Ireland, was slain by McLoughlin (Donnell) and the Kenel Owen, and McLoughlin assumed the lordship.

1239: The battle of Carnteal was fought by Donnell McLoughlin, in which Donnell [? an tamny] O'Neill, McMahon, O'Gormly and others were slain. After this battle McLoughlin assumed the lordship, but lost it soon after.

1241: O'Neill (Brian), after having been expelled by McLoughlin, went to O'Donnell, who marched with an army to aid him, and they gave battle to McLoughlin, Lord of Tyrone, who was aided by 10 of his own tribe and all the chieftans of the Kenel Owen. A battle was fought between them at Cam-eirge, in which Donnell O'Loughlin was slain, upon which Brian O'Neill was inaugurated Lord of Tyrone.

1246: Brian O'Neill was Lord of Tyrone, also in 1248, 1252, 1253, 1258.

1259: Hugh Boy O'Neill seems lord.

1260: Dermot McLoughlin fell in the battle of Drumderg, near Downpatrick.

1261: Hugh Boy O'Neill expelled and Niall Culanach set up in his place.

1262: Hugh Boy O'Neill again elected and his rival expelled. Killed 1293.

1281: Hugh Boy O'Neill, Lord of Tyrone, and Enna O'Gormley, chief of Kenel-Moen.

Miscellaneous Papers

1291: Niall Culanach O'Neill set up.

Fourteenth Century Annals

1303: Mortagh McLoughlin slain by Hugh O'Donnell.
1319: Donnell O'Neill Lord of Tyrone.
1343-45: Hugh Reamhar O'Neill.
1345: Cormac, the son of Mortagh McLoughlin was slain by the sons of Malgarg, who was son of Fergal O'Rourke.

Fifteenth Century Annals

AD 1490: O'Gormley (Mortagh, the son of Henry, who was son of Connor Roe, who was son of Giolla-Patrick Maguire) died [queried].
AD 1493: Mac-Conmidhe (Teige, the son of Connall Roe, who was son of Eachmarcach), a learned poet and a Latin scholar ([Irish letters] fogh lainnteach), was slain by a labourer, one of his own people, viz. Mac-Ui-Chlumain.

Sixteenth Century Annals

AD 1507: O'Donnell (Hugh Oge, the son of Hugh Roe) marched with an army to Tyrone, where he pitched his camp around O'Neill's castle of Dungannon, and slew numbers of the people of the town, besides the son of Giolla-ruad (Brian). O'Neill on this occasion made peace with O'Donnell, who proceeded to the lord chief justice's house. After his departure O'Neill plundered Kenel Moen, and slew Brian, the son of O'Gormley.
AD 1508: Edmond, the son of Magnus O'Gormley, was slain by Con, the son of Niall Bearnach, who was son of Henry, who was son of Owen; and Con himself was slain in the same month by Brian, the son of Con, who was son of Henry, who was son of Owen.
AD 1516: MacCoinmhidhe (Brian Oge, the son of Brian Roe) died.
AD 1523: MacConmidhe (Melaghlin) died.
AD 1525: The deacon, the son of Brian Roe MacConmidhe, who had maintained a house of general hospitality, died.
AD 1537, page 655 q.v. (Bills).
AD 1542: MacConmidhe (Brian Doragh, the son of Solomon), a man versed in poetry and literature, and a rich and prosperous man, who had maintained a house of general hospitality for all, died about the festival of Saint Columbkille, through the miracles of God and Saint Columbkille and the curse of O'Robhartaigh (Rafferty), for he before that time violated and dishonoured (condemned) the great cross, for he struck it.

Letter from James Spiller to James Sinclair, 18th June 1824

MEMOIR WRITING

Letter detailing Proposed Canal

[From Memoir of Aghalurcher].

Omagh, Tyrone, 18th June 1824. My dear Sir, The line of the intended canal, as it appears on the map laid before me by Mr Bransan, seems not to define the townlands with accuracy through which it is intended to pass. I can only name the tenants in the townland of Lord Belmore's through which it seems to pass. To have the thing done with accuracy, a person should follow the line and take down the tenant's name and farm through which it would pass. I know nothing of the paper that was sent to Lord Belmore until he handed it to me in Dublin, and I gave it to Mr Marshall the moment I came to the country. Yours, my dear Sir, most sincerely, [?] James Spiller [to] James Sinclair Esquire. [Cover of letter] for James Sinclair Esquire, Hollyhill, Strabane.

Ballygoan near Omagh, the property of the late John Church Esquire, lately sold in Dublin and bought, it is supposed, for one of the McCluwher [? McClincher] family; barony Omagh and parish Drumragh. It goes near but does not seem to touch on Garvagh, Lord Belmore's property.

Donamona, Major Crawford, same parish and barony.

Tattycor, Lord Belmore, same barony, parish Dromore. Tenants' names: Patt Slevin, Hugh Johnston, Robert Warnock [? Winarsh], John Slevin Junior, Thady <Tady> Slevin, John Slevin Junior, Michael Slevin, Harry McGuigan, Owen McGuigan, James McGuigan, Patt McGuigan Junior, Hugh and [?] Connor McCusker, Pat [?] McKeagney, Pat McGuigan and Messrs McCluny.

Galbolly, General Archdall, parish Dromore, barony Omagh.

Magherylough, Mr Blacker.

Ballynamallard, Fermanagh, Andrew Crawford Esquire.

Ballycassidy, Fermanagh, Edward Archdall Esquire.

www.ingramcontent.com/pod-product-compliance
Lightning Source LLC
Chambersburg PA
CBHW051211290426
44109CB00021B/2416